W9-AOI-398

The ABC's and All Their Tricks

THE
Complete Reference Book
of
PHONICS and SPELLING

The ABC's and All Their Tricks

By **Margaret M. Bishop**

MOTT MEDIA
Fenton, Michigan 48430

THE ABC'S AND ALL THEIR TRICKS

Copyright © 1986 by Mott Media

Manufactured in the United States of America.

ISBN 0-88062-149-4

Acknowledgments

The word counts presented in this book are based on the print-outs published in *Phoneme-Grapheme Correspondences as Cues to Spelling Improvement*, by Hanna, Hanna, Rudorf and Hodges, a 1966 publication of the United States Office of Education, Department of Health, Education and Welfare. The work of this research group is described in Appendix D.

For the way in which the material is presented and explained, I am greatly indebted to the Fortune Society, an association of ex-offenders in New York City. For nine years, I trained volunteer tutors and also tutored students of my own in the Adult Basic Education program which the Fortune Society maintains for its illiterate members. Both the volunteer tutors and the students taught me what I know about how to make the ins and outs of the English writing system clear to adults who are not already familiar with these matters.

Finally, I am very deeply indebted to my husband, whose patience has permitted me the many hours of concentration required to pull it all together.

Any errors, factual or conceptual, which appear in these pages are, of course, entirely my own.

September, 1985
Margaret M. Bishop

Contents

To The Teacher

We all know that there are many irregularities in English spelling. Many of our most common words are not pronounced exactly the way the letters of the words would suggest. For example, the word **said** is really pronounced with a short E sound. But the letter combination AI is normally used to show a long A sound. Peculiar spellings of this kind appear in many other words as well.

Towards the middle of the last century, educators began to believe that there were so many of these irregularities that they were making problems for children learning to read. Educators began to feel that direct training in the regular letter-sounds was causing confusion in the children's minds. So they developed systems of reading instruction which emphasized visual memorization of whole words. It was assumed that by learning to recognize words at sight, the children would absorb enough knowledge of the letter-sounds to become independent readers. Such systems postponed until later grades any formal work on letter-sounds.

These systems began coming into widespread use in the public and private schools during the 1930's. They continue to be very widely used to this day.

The Regular Letter Sounds

Meanwhile, however, certain leading linguists began to express alarm over the abandonment of early emphasis on letter-sounds. Leonard Bloomfield, the father of modern American linguistics, worked out a system for teaching the regular letter-sounds to children directly, and having the children use these letter-sounds to figure out the words. But the trend in the schools against this idea was so strong that Dr. Bloomfield could not get his material published during his lifetime. Indeed, his system did not become available until several years after his death, when his protegé finally got it published in 1961.[1]

1. Let's Read: *A Linguistic Approach*, Clarence L. Barnhart, Inc., Bronxville, New York.

In the early '60's, three different research groups were working on the question of how much emphasis really should be put on letter-sounds in teaching beginning reading. Two of these groups were at Stanford University, and one at Harvard. The results of the two Stanford studies were published in 1966 by the United States Office of Education, Department of Health, Education and Welfare.[2] The results of the Harvard study were summarized in *Learning to Read: The Great Debate*, by Jeanne S. Chall, published by McGraw-Hill in 1967.

Dr. Chall's study was devoted to an examination of all the research projects which had compared the reading performance of children learning by word-memorization methods to the performance of children learning by methods emphasizing regular letter-sounds from the beginning. She found that children taught to use letter-sounds from the beginning were more successful as readers than the children taught mainly by whole-word memorization.

The Stanford studies help to explain how this comes about. One of these studies was done by a group of linguists among whom Dr. Richard L. Venezky was prominent. This study showed that letter-sounds in English are not nearly so unreliable as earlier scholars believed. It reveals, however, how important it is to help children understand how certain letters are used to influence the sounds of other letters in a word.

For example, the extra P in **hopping** is silent, but it is there to show that the O is short, like the O in **hop**. Another example is the E in **hope**, which has no sound of its own, but shows that the O is long. Still another example is the influence of the letters E, I and Y on the letter C. The letter C shows an S sound when the next letter is E, I or Y, as in **cent**, **city** and **fancy**. Whenever C appears before any other letter, however, it shows a K sound, as in **cat**, **cot**, **cut**, **clap**, **crib**, **act** or **accent**.

The other Stanford study was conducted by a group under the leadership of Dr. Paul R. Hanna, He was a professor of Education, interested in helping high school students with spelling problems.

2. Richard L. Venezky and Ruth H. Weir, *A Study of Selected Spelling-to-Sound Correspondence Patterns.*

Paul R. Hanna, Jean S. Hanna, Richard E. Hodges, and Edwin H. Rudorf, Jr., *Phoeme-Grapheme Correspondences as Cues to Spelling Improvement.*

This group also showed the importance of interaction between the different letters in a word. Although there are small differences in detail between the two Stanford studies, they both came up with the same set of rules for letter-sounds and how they are affected by interactions between letters.

The conclusion to be drawn from these two studies is that letter-sounds alone may well be confusing to children. But letter-sounds combined with a few fairly simple rules about letter interactions can eliminate most of this confusion. **Phonics** is the term which describes this combined teaching of letter-sounds and basic spelling rules at the very beginning of school.

Educators who still believe that it is best to start with whole-word memorization distrust the phonics approach in spite of these findings. They believe that there are too many exceptions to all the letter-sounds and all the letter interaction rules that children can learn. But one of the major findings of the Venezky and Hanna studies was that there are not nearly so many exceptions as most educators think there are.

Teaching With Phonics

Teachers who do use phonics from the beginning find that the exceptions which occur in the common words that children need for reading do not actually cause much confusion if the children are secure in their knowledge of the regular letter-sounds. If you teach the children to pronounce AI with a long A sound, and then tell them frankly that **said** is a funny word because the AI in it is funny, they can handle **said** perfectly well. Fortunately, most of the irregular words contain only one feature showing an irregular sound, while all the other letters in the word are behaving perfectly normally.

But children who are left to derive the letter-sounds and phonic rules for themselves are so confused by the letter-interactions, that they form the idea that all the letter-sounds are very unreliable. As a result, they have very little confidence in the letter-sounds they do figure out. They therefore do not learn even these sounds very thoroughly. Even when the school begins teaching something about letter-sounds and letter interactions in the later grades, this does not help the children very much, because it is not enough to overcome their acquired distrust of the letters.

Teaching phonics from the beginning of first grade involves teaching the regular sounds of the 26 letters of the alphabet; teaching the regular sounds of the standard letter combinations like SH, CH, EE, AI, AW, etc.; teaching the basic rules about how some letters influence the sounds of other letters; and helping the children to make the most of the reliable letters in the common irregular words.

Of course, since you are not teaching the children to memorize words as individual visual units, the only way they can identify words is by sounding them out. At first, they often need a good deal of help in mastering the trick of blending the letter-sounds of a word smoothly enough to realize what it means. Children seem to vary a great deal in how easily they can learn this trick. But once they learn it, they can use it very easily. Then they soon begin to recognize the common words at sight, simply because they have sounded them out successfully so many times. This is the experience of classroom teachers who are accustomed to using phonics teaching methods.

Many parents have had similar experiences in successful teaching with phonics methods. Very often, when a child is obviously memorizing a few words, but cannot read anything except the school reader, a parent becomes dissatisfied with the school teaching. Parents who are themselves good readers often teach such a child to read quite easily. Sometimes the parent obtains a simple phonics textbook and uses it to teach the child. Sometimes the parent simply draws on his or her own knowledge of phonics to teach the child. Sometimes a parent teaches a child, without even realizing it, simply by answering questions about letter-sounds and letter interactions, and modeling the trick of sounding out.

Public Demand For Phonics

A great many parents are alarmed by the poor reading and spelling performance of their children. When they hear about the millions of adult illiterates who crowd our unemployment lines, our soup kitchens, and our prisons, they begin to feel that something is wrong with the school system. Many of these parents are beginning to demand that phonics methods of reading instruction be installed in the schools instead of the word-memorization methods. As a result, many public schools, and many independent schools as well, are beginning to do their best to comply with this demand.

Teachers And Phonics

At first glance, it seems that changing from word-memorization-first to phonics-first should not be very difficult. After all, word-memorization methods do bring phonics in eventually; and phonics methods do produce word-memorization eventually. Besides, the public naturally assumes that our professionally-trained teachers know how to teach whichever method a school board chooses to use.

Unfortunately, it is not so easy to make this change whenever the parents want it. The teachers' colleges have for many years concentrated on courses that are needed by teachers who will be working with word-memorization first. These courses include a great deal on how to diagnose reading difficulties, and statistical methods for measuring class performance. They include a great deal about how to teach arithmetic, history and science without any heavy reliance on children's reading ability. They include a great deal about how to motivate children to try to memorize their words.

But most teachers' colleges teach very little about phonics iteslf. They do not teach which letter sounds are the easiest ones for children to start with, or which letter-sounds are the most important ones for children to learn early, or which letter-interaction rules are essential, and which ones can be postponed for a little while. They do not have teacher candidates study the history of written English to understand how the letters came to have their present sounds and interactions. They do not teach teachers how to help children learn the trick of sounding words out well enough to understand them, or how to help the children with the truly irregular words.

Furthermore, most of the teachers now in the schools, public or independent, themselves grew up in word-memorization classrooms. Thanks to informal help from parents, they are able to read. But many of them lack confidence in their own spelling ability. And, because they themselves did not receive formal training in phonics, either in first grade or in college, they have little confidence in the wisdom of using the phonics programs the parents are now demanding. They really cannot put their hearts into the task. As a result, the children do not do as well as expected; everyone is disappointed; and often the school goes back fairly soon to the word-memorization method with which the teachers are more familiar.

How Reliable Are The Regular Letter-Sounds?

Most teachers really do believe that children need to acquire some knowledge of letter-sounds sooner or later. But there is one idea which is extremely influential in making them distrust methods that are based on teaching phonics first. They believe that all the phonics rules that the children can learn have a great many exceptions. They believe that the exceptions make the rules very hard for the children to learn, and very unrewarding for them. If this were true, then phonics methods really *would not* work, even in the hands of a teacher well-trained in using such methods.

The fact is, however, that there are really very few exceptions to each rule. But teachers are not going to believe this unless they see the evidence for themselves. Until 1966, when the Venezky and Hanna studies were published, this evidence was never available. Unfortunately, neither of these studies presents the evidence in a way which makes it easy for teachers to use.

The published results of the Hanna study, however, are presented in such a way that the evidence can be put into a form which is as easy to use a dictionary. This is what the present volume is intended to do. (For details about how the Hanna study was done, see Appendix D.)

Both Venezky and Hanna give estimates of what percentage of English words are regular. But when such percentages are quoted, there is always someone around who will challenge the definition of regularity which was used to classify words as regular or irregular. In any case, the over-all percentage of regularity is not what worries the elementary school teacher. She is concerned with getting down to cases. She sees that her textbook expects her to teach a certain rule about a certain letter. She wants to know how reliable that particular rule is, and how often the children will encounter places where this rule does not work.

Take the rules about C, for example. As was mentioned earlier, C is soft, and therefore sounds like S, before the letters E, I and Y. Anywhere else, C is hard, and sounds like K. This is one of the letter interaction rules taught in phonics programs. The teacher needs to know how reliable this specific rule is. The Hanna study shows that C before E, I or Y sounds like S in 1,295 words. In 3,915 words, where C is not followed by E, I or Y, the C sounds like K. So the rule works for 5,210 words. There are only 10 words in which the rule does not work. Since the Hanna study is based on a total of 17,310 words, one can see that more than a quarter of the vocabulary consists of words where it is extremely helpful for the reader to understand what makes C sound like S and what makes it sould like K.

What about the sound of AI? When the subject of irregularity is raised in professional magazines for teachers, AI is often mentioned as a cautionary example. The fact is that AI can have five different sounds. The Hanna study shows that this is true. But it also shows that, as a matter of common sense, this variety of sounds is not a very serious problem for children. AI occurs in 314 words out of the 17,310 of the Hanna study. In 271 of those words, it has the long A sound, as in **rain**. This is the sound that teachers are expected to teach for AI. In another 37 words it occurs in an unstressed syllable, where the vowel sound is severely muffled, as vowel sounds usually are when they are not emphasized.

But, as the teachers' magazines point out, AI can also sound like short E, short A or long I. Doesn't this make AI very difficult? Not when you consider the specific words that are involved. AI has the short E sound in four words, **said**, **again**, **against** and **aforesaid**. Children must learn **said** and **again** as exceptions. They can easily handle **against** but analogy with **again**, and **aforesaid** is hardly likely to occur in their reading. Then, there is one single word where AI has a short A sound, the word **plaid**. (Incidentally, Scotsmen pronounce this word with a long A, "plade.") Finally, there is the single word **aisle**, where AI has a long I sound and the S is silent. But the words **plaid** and **aisle** do not crop up in children's reading often enough to shake their faith in AI for long A, **unless** their teacher seems uncertain about it.

The facts about AI can be summed up by saying that AI is regular in 308 words, and irregular in six words. Thus, it is regular 98% of the time. Common sense suggests that this is a high degree of reliability. Common sense matters because common sense is the yardstick by which children assess what is important and what is too silly to bother their heads about.

This ABC book is designed to enable teachers to judge for themselves the reliability and usefulness of any letter sound, any letter combination, or any letter-interaction rules presented in the phonics method they are trying to use.

Finding The Facts About Letter Sounds

The main body of this book devotes one page to each letter of the alphabet, and one page to each basic letter combination. If a letter or letter combination can have more than one sound, there is an extra page for each extra sound. Each page has an explanation of whatever letter interactions influence the letter sound treated on that page.

The pages for letters and letter combinations are arranged in alphabetical order for easy reference. The letter or letter combination for each page appears in the upper outside corner, like a dictionary guide-word.

Each page presents lists of words which illustrate the letter sound for that page. These lists are divided into three groups. The group in the upper third of the page illustrates the letter sound in words of interest to young children who know how to use letter sounds. Certain words in the children's section may seem rather adult, but they are words which occur frequently in fairy tales or children's adventure stories.

The group of words in the middle section of the page contains words more likely to occur frequently in books for older children or for the ordinary reader of any age. These words, however, are also important for the younger children. Children who are taught to read with phonics will be very familiar with the types of words presented in the first and second groups long before they enter secondary school.

The words in the lowest section of the page are the most unfamiliar and least frequently-used words in English which use the letter-sound treated on the page. Words of this difficulty are presented with the idea that the good reader would first encounter them during high school or college, or later in adult life. The reader would still need to know the letter-sound on the page regardless of the age at which he or she happened to encounter these words.

In each of these major groups of words, there are three columns. The first column usually presents one-syllable words. The second column presents two-syllable words, and the third one presents longer words.

On each page, below the word lists, there is an explanation of the letter-sound treated on the page and any letter-interaction rules which affect that particular letter-sound.

Below this is a statement of how many times the letter-sound conforms to the rules. If syllable-stress makes a difference to how the letter is pronounced the figures show how often it occurs in a stressed syllable, and how often it occurs in an unstressed syllable.

In the earlier discussion, the word-counts for hard and soft C, and for AI were given. These counts showed that C occurs in 5,210 words, while AI occurs in only 314 words. A teacher may well wonder how important it is to teach AI if it affects such a small number of words. This is why the lists on each page are divided into children's sections and a grown-up section. By reading over the lists on any page, and thinking of other words similar to the ones that are given, the teacher can judge for herself how important such words are for children learning to read.

If a certain letter combination does not occur very often in books of special interest to young children, then the lists in the upper third of the page may contain only one or two items altogether. The teacher can then see why this letter combination is not introduced in the early part of the phonics method she is using. (See the page for EY, for instance.)

Finally, young children will encounter certain letter combinations which are not really English letter combinations at all. For example, toward the end of first grade, children taught with phonics can enjoy reading Aesop's Fables for themselves. These children are likely to be very sensitive to unusual letter combinations, and they may ask why you have not taught them AE for long E. The AE page in the ABC book will show you that AE occcurs only in 12 words, that in eight of them it stands for long E, in three for short E, and in one for long A. Furthermore, most of these words are strictly adult in nature. That's why your phonics method does not include AE as a combination to be taught in first grade, and that is what you can tell the children.

What Words Are Irregular?

But the teacher wants to know more about the irregular words themselves and how they will affect the children. That is what the gray panel in the inner margin of each page is all about. The gray panel presents a list of **all** the basic words in which the letter or letter combination for the page has a sound different from the regular sound. Take the page for short U as an example. There, the main section of the page shows that U is short in 1,027 stressed syllables and in 518 unstressed syllables, all of them having one or more consonants after the letter U. The gray panel lists 4 words where U followed by consonant letters is long instead of short. These words are **Ruth**, **truth**, **Duluth** and **impugn.** Any child needs to be able to read **Ruth** and **truth**, of course, and those living near **Duluth**, need to know that word, also. Moreover, they need to know that the way U sounds in these words is **not** the way it normally sounds before a consonant. We do not want little Ruth relying on her own name to remember how short U sounds.

This is one reason the irregular words are so important. It often happens that the very most familiar word which uses a certain letter is the worst word to use as an example of how the letter is supposed to sound.

But this list is typical of the irregular words. Whatever the letter sound, it is often irregular in two or three words which are absolutely indispensible in children's reading. Then, the rest of the irregular words are very adult in character, like **impugn**. Since these adult words hardly ever occur in writing for children, they do not shake the children's confidence in the letter-sound they are learning. Later, when such children have grown old enough to encounter those words, they will automatically notice the peculiar spelling as being exceptional, and again suffer no damage as a consequence.

The list in the gray panel does not include every single word where the letter sound is irregular. But it always lists all the **basic** irregular words. For example, in addition to the four words in the gray panel on the short U page, one could also think of the following words: **ruthless**, **ruthlessly**, **truthful**, **truthfulness**, **untruthfulness**, **truthfully** and **untruthfully**. Since these are only more elaborate forms of the basic words already noted they are not included on the list of exceptions.

Related Letter Sounds

In addition to the basic irregular words, the gray panel presents one other type of information. At the top of the panel there are cross-references to other pages. Sometimes these pages involve other letters for the same sound, and sometimes they involve a different sound for the letter or letter combination treated on the page you are looking at. For example, short U sometimes has the sound it has in **put** instead of the sound it has in **but**. On the short U page, you are referred to the next page, which deals with words like **put.**

Letters With Several Sounds

We all know that in English many of the letters have more than one sound. Thus, any vowel letter can be either long or short; C can be hard or soft, and G works the same way; CH can stand for three sounds, the first sound in **chicken**, the first sound in **Christmas**, or the first sound in **chef**. Y is a consonant some of the time and vowel the rest of the time. And so on.

This is one reason it is so important to teach phonics to children in a systematic way, instead of waiting for them to figure the letter-sounds out for themselves. With so many letters doing double or triple duty, anyone, child or adult, needs help in sorting out the letter-sounds. What is more, the closer you look at the letter-sound system of written English the more tricky little details you discover.

When you look in detail at the letter A, for instance, you find out that long A and short A are not the whole story. The letter A can also be broad as in **fa la la**. Besides, it can appear in letter combinations like AR (**car**), AI (**rain**), AY (**pay**), AU (**cause**), AW (**saw**), EA (**meat**), OA (**boat**) and ALL (**ball**). You begin to wonder whether you really know everything you need to know to help the children with the letter A. How many more little tricks does this letter have up its sleeve? And when the children ask about these tricks, what can you tell them?

The ABC book has a feature designed to help teachers with such questions. For every letter which has a variety of sounds, there is a summary, listing and explaining all the ways in which that letter can be used.

These summary pages may be found immediately before the separate pages which deal, one by one, with the different uses of the letter in question. Thus, the pages summarizing the uses of A come right before the separate pages on long A, short A, broad A, A__E, AE, AI and so on.

These summaries may appear a bit intimidating at first glance, but if you compare the vowel pages among themselves, you will find that the story for each vowel letter is very similar to the stories for all the other vowel letters. If you compare the summaries for C and G, you will find that the stories on each of these letters are very similar. Or you might be reminded of OR and ER by what the A summary says about AR. A glance at the R summary will show that, yes, what R does to the vowel before it is most of the story on the letter R.

These pages are provided to help the teacher see that, although the way we use the letters in English is complicated, there is a pattern to it. Most important, there **is an end to it.** When children have learned the pattern, they are finished, and they will be able to read anything they want to read.

Words Of Many Syllables

But the best possible information about letters and sounds does not really tell all one needs to know about the long, fancy words of the adult vocabulary. In these words, single and double consonants between vowels work a little differently from the way they work in the simpler words. Appendix B deals in detail with such questions.

These are problems which are not of very great concern to the first grade teacher. Her children will be dealing mainly with words of only one syllable, and with one-syllable words lengthened by the addition of familiar endings like -**ing**, -**ed**, -**er**, -**y**, etc., as in **hopping**, **liked**, **baker** and **sunny**. They will also be dealing with simple two-syllable words like **little**, **table**, **hammer**, **pocket**, **lady** and **happy**. In all such two-syllable words, it takes two consonant letters between vowels to show that the first vowel is short, while one consonant between vowels shows that the first vowel is long. This is one of the most important letter-interaction rules of English. Children need to know about this rule and master it very thoroughly. Otherwise, whenever they see a word with two syllables and only one vowel letter in the first syllable, they will have to guess whether that vowel sounds long or short.

However, we also have thousands of fancier words where the first vowel is short even though there is only one consonant letter before the next vowel. **Family** and **elephant** are examples of such words. They come down to us from Ancient Latin. The Romans had only one sound for each vowel letter, so they did not need fancy tricks like doubling consonants to keep a vowel letter short. But we still spell these words the Roman way.

There are a few of these words in materials written for children. **Animal**, **magical**, **general**, **enemy** and **natural** are other examples. Children who are learning reading with phonics seem to take such words in stride without any trouble. It is quite rare for a child to ask how the A in **family** can be short when it has only one M after it. If they do ask, they seem satisfied with the answer that this is a fancy word like **animal**, and works the same way. But by the time they get far enough to encounter these words, they are usually too interested in the story to worry about the spelling peculiarity.

It is only in the later grades, when they are reading about more adult subjects like geography, history and general science that they begin to meet a lot of those Latin-style words. Then they are dealing with lots of words like **hemisphere**, **population**, **federal**, **democratic**, **civilian**, **military**, **physics**, **chemistry**, **element**, **acidity** and **soluble**. In addition, they will be reading words where doubled consonants do not seem to be doing a good job of keeping the vowel before them short, words like **abbreviation**, **addiction**, **commercial** and **offensive**.

These complexities are dealt with in Appendix B. Although these tricky spellings do not seem to bother children much when they read, there are two reasons for including the material in this book. First, the complexities will probably worry first grade teachers who are trying to do their best for the children. And second, in a school where first grade phonics produces second, third and fourth grade children who are good readers, the early phonics work needs to be backed up by the teachers in these later grades. They will have the problem of making sure the children can spell the fancy words.

The very fact that the children read those words easily reflects a casualness in their attitude to the letter-peculiarities the words exhibit. And this casual attitude can play havoc with their spelling. It is much easier to get their spelling into shape if the teacher can explain the consonant doubling rules which actually do apply to the Latin-style adult vocabulary.

Spelling

On the question of spelling, a few special remarks are in order. When you are teaching a phonics program, you need to teach spelling right along with the reading. As each new letter sound, letter combination, or letter-interaction is introduced in first grade, you need to have the children writing the words which use that item. They should be using it actively in spelling work and in story-writing. This does not mean copying or spelling out loud by naming letters. It means writing the words by pronouncing them and putting down letters to match the pronunciation.

It is easy to assume that, since your children are learning letter-sounds for reading, they will be able to use them in writing without a lot of emphasis on spelling practice. Unfortunately, it does not work out that way. Using phonics for reading does not automatically help children spell reliably. Indeed, experience in phonics classrooms shows that it works the other way around. What children learn by applying phonics to spelling strengthens their reading ability very noticeably. But the phonic skills do not transfer to spelling ability without special attention to spelling practice.

Some phonics textbooks give teachers ample guidance on this score, suggesting spelling activities at every step of the way. But others do not emphasize spelling at all. It doesn't matter. If you yourself adopt spelling as one way of teaching each item that comes along, the children's **reading mastery** will develop more quickly and be much more thorough than would otherwise be the case. And they will have the added advantage of self-confidence in spelling.

Of course, the irregular words make for spelling problems. At first, the children will spell **said** as "sed" and **was** as "wuz." When beginners do this kind of thing they should first be praised for using letters which match the word's pronunciation. But then they should be reminded that this is not the way the word looks in the book, because it is a funny word (or a crazy word, or an "outlaw word," or whatever term your textbook suggests). The point is not to ridicule **the children** for such mistakes. Ridicule the **irregular words** instead, and in this way stimulate interest in mastering the irregular spellings.

Dyslexia

There remains one other issue which should be dealt with in this introduction, the problem of **dyslexia.** This is a condition which was investigated and named by Dr. Samuel T. Orton in the 1920's. The symptoms are a tendency to do mirror-writing; to make a lot of reversals in reading, seeing **was** as **saw**, for instance; being very slow and hesitant in reading, and misunderstanding much of what is read.

Dr. Orton was a neuro-surgeon at a time when a great deal of work was being done on the study of visual, auditory and motor functions of the brain. Researchers were discovering the speech center and the different characteristics of the right and left hemispheres of the brain. It was also the time when the visual-memorization approach to reading instruction was just coming into widespread use.

Dr. Orton saw many patients whose major complaint was difficulty in reading. He concluded that in some of the worst cases there was probably a connection between dyslexia and small, undetectable irregularities in the brain functions of the individual. But he found that most of them were simply cases of people who did not understand how reading was supposed to work. He treated **all of them** by having them tutored with very careful, highly structured **phonics** lessons.

Most of the patients he treated in this way learned to read very well, and their dyslexic symptoms disappeared. All of them improved their reading ability greatly, although some never completely overcame their reversal tendencies. Dr. Orton concluded that most of the cases brought to him with reading problems had never been dyslexic at all. Instead, they were people who had become confused by the word-memorization approach to reading. He believed that only a few of the worst cases had any brain dysfunction problems. He believed that most of the cases he treated would never have developed if the sufferers had been taught with phonics in the first place.

Dr. Orton's conclusions led to the establishment of the Orton Society. This is an organization which teaches teachers in the extra-careful phonics work which is needed to straighten out the confusions of readers who have been disabled by the word-memorization approach. These teachers are also qualified to reduce very greatly the reading difficulties of the few who are truly dyslexic.

The work of the Orton Society (recently renamed "The Orton-Dyslexia Society) has also produced many fine teachers of first grade phonics. These teachers take the same phonics principles that are needed for remedial reading students, and use them to **prevent** the development of reading problems. The principles they use are the same ones used in any systematic phonics program for first grade. The only fundamental difference between the Orton-inspired programs and other phonics programs is that Orton-inspired programs emphasize spelling practice very heavily, while others tend to neglect spelling as a way of strengthening reading ability.

Orderliness At School

Any school which teaches phonics from the beginning is likely to earn a reputation as a good school, because the children really learn to read and spell very well. Since their reading skills are good, the children have much less problem with study skills than other children. They do not need the dictionary so often as other children do, but when they do need it, they can master its use very readily. They see the usefulness of titles, tables of contents and indexes, and they can master graph-reading, and table-reading easily. Most of all, they can understand the textbooks used in the upper grades, and they can learn to express themselves effectively in writing assignments.

As a result, school is more interesting for them than it is for children with reading disabilities. Furthermore, the schoolwork they need to do, and the recreational reading they can do, absorb a good deal of the children's natural energy. This means that the children are fairly orderly in the classroom, because they get some advantage by paying attention and doing the assigned exercises. Discipline is usually much less of a problem in these circumstances than it is when many of the children are reading below grade level. So the school gets a good reputation for orderliness, as well as having a good academic reputation.

On the other hand, in schools where word-memorization is emphasized, many of the children soon realize that they are not learning to read. For any child in our society, this is a very frightening realization. Some react by withdrawing, some by acting out their frustration, and others by becoming class clowns to distract attention from their failures. This is one of the chief sources of discipline problems in these classrooms.

Parents who can afford it often transfer a child with reading problems from such a school to one with a better reputation for discipline and academic success. If your school is using a phonics approach effectively, your school may be the one such parents will choose. Each year, a few children will transfer to your school, entering second or third grade, the upper elementary grades, or any one of your high school classes, if your school goes beyond the elementary level.

Some of these transfer pupils will be entering your school because they could read a lot better than most of the children at their former school, and they have always been bored with schoolwork which was too easy for them. Such children may receive a shock when they find out that they are not, after all, the smartest children in the whole world. But after a reasonable period of adjustment, they can usually fit in quite well.

But many of the transfer pupils will be children with a very low reading level, children who cannot possibly keep up with the work your own pupils can easily do. These children cannot be expected, to "catch on" to reading without special help. Almost always, their reading level is low because they know nothing about phonics except what they have figured out for themselves. What they have figured out usually involves a certain amount of accurate understanding of the one-letter consonant sounds, a few gross misconceptions about other consonant sounds, and a hodge-podge of bizarre ideas about vowel sounds. Most important, they have no realization that it is either possible or permissible to sound words out by their letter-sounds, and no notion of how to go about blending letter-sounds in order to sound out.

These children need special tutoring in phonics, or special classes in phonics if there are two or more of them in a given grade at your school. At different ages, these remedial pupils need slightly different types of handling, because children go through distinct developmental changes in their attitudes about their reading difficulties.

If you are in a position of having to deal with remedial students, you may have special questions about how to help them. Appendix C presents a few guidelines to help you plan suitable work for these pupils. In addition, you will find many specific comments in the body of the book, highlighting the details which present special problems for remedial students.

Conclusion

To sum up, the schools have for many years been teaching reading by way of word-memorization first, instead of phonics first. One of their major reasons for preferring word-memorization is the erroneous impression that spelling irregularities in English make it too difficult for children to learn reading by a phonics method. But as we have seen, research shows that the irregularities are not so numerous if we take account of the regular letter and letter-combination sounds, and the regular letter-interactions.

Furthermore, research comparing word memorization classrooms with phonics classrooms shows that the children taught with phonics first read better than the others. Finally, detailed medical research with persons who have dyslexic symptoms shows that most of them can learn to read perfectly well through remedial lessons based on phonics.

This book is designed to help teachers who are teaching phonics understand how the letter-sound system of English works, and how to evaluate the importance of each phonic element as it crops up in the phonics textbook they are using. It is hoped that the book will help teachers understand a subject which was neglected at the time of their training. For only the teacher who understands a subject well can really do a good job of getting that subject across to the children.

Letter Names and Letter Sounds

An alphabet letter has two aspects: It has a **name**, and it has a **sound**. The **name** is what we call the letter when we talk about it. The **sound** is what the letter stands for, and the phrase letter-sound implies not only the sound the letter represents, but also the mouth position and vocal effort that are used in pronouncing that sound.

It might seem as though these statements are too obvious to be worth mentioning. Unfortunately, confusion between letter-names and letter-sounds can easily arise in the minds of children learning to read. Such confusion is very common among remedial students.

A major source of this confusion is the fact that the long sounds of the vowels are the **same** as the vowel letter-names. Thus, when you say the word **he**, you pronounce the **sound** of H, and then you blend that **sound** to the **name** of E. When you say the word **so**, you blend the **sound** of S to the **name** of O. When beginning or remedial readers know how to spell **he** or **so**, they can have trouble understanding why one cannot spell **tar** as "tr," putting down T for the T sound and R for the rest of the sound in the word. They will likewise use "mlt" for **melt**, using M for the first sound, T for the last sound and L for the middle sound.

With remedial students, who have only the vaguest ideas about letter-sounds, this confusion can be deep-seated and persistent. For them a great deal of work may be required to overcome this sort of confusion. With children just beginning to learn reading, it is important for the teacher to recognize the source of this kind of confusion whenever it comes up. Then the teacher can help the child sort out letter-names and letter-sounds and prevent the confusions between them from developing into learning problems.

Vowels and Consonants

There are two kinds of speech sounds — vowel sounds and consonant sounds. Words are spoken by combining these two different kinds of sounds in varied patterns. The vowel sounds are pronounced by opening the mouth in different ways. They allow the voice to come out. The consonant sounds are pronounced by closing the mouth in different ways. They restrict the voice, or interrupt it completely. Consonants are co-sounders, that are pronounced along with the vowels. Vowels can be pronounced alone, or they can carry consonants along with them.

The vowel and consonant letters represent the vowel and consonant sounds. In an ideal alphabet, there would be one letter for each sound, and each letter would represent only one sound. The Latin alphabet was very nearly ideal when it was fitted to the Latin language of ancient Rome.

It is the Latin alphabet that is used for writing Modern English. However, this ancient alphabet is not ideal for our modern purposes. The Latin alphabet has only six vowel letters (A, E, I, O, U, Y), whereas English has sixteen vowel sounds. And the Latin alphabet has only twenty-one consonant letters, while English has twenty-five consonant sounds, counting Y as a consonant, also. (Some linguists count even more different sounds.)

This alphabet must therefore be stretched extensively to fit the English language. We do this by using letter combinations like OY and CH for the extra vowel and consonant sounds. In this book, such letter combinations are called vowel or consonant **teams**. (See "Vowel Teams," p. 35 and "Consonant Teams," p. 51.) By using teams, and by constructing syllables in special ways, we make the old Latin alphabet represent all the speech sounds of Modern English. (See "Syllables, Stress and Word Structure," Appendix B, p. 299.)

Two Styles of Spelling

As has been mentioned elsewhere in this book, Modern English incorporates two subtly different styles of spelling. This results from the way in which Modern English became a written language.

We borrowed the Latin alphabet for writing English because Latin was still an active, spoken language for educated Englishmen when people first began wanting to write extensively in Modern English. Since all educated Englishmen read, wrote and spoke Latin, many of the Latin words had come into active use in spoken English, as well. We continued to spell most of these words according to the standard Latin spelling patterns. For many other Latin words, we used spelling patterns that the words had picked up as they gradually migrated from Italy, through France, into England.

Most of the borrowed Latin words were connected with cities, government, law, art, philosophy, science, commerce and the military. But the words of home, childhood, farm, forest and seafaring continued to be the native English words. These had come down to us from Old High German, through half-a-dozen Old English dialects. For these words a whole new spelling system was invented, with spelling patterns which differ from those of the Latin words.

We thus have two different styles of spelling in Modern English, the native English style, which applies to words of German origin, and the Latin style, which applies to words which came to us directly from Latin, or by way of its daughter languages, Italian and French.

The native English style of spelling affects all of our one-syllable words, regardless of origin. It also affects the vast majority of the two-syllable words which occur in first and second grade school materials. This is the style of spelling that children study when they learn to read with phonics. It is only in the later grades that children begin to encounter large numbers of words affected by the Latin style of spelling.

The differences between the two styles, and pointers to help the reader or speller know which style governs any given word, are fully dealt with in Appendix B, p. 299.

Syllables

A **syllable** is a word-part. It is composed of a vowel **sound** and all consonant **sounds** that are pronounced with that vowel. Most people find it quite easy to tell how many syllables there are in a spoken word. You simply say the word slowly, and notice how many "bites" it seems to have.

Most children learn to count syllables quite easily, and most remedial students, too, can count spoken syllables. Many remedial students can also tell you that "a syllable is a part of a word containing a vowel sound." This is the definition which is usually taught in school.

Superficially, this seems like a perfectly good re-statement of the definition given above. But it turns out that most remedial students have interpreted this definition to mean that **syllable** is just a fancier word for **vowel**. When they have read a word like **cold** correctly, and said that it has one syllable, and you ask them to pronounce that syllable, they will answer by pronouncing the O alone.

Of course, there are syllables which are composed of a vowel only, like the first syllable of **o**-cean. There do not happen to be any consonants to pronounce with the O of **ocean**. But there is an N sound to pronounce with the O of **no**-tion, three consonant sounds to pronounce with the O of **cold**, and five to pronounce with the O of **scolds.**

Because of the way letter-interactions work in English spelling, it is important for students to understand clearly that a syllable is a vowel sound **and** whatever consonants are pronounced with it. They also need to understand the ways in which spoken words break up into different syllables when they contain more than one vowel sound.

To understand this, it is necessary to be familiar with another aspect of syllables—that most of them **begin** with consonant sounds. There are, of course, some one-syllable words that begin with vowels. But these tend to be confined to a few of the pronouns, like **I, us** and **our**; the conjunctions **and** and **or**; exclamations like **ah, oh** and **aha**; and about a third of the prepositions, like **in**, **out**, **of**, **under**, **after**. But the words which express main ideas, the nouns, verbs, adjectives and adverbs usually begin with consonants, as in **house**, **run**, **brown** and **very**. Only a very few of these begin with vowels, as in **art**, **eat**, **itch**, **old** and **use**.

The main-idea words, of course, form the overwhelming bulk of the vocabulary of any language. The tendency for these words to begin with consonants is general throughout the Latin and Germanic languages from which English comes. If the longer main-idea words begin with vowels, it is usually because they are composed of a preposition beginning with a vowel prefixed to another word, as in **in**side, **out**put, **under**take and **after**thought.

In English, most of the main-idea words which begin with vowels have prefixes which go back to the Latin prepositions which began with vowels. Examples are **ad**jective, **e**ject, **in**ject, **ob**ject and **inter**jection.

When one turns from the first syllable of a longer word to the later syllables, the fact that most syllables begin with consonants has important consequences. Consider the word **conductor**. This word involves the prefix **con-**, the root **duct**, and the suffix **-or**. This suffix begins with a vowel. But it is not a syllable in its own right. It becomes a syllable by borrowing a consonant from the end of the root. We do not say con-**duct**-or. Instead, we say con-duc-**tor**, pronouncing the T from **duct** with the **or** of the suffix.

Even more striking examples of this phenomenon can be found in words where the suffix begins with I followed by another vowel, suffixes like **-ion** and **-ial**. In **pro-duc-tion**, the T from **duct** goes off with the **-ion**, and is converted in the process into an SH sound. The same thing happens to the T from **part** when **-ial** is added to make **par-tial**. If these T's were not being removed from the root and pronounced with the suffix, they would not be so profoundly affected by the suffix.

Most of our suffixes, both the native English suffixes and the Latin ones, begin with vowels. They routinely become syllables by removing the consonant from the end of the word to which they are added, forming a final syllable beginning with a consonant. An understanding of this can be very helpful to teachers who are trying to teach the consonant-doubling rule, whereby the P's must be doubled in words like **hop-ping**, and left single in words like **ho-ping** and **jum-ping**.

The above analysis reflects the facts about how we **pronounce** words and the syllables they contain. It does not reflect the system of syllable division which is employed in dictionaries. For an explanation of the dictionary system, see Appendix A, "Dictionary Division of Syllables," p. 297.

Root Words and Longer Words

The **root** of a word is the syllable which supplies the word's basic meaning. When a word has only one syllable, that syllable is a **root word**. Root words can be lengthened by the addition of various affixes. **Affixes** are word-parts added before or after the root to supply alterations to the basic meaning. When affixes are added before the root word, they are called **prefixes**, as in **un**lock and **re**lock. When affixes are added after the root, they are called **suffixes**, as in lock**s**, lock**ed**, lock**ing**, lock**er** and lock**et**.

On the Latin side of English, there are many roots which cannot stand alone as separate words. An example is the root **-ject-**, which is a form of the Latin word for **throw**. Although these Latin roots are unfamiliar as independent words, they are very familiar to modern speakers as parts of long words. They can take prefixes, just as the simple root words can, as in **e**ject, **in**ject, **ob**ject, **pro**ject, **re**ject and **sub**ject. And these words can take suffixes, as in object**s**, object**ing**, object**ed**, object**ive** and object**ion**.

Prefixes change the meaning of a root in a specific way. Thus, when you **un**lock a door, you reverse the proces of locking it. When you **re**lock the door, you lock it all over again. When you **e**ject something, you throw it **out**; when you **in**ject medicine, you throw it into the patient; when you **ob**ject to something, you throw up barriers **around** it; when you **pro**ject a plan, you throw it **forth** into the future; when you **re**ject something, you throw it **back** at the giver; and when you **sub**ject something to study, you throw it **under** the attention of the student.

Suffixes, on the other hand change the **form** of the word, either to make it conform to the grammatical requirements of sentences, or else to change it to a different part of speech. An example is the suffix **-ed**, which forms the past tense of the verb. Most of our past tenses are formed with **-ed.** However, we also have many past tense forms which are produced by changing the vowel of the root word, instead of by adding a suffix, as in run/ran, hide/hid, ride/rode, sleep/slept, mean/meant and sing/sang.

The suffix **-ed** is a native English suffix. Others are **-s**, **-es**, **-ing**, **-er**, **-est**, **-th** and **-eth**. The suffixes **-s** and **-es** form the plurals of nouns, or the third person, present tense of the verb, as in cat**s**, dish**es**, jump**s** or fix**es**. The suffix **-ing** indicates action in progress, as in "is jump**ing**" or "were fix**ing**." The suffixes **-er** and **-est** form the comparative and superlative of adjectives, as in bigg**er** and bigg**est**. The suffixes **-th** and **-eth** change numerals from cardinal to ordinal, as in six/six**th** and sixty/sixti**eth**. These are all essentially grammatical arrangements.

But **-th** can also change an adjective into a noun, as in wide/wid**th**, long/leng**th** and deep/dep**th**. In grow**th**, **-th** changes a verb into a noun. Indeed, most suffixes in Modern English change the part of speech instead of handling basically grammatical changes. For example, although **-en** often forms a past participle, as in hidd**en**, ridd**en** or wov**en**, it can also change an adjective into a verb, as in wid**en**, "to make wide;" sharp**en**, "to make sharp;" and gladd**en**, "to make glad." And **-er** can change a verb into a noun for the agent of the action, as in dust/dust**er**, camp/camp**er**.

The suffixes illustrated above are native English suffixes. The Latin suffixes always make changes in the part of speech. Thus, **reflect** is a verb. Reflect**or** is the agent of that action, reflect**ive** is the adjective form of the word, and reflect**ion** is the noun meaning "the process of reflecting."

An understanding of roots, prefixes and suffixes and how they interact can be very helpful to children in the later grades who are trying to perfect their spelling skills. This understanding can also contribute very substantially to vocabulary-building.

The details of how roots, prefixes and suffixes work are supplied in Appendix B, "Syllables, Stress and Word Structure," p. 299.

Vowel Sounds and Vowel Letters

English employs sixteen different vowel sounds, all of which must be spelled with the vowel letters A, E, I / Y,* O and U. We stretch these few vowel letters by using special spellings for the five short vowel sounds, the five long vowel sounds, and the six special vowel sounds that are peculiar to Modern English.

1. We show that a vowel sound is short by putting a single vowel letter in the middle of the syllable, as in

   bat, **bet**, **bit**, **gym**,* **got**, **but**

2. We have three different ways of showing that a vowel sound is long:

   a. By putting a single vowel letter at the end of its own syllable, as in

      pa-per, **e**-ven, **ti**-ger, **ty**-rant,* **lo**-cal, **stu**-dent

   b. By using the pattern vowel-consonant-silent-E, as in

      tape, **these**, **time**, **type**,* **tone**, **tube**

   c. By using a variety of letter teams (two or more letters representing a single speech sound), as in

      Long A: **ray**, **rain**, **they**, **their**
      Long E: **meet**, **meat**, **chief**, **movie**, **chimney**
      Long I: **tie**, **night**
      Long O: **show**, **toe**, **boat**, **soul**,
      Long U: **few**, **due**, **fruit**, **feudal**

3. We represent the six special vowel sounds by using special letter teams (two or more letters for a single speech sound), as in

   a. **saw**, **cause**
   b. **boy**, **boil**
   c. **cow**, **shout**
   d. **boot**
   e. **foot**
   f. **her**, **sir**, **myrrh**,* **fur**

---

* Notice that Y within the word spells the same sound as I in the same position.

This is the basic pattern of our spelling system. For historical reasons, however, there are many variations on this system. The details of these variations are presented on the individual vowel pages. In addition, before the individual pages for each vowel letter, there is a summary of the ways in which that letter is used.

"Long" and "Short"

What is "long" about a long vowel sound; and what is "short" about a short vowel sound? These terms, **long** and **short**, are not arbitrary labels for the contrasting sounds of vowels spelled by the same letter. It can be helpful to understand what these terms really mean.

The following words **begin** with the five **short** vowel sounds:

apple, Eddie, Izzie, operate, upper

If you pronounce each short vowel sound separately, your mouth will make **only one movement** while producing each sound, and each one will leave your mouth open.

The following words **end** in the five **long** vowel sounds:

day, see, pie, toe, cue

If you pronounce each long vowel sound separately, your mouth will make **two movements** while producing each sound. For each one, your mouth will open to begin the sound, and then glide shut to end the sound. The sounds of long A, E and I all glide shut with a Y sound at the end; and long O and U both glide shut with a W sound at the end. Therefore, the long vowel sounds do not leave your mouth open.

A short vowel is "short" because it involves **only one** motion of the mouth—opening. A long vowel is "long" because it involves **two** motions of the mouth—opening, and then closing. The technical term for a two-part vowel sound of this kind is **diphthong**.

This contrast between the long and short vowel sounds is a fundamental element in the phonetic structure of the English language. It is linked to one of the basic characteristics of the language—that English words end with the mouth closed whenever possible. We do have a few words that end with the mouth open, as will be seen below. But the habit of closing the mouth at the end of every word is extremely strong among native speakers of English.

If the mouth must close at the end of every word, it follows that the short vowel sounds, which leave the mouth open, cannot be used at the ends of words. And the fact is that short vowels do not occur at the end in English. After a short vowel sound, we regularly use a consonant sound to close our mouths for us. This is the basis of the spelling rule that vowels are short **within** the syllable, as in **can**-dy. A vowel can be short only if it has a consonant or consonant blend coming along in the same word to close our mouths for us. This is an example of how letter-interactions work in English. (See Vowels and Consonants, p. 21.)

On the other hand, the long vowel sounds can and do come at the ends of words, because each one has a built-in mouth-closing glide at the end, the extra motion which makes it long. This is the basis of the spelling rule that vowels are long at the end of the syllable, as in **pa**-per.

Many of the one-syllable words which contain short vowels end in two different consonant sounds, as in

> ha**nd**, be**nt**, ri**sk**, po**nd**, du**st**

In pronouncing these words, the mouth begins in whatever closed position is indicated by the beginning consonant. The mouth then opens for the vowel sound, and closes for the first of the two final consonant sounds. The last consonant sound is then whispered, with a certain amount of deliberate effort, by careful speakers. If you pronounce the sample words slowly and distinctly, you can observe these events taking place.

One-syllable words which contain long vowel sounds and end in consonant sounds work in a similar way, as in

> ta**me**, fee**t**, li**ke**, boat, ru**de**

Here, the mouth begins in the closed position of the first consonant, opens for the first part of the long vowel sound, and closes with the second part of the long vowel sound. The final consonant sound is then added, and is pronounced distinctly by careful speakers. In the long-vowel words given here, it may not be easy to observe the closing of the mouth before the final consonant sound. But when the final sound is L or R, it is easier to observe that the consonant is added separately, almost as though it were a separate syllable, as in

> pile, file, tire, fire, hire

These words are pronounced almost as though they had two

syllables, as witness the fact that **pile** and **file** rhyme with the two-syllable words **di-al** and **tri-al**, while **hire** sounds exactly like **higher**. Indeed, when we add the suffix **-y** to **fire**, we spell the result as three syllables — **fi-er-y**.

This phenomenon is not quite so striking with the other long vowels, or with other final consonants. But notice how close the following pairs come to rhyming—detail/betrayal, care/mayor, dear/seer, enroll/bestowal, rule/jewel, cure/sewer, fine/lion, moon/ruin. These are not perfect as rhymes, but the significant point is that, without loss of meaning, the long vowels that are within syllables can be dragged out to rhyme perfectly with their two-syllable counterparts.

This has great significance for reading students of any age. When they are trying to decode a word that contains a long vowel sound and ends in a consonant sound, they must be warned to give the vowel its full length, and let it close the mouth, before trying to add the final consonant sound. This is the strategy that will bring them closest to the meaning of the target word. Once the word has been understood, of course, it can then be repeated with a more normal pronunciation. The student who hurries to the final consonant sound without giving the long vowel its full length is likely to sound **sail** like **sell**, **peel** like **pill**, **fire** like **far**, and so on. Such confusions often arise when students are first learning to sound out long vowel sounds.

In addition to the single vowel letters, all of which can be long or short, there is one vowel team which has both long and short sounds, the team OO. It is short in **foot**, and long in **boot**. Short OO is always followed by a consonant sound, while long OO can come at the end of the word, as in **too** and **zoo**. The long sound ends with a W sound. As with the other long vowel sounds, the student must give the long sound of OO its full length before adding a final consonant sound, as in **pool** and **tool**. Otherwise, **pool** may sound like **pull**. The words ending in **-ool** rhyme with **jewel** and **rule**.

We have two other teams that represent sounds which behave like long vowels because they are diphthongs. These two are OY and OW, as in **boy** and **how**. The sound of OY ends with a Y sound, and OW ends with a W sound. Again, students must be

careful to give these vowel sounds their full length to avoid confusion, especially before L and R sounds. These sounds occur
within such words as

boil, moist, point, howl, town, shout, proud, sour

Notice how well those ending in L and R rhyme with two-syllable
words—boil/royal, growl/vowel, sour/shower, hour/tower.

As was mentioned earlier, we do have a few sounds which are
short, and yet come at the ends of words. One of these is the
sound represented by the team AW, as in **jaw**. This is a vowel
sound which opens the mouth with one motion, and leaves it open.
Perhaps it is because this goes against the grain for English
speakers that in some regions an R is used to close the mouth
when a word ends in this sound. In these regions, there is much
confusion of pairs like saw/sore, raw/roar, law/lore, etc.

Another short vowel sound which can come at the end of the
word is the broad sound of A, as in **fa la la**. This sound of A is
equivalent phonetically to the short sound of O as in **hot**. There
are only a few one-syllable words that end in this sound, and these
are not words of the usual sort. Instead, they are imitations of en-
vironmental sounds of music, laughter, and infant babbling.
Perhaps as a result of this, there does not seem to be any tendency
to add R sounds to these words.

But we also have a great many words in which A is a suffix and
is unstressed, as in

soda, tuna, idea, pneumonia, Anna, and Cuba

Like so many unstressed vowel sounds, these A's take on the
sound of an unstressed short U. Of all our vowel sounds, this one
opens the mouth the least, so it should not be too much of a problem as a final sound. Nevertheless, the same regions which pronounce **saw** like **sore** pronounce **Cuba** like **Cuber**.

Finally, we have the sound of the suffix **-y**, as in **happy**, which
many dictionaries identify as a short I sound. However, in many
regions, this suffix is pronounced with an unstressed long E sound.
Indeed, I myself have heard the short I version of **-y** only as one
element of a marked Southern accent. Since the standard sound
of **-y** seems to be long E, I cannot see it as a wide-spread exception to the general habit of closing the mouth at the end of the word.

Vowel Teams

As has been seen under "Vowel Sounds and Vowel Letters," p. 29, English uses a variety of vowel letter-combinations for its five long vowel sounds and for its six special vowel sounds. We even use one for short E.

There are historical reasons for this variety of spellings. But the net result is that students must master this variety, and the task can be confusing. Since there is no avoiding it, teachers must do their best to make the task as simple and straightforward as possible.

The vowel letter-combinations of English are as follows:

1. For short E
    EA as in h**ea**d

2. For the long vowel sounds
    Long A - AY, AI, EY and EI, as in p**ay** p**ai**n, th**ey** and th**ei**r
    Long E - EA, EE and IE, as in m**ea**t, m**ee**t, chi**e**f and mov**ie**
    Long I -IE and IGH, as in p**ie** and n**igh**t
    Long O - OW, OA and OE, as in sh**ow**, b**oa**t and t**oe**
    Long U - EW, EU, UE and UI, as in f**ew**, E**u**rope, d**ue** and fr**ui**t

3. For the special English vowel sounds
    AW and AU, as in j**aw** and p**au**se
    OY and OI, as in b**oy** and b**oi**l
    OW and OU, as in c**ow** and sh**ou**t
    OO as in b**oo**t
    OO as in f**oo**t
    ER, IR, UR and EAR- as in h**er**, s**ir**, f**ur** and h**ear**d

At the Fortune Society, where the information and ideas in this book were tested for ten years, we use the term **letter team** for any letter-combination which stands for a single speech sound. If the combination stands for a vowel sound, we call it a **vowel team**, even if there are consonant letters in the combination, as in IGH, one of the teams for long I. All of the above letter combinations are **vowel teams**.

The term **vowel team** is important because many people are under the erroneous impression that whenever two vowels come together in a word, the first vowel is long and the second one is silent. An examination of the teams listed above shows how misleading this rule is.

In the first place, the rule does not give any hint that Y, W, R or GH can be parts of vowel letter-combinations. Thus, it ignores the vowel teams AY, EY, OY, AW, EW, OW, ER, IR, UR, EAR- and IGH, eleven of our twenty-five standard vowel teams. If we go along with the rule, ignore these eleven, and consider only the remaining fourteen, it turns out that the rule is really useful only for the following six teams:

AI, EE, OA, OE, UE and UI, as in

r**ai**n, m**ee**t, b**oa**t, t**oe**, d**ue** and fr**ui**t

At first glance, the rule seems to be useful for EA. But, in reality, it holds true only for two-thirds of the EA words, as in m**ea**t. In most of the remaining third, the E is short instead of long, as in h**ea**d; and in the rest it is part of the EAR- team, and sounds like ER, as in h**ear**d.

For the team IE, the rule is true less than one-tenth of the time. In a very small number of words like p**ie**, the I is long and the E is silent. But in most words, the E is long and the I is silent, as in ch**ie**f and mov**ie**.

The rule is always false for the following six teams:

AU, EI, EU, OI, OO and OU, as in
p**au**se, th**ei**r, **Eu**rope, b**oi**l, b**oo**t, f**oo**t and sh**ou**t

The following nine pairs of vowel letters can also appear together in English words:

AE, AO, EO, IA, IO, IU, UA, UO and UU as in

pha-**e**ton, cha-**o**tic, ge-**o**graphy, gi-**a**nt, radi-**a**te, bi-**o**logy, radi-**o**, tri-**u**mph, radi-**u**m, gradu-**a**te, continu-**ou**s, continu-**u**m

In all of these words, the two vowels are in different syllables, and the second one has the sound required by the syllable to which it belongs. In most of these examples, the first vowel is indeed long, but that is because it is at the end of its own syllable. When the first of the two vowels is I, however, it is long only in the root syllable of a word. If the I is farther along in the word, it has a long E sound, like **-y** as a suffix. Compare Y and I in fu**ry** and fur**i**ous.

Clearly, the rule that when two vowels appear together, the first is long and the second silent, is a very unreliable rule. This unreliability can cause great confusion for remedial students. It often leads such students to read **boot** as "boat," **cause** as "case," or **boil** as "bowl." Even first-graders in schools where reading is taught by a phonics-first approach can exhibit such confusions. Many of them pick the rule up from parents who learned it in school and passed it on when the children first began asking questions about letters and sounds.

This rule is so widely known for three reasons. First, it holds true for enough of the most common words so that it is very learnable. Second, aside from the simplest consonant sounds, it is almost the only "phonics" which is taught in schools which emphasize word-memorization. And third, it is often taught even in schools which use otherwise excellent phonics programs. Indeed the flaws in this rule supply the chief arguments for those who maintain that phonics should not be taught first. And at the same time these flaws shake the confidence of those who are just beginning to believe that phonics should be more strongly emphasized.

As was mentioned earlier, the great variety of vowel teams that we do have in English makes the mastery of the vowels confusing to begin with. Compounding the confusion by invoking such an unreliable rule is hardly the way to ease the task.

As a matter of fact, however, there **are** patterns which can be highlighted to bring order into the apparent chaos of the vowel letter-combinations. In teaching these patterns, the first step is to establish the term **team** for any combination of letters which is normally used to represent a single speech sound. Then explain to the children that they need to learn to **see** each team as a **unit**, and to learn the sound or sounds for each one just as well as they know the sounds for single letters, like T or C.

It is also helpful for the teacher to realize that letter teams occur chiefly in the native English style of spelling. Vowel teams do crop up occasionally in the Latin style of spelling, as in del**ay**, ma**in**tain, obey, surveillance, appeal, esteem, relief, approach, pneumonia, royal, rejoice, allow, propound, determine, circus and purpose. But in the Latin style of spelling an apparent vowel team often breaks up, and the two vowels are in separate syllables, as in mosa-ic, re-inforce, re-ality, pre-emptive, di-et, conveni-ent, co-alesce, po-etic, du-et, ru-in, co-incidence and co-operate.

The next step is to work with the two teams where both letters are the same, EE and OO, as in

>   see, meet, too, boot, and foot

These two teams are very easy for children and remedial students to master, if they are taught **as teams**. Students must, of course, learn two sounds for OO.

The next step is to emphasize that for most of the vowel teams, the position the team has in the word is very important. A great deal depends on whether the team is **in the middle** of the root word, like AI in pain, or whether it represents the **last sound** in the word, like AY in pay. With this in mind, the remaining teams can be considered in groups classified according to the **last letter** of the team, as follows:

1. Teams ending in A — EA and OA, as in

>   sea, meat, head and boat

   EA and OA are teams for long E and long O. OA is for long O in the middle of the root word. EA is for long E either in the middle of the root word or at the end. When EA is in the middle of the word, it can also represent short E. But quite a few of the words which have EA as short E are longer forms of root words where EA is long, as in mean/meant, leap/leapt, heal/healthy, clean/cleanser.

2. Teams ending in E — IE, OE, and UE, as in

>   pie, chief, movie, toe and due

   When these teams come at the end of the **root** word, they stand for long I, O or U. In such words, they can be considered as special cases of the long-vowel spelling pattern, vowel-consonant-silent-E. **Pie** works like **pipe** with the second P omitted. **Toe** works like **tone** with the N omitted. **Due** works like **duke** with the K omitted.

In a word like chief, however, since the E is not final, this parallel is not valid. IE in the middle of the root is a team for long E.

In a word like movie, the IE is not at the end of the **root** word. Here, the root word is **move**, and the -ie is a suffix which works like the suffix -y, as in baby. For the behavior of IE in the suffixes -ies and -ied, see p. 161.

3. Teams ending in I or Y — AI, AY, EI, EY, OI, OY, as in

   pain, pay, their, they, boil, boy

These six teams involve three complementary pairs, AI/AY, EI/EY and OI/OY. In each pair, the team ending in I is for the **middle** of the root word, while the team ending in Y is for the **end** of the root.

The AI/AY and EI/EY pairs both represent the long A sound. This sound is termed **long** because two motions of the mouth are needed to pronounce it. (See " 'Long' and 'Short,' " p. 31.) Long A is pronounced by opening the mouth and letting it glide shut with a sound like the consonant Y. OY, as in boy, is a special English vowel sound. This, too, is pronounced with two motions of the mouth—first opening, and then gliding shut with a Y sound. It therefore makes phonetic sense to have teams ending in Y for all three of these pairs. When suffixes beginning with vowels are added to words containing these teams, the Y takes on a quite marked consonant sound, as it furnishes a consonant sound to begin the last syllable: player, playing, conveyor, obeying, royal, toying.

But it is a convention of English spelling that the letter Y is not used as a vowel letter inside the word except in Greek spellings like gym, type and typhoid. If a **final** Y spelling moves inside the word, it must change from Y to I: cry/cried, carry/carried, happy/happily. The AI, EI and OI versions of these teams are simply examples of this rule in operation.

4. Teams ending in O. The team OO, which was dealt with above, is the only team ending in O.

5. Teams ending in U or W—AU, AW, EU, EW, OU, and OW, as in

   pause, paw, feud, few, shoulder, show, proud and prow.

Here again, as with teams ending in I or Y, we have pairs of complementary teams. Those ending in U are for the **middle** of the root word, and those ending in W are for the **end** of the root. This makes sense if you stop and listen closely to the name of the letter W—"double U." If you take W as a **double** U and the letter U itself as a **single** U, you can appreciate the equivalence of these two letters. However, the situation with these teams is not quite as clearcut as it is for those ending in I or Y.

In the first place, AU/AW stands for a special English vowel which is not a two-motion vowel. Instead, it is a **pure** vowel sound, which opens the mouth and leaves it open. This is uncomfortable for English speakers, with the result that in many regions an R sound is added to words ending in this sound. Then there can be much confusion between pairs of words like **saw** and **sore**, **paw** and **pour**, or **law** and **lore**.

The remaining teams in this group, however, represent long U, long O, and the special English vowel sound of **cow**. All of these are two-motion vowel sounds, and all of them end with a W sound. When suffixes beginning with vowels are added to these words, the W sound goes off with the suffix, furnishing a consonant sound to begin the last syllable, as in chewing, fewer, showing, plowing, avowal, shower and towel.

A peculiarity of the teams ending in W is that they often appear in the middle of a root word, especially before final N or final L, as in d**awn**, **crawl**, str**ewn**, **own**, b**owl**, d**own** and gr**owl**. AW can also appear before K, as in h**awk** and **awk**ward. And OW as in c**ow** can appear before D, as in cr**owd** and p**owd**er. But if there is a second consonant after the N, the W becomes U, as in j**aunt**, l**aunch**, p**ound** and c**ount**.

It should also be noticed that OW occurs fairly frequently with the long O sound as a suffix, as in pill**ow** and foll**ow**.

Finally, there is one more point to be noticed about the OU/OW teams. Although OW has two regular sounds, it is the most reliable vowel team in the language. OW appears in 253 words, about half of them with the long O sound, and the rest with the sound of **cow**. Of the 253 words, only one, the word knowledge, has OW with any other sound, and since the sound of the root word know echoes for us in the background of the word knowledge, we are hardly aware of this abnormality.

OU, on the other hand is the most unreliable of all our vowel teams. Almost all the other vowel teams have exceptional sounds in an occasional word, as in said, sew, great and choir. But although OU has its normal sound, as in shout, in 279 words, and in a few of the OUGH words, and its long O sound in 37 words, it also appears with other sounds in sizeable groups of words. It has the sound of OO, as in boot, in soup and 36 other words. Before R and a different consonant, it sounds like ER, as in journey. This involves 49 words. And it sounds like short U in young and 25 other root words, and also in the 350 adjectives formed by the suffix -ous, as in famous and tremendous.

6. Teams ending in R — ER, IR, UR and EAR-, as in

    her, sir, fur and heard

All four of these vowel teams represent the special English vowel sound of ER. EAR- represents this sound only when the R is followed by a different consonant letter, as in learn, pearl, early, hearse and earth.

All of the others can come at the end of the word, and -er is very heavily used as a suffix. They occur mainly in root words before other consonants, as in curb, bird, serf, urge, clerk, girl, firm, turn, chirp, nurse, hurt, curve, person and circus. (See "The Letter R," p. 216 and "Homonyms and Other Optional Spellings," p. 65.)

7. Teams ending in GH

The only real team ending in GH is IGH as in night. IGH is a team for long I. It occasionally occurs at the end of the root word, as in high, but it occurs mainly in root words that end in T, as in light, sight, bright, slight, etc. Here the GH part of the team is the only indication of a long vowel sound.

One might argue that AIGH, EIGH and AUGH, as in straight, weigh, freight, caught, daughter, and a few other words should also be considered as teams. However, in these words, the

AI, EI and AU all have their normal sounds. The GH is merely a written relic of an obsolete consonant sound. Since the GH has no special effect on the vowel sounds, it seems overly fussy to identify these combinations as special vowel teams.

OUGH, however is a different matter. In most words containing OUGH, the GH itself is silent. But it indicates a variety of sounds for the OU teams.

Only 38 words contain this team. These words include the following 23: thr**ough**, where the team represents the long OO sound; b**ough**, d**ough**ty, dr**ough**t and sl**ough** (a marsh), where the OU has its normal sound as in sh**ou**t; th**ough**, d**ough**, bor**ough**, furl**ough** and thor**ough**, where the team has a long O sound; en**ough**, r**ough**, t**ough** and sl**ough** (what a snake does with its skin), where the team is for **-uff**; c**ough**, where it represents **-auf**; and **ough**t, b**ough**t, br**ough**t, f**ough**t, n**ough**t, s**ough**t, th**ough**t and wr**ough**t, where the team represents an AU sound. The remainder of the 38 OUGH words are longer forms of those already listed, like al**though**, **thorough**fare, **rough**en, **thought**less and over**wrought**.

OUGH thus represents six different sounds randomly scattered among 23 basic words. At the Fortune Society, we teach that OUGH is a team that should be seen as a unit. But we also teach that it is a **wild** team (like a **wild card** in a card game). We advise students not to try to learn any specific sound for OUGH, but to sound out the other letters in the word and let context suggest the appropriate sound for the OUGH.

The vagaries of OUGH are favorite grounds of complaint among people who believe that phonics is too complicated to be useful. But it is the experience of teachers who rely on phonics that OUGH creates very little problem. It occurs in so few words, and its variability makes it so noticeable, that children who know the regular phonics handle it easily.

The above analysis of English vowel teams does not, of course reflect the order in which the various teams should be taught. You should stick to the order of presentation reflected in the phonics materials you are using. Different programs present the teams in different orders. In general, they do the sensible thing, and bring in first the ones which appear most frequently in the vocabulary of children. But it is hoped that the analysis here will help teachers to integrate new teams with more familiar ones as the lessons go forward.

Silent Vowel Letters

Final Silent E

One of the devices used for stretching the Ancient Latin alphabet to fit Modern English is the use of final silent E. The letter E is regularly silent when it is the last letter in the word, and there is any vowel earlier in the word. Of course, if E is the last letter of the word, and there is no other vowel in the word, the E must sound, as in **be**, **he**, **me**, **she**, **the**, **we** and **ye**. But in longer words, instead of having any sound of its own, final E interacts with other letters in the word, giving the reader essential information about the affected letters. Both young children and remedial students understand this best if you explain that the silent E "has an important job to do," even though we don't pronounce the E at all.

Final silent E does a variety of "jobs," as follows:

1. "One-job E's"
    a. It makes the vowel before it long, as in

    ca**ke**, th**ese**, bi**ke**, ty**pe**, ro**pe**, tu**be**

    b. It makes a final C or G soft, as in

    chan**ce**, for**ce**, sau**ce**, hin**ge**, lar**ge**, gou**ge**

    c. It shows that a final S or Z sound is part of the root word, and is not the suffix **-s**, as in

    den**se**, pur**se**, hou**se**
    chee**se**, prai**se**, pau**se**
    bron**ze**, snee**ze**, oo**ze**

    (See "The Letter S," p. 222, and -ZE, p. 292.)

    d. It prevents V from being the last letter of the word (keeping the V from falling over?), as in

    ha**ve**, nati**ve**, twel**ve**, car**ve**, lea**ve**, groo**ve**

    e. It adds length to a word containing only one or two sounds, making the word look important enough to be a main-idea word, as in

    or**e**, ew**e**, aw**e**

(See "Very Short Words," p. 295.)

f. In the suffix **-le**, it makes the letter L behave like a vowel, as in

ap-p**le**, sta-p**le**, bun-d**le**, bu-g**le**

Notice that in the second syllable of each word the voice comes out with the L sound.

2. "Two-job E's"

In the following words, the final silent E is doing two "jobs" at the same time:

a. **pace**, **page**, **rice**, **huge** (making the first vowel long; making the C or G soft)

b. **base**, **rise**, **doze** (making the first vowel long; showing that the S or Z sound is part of the root)

c. b**rave**, d**ive**, dr**ove** (making the first vowel long; keeping the V from coming last)

d. **pie**, t**oe**, **due** (making the first vowel long; adding length to a very short word)

3. "No-job E's"

There are also a very few extremely common words in which final silent E is doing nothing at all. These are:

ar**e**, wer**e**, ther**e**, wher**e**, gon**e**

In **are** and **were**, the vowels are changed by R, just as if there were no E at the end. In **there**, **where**, and **gone**, the first vowel in each word is short instead of long.).

We also have a number of borrowed words, like **grille**, **horde**, **plaque**, and others, where final silent E is doing nothing in English. In the French, from which these words come, final silent E shows that the final consonant sound should be pronounced. In English, with our anxiety to get our mouths closed at the end of every word, we have no need of any special letter to tell us to pronounce the final consonant sound.

Silent U

The letter U is silent when it comes between G and E, I or Y, as in

> guess, plague, guide, guy

In words like these, the E, I, or Y would make the G soft if they were allowed to come right after the G. Then the G would sound like J. (See " 'Hard' and 'Soft' ", p. 50.) The U has no sound of its own, and only serves to keep the G hard.

Final silent E, with its various "jobs," and silent U acting to keep a G hard, are the only silent vowel letters in English. But many people believe that in any vowel letter-combination the first vowel is long and the second one is silent. This rule has very little validity. Its unreliability is discussed in detail under "Vowel Teams," p. 35. Here, it is only necessary to say that the unreliability of this rule means that it is best to discard the rule completely, and to teach children that the only silent vowel letters are the E's and U's mentioned above.

Consonant Sounds and Consonant Letters

English employs twenty-five different consonant sounds, but the Latin alphabet which we use contains only twenty-one consonant letters. Worse still, three of the Latin consonant letters duplicate the sounds of other letters. C duplicates the sounds of S or K, as in **cent** and **cat**; X duplicates the blended sounds of KS, as in **tax**; and Q before U duplicates the sound of K, as in **queen**. We stretch the available letters by using letter teams to represent consonant sounds which did not occur in Ancient Latin.

The consonant sounds and their ordinary spellings are as follows:

/b/*	as in **b**oy	/t/	as in **t**op
/d/	as in **d**og	/v/	as in **v**ine
/f/	as in **f**ire	/w/	as in **w**ing
/g/	as in **g**oat	/y/	as in **y**ard
/h/	as in **h**and	/z/	as in **z**ebra
/j/	as in **j**ump or **g**ym	/ch/	as in
/k/	as in **c**at or **k**ing		**ch**ildren
/l/	as in **l**eaf	/sh/	as in **sh**ip
/m/	as in **m**an	/th/	as in **th**is
/n/	as in **n**est	/th/	as in **th**ing
/p/	as in **p**ig	/wh/	as in **wh**en
/r/	as in **r**ing	/zh/	as in vi**s**ion
/s/	as in **s**it or **c**ent	/ng/	as in lo**ng**

These are the basic spellings of our consonant sounds. For reasons connected with language history, there are variations on these spellings. The details of these variations are presented in the individual consonant pages. The variations are most numerous for the letters C, G, H, L, P, R, S, T, W and Y. Before the individual ABC pages for each of these letters, there is a summary of the ways in which the letter is used.

---

* Slashes enclosing a small letter mean "the sound of" that letter.

Unvoiced, Voiced and Nasal Consonants

Consonant sounds are pronounced by closing the mouth and restricting the voice, or interrupting it completely. This is what makes them different from the vowel sounds, which are pronounced by opening the mouth and letting the voice come out freely. But a slight use of the voice does accompany some of the consonant sounds.

The consonant sounds differ among themselves according to the degree to which the voice is used in pronouncing them.

A consonant sound is **unvoiced** when the voice is not used at all in pronouncing the sound, and only the breath is used. Students get this idea best if they are told to **whisper** the consonant sound. The P sound is an example of an unvoiced consonant sound.

A consonant sound is **voiced** when the voice is used while pronouncing the sound. Students get this idea best if they are told to **grunt** lightly as they pronounce the sound. The B sound is an example of a voiced consonant sound.

A consonant sound is **nasal** when the mouth is held closed, and the voice carries the sound out through the nose. Students get this idea best if they are told to **hum** the consonant sound. The M sound is an example of a nasal consonant sound.

Notice that P, B and M all involve the same mouth position, with the lips pressed firmly together. By using this one mouth position, and making it unvoiced, voiced or nasal, we pronounce three distinctly different sounds, as in **pat**, **bat**, **mat**, or in **rip**, **rib**, **rim**.

The table of consonants on the opposite page shows which consonants have which type of sound.

Table of Consonants

Unvoiced	Voiced	Nasal
P	B	M
T	D	N
K	G	NG
F	V	
S	Z	
CH	J	
SH	ZH	
WH	W	
TH	TH	
(thing)	(this)	
H	R	
	L	
	Y	

It is sometimes helpful for students to understand these differences among consonant sounds, especially in connection with voiced and unvoiced TH, and in connection with L and R. The consonant sounds L and R are so heavily voiced in English that problems result, especially when these consonant sounds follow a vowel sound. (See "The Letter L," page 170, and "The Letter R," page 216.)

Hard and Soft C and G

The terms **hard** and **soft** apply to the letters C and G. When C is **soft** it represents the same sound that S represents. When G is **soft**, it represents the same sound that J represents. **Hard** C represents the same sound as K, and **hard** G represents the first sound in **goat**.

Both of these letters are soft before the letters E, I or Y, as in

ce**n**ter, ci**t**y, i**ce**, i**cy** and **ge**neral, **gi**ant, ca**ge**, ca**gy**

When C or G appears anywhere else, it is hard, as in

cat, **co**t, **cu**t, **cl**ap, **cr**ib, pa**ck**, fa**ct**, a**cc**ent, plasti**c**, **ga**s, **go**t, **gu**n, **gl**ass, **gr**ass, si**g**nal, ma**g**ma, bi**g**

These are examples of letter-interactions. The details of how C and G work are given in the summary for the letter C, page 89, and in the summary for the letter G, page 132, and on the individual pages for C and G.

The point to be made here is that C and G are the only letters which can be either **hard** or **soft**. This needs to be emphasized because many people confuse these terms with the terms **voiced** and **unvoiced**, especially in connection with the two sounds represented by TH.

TH is voiced in **th**is and unvoiced in **th**ing. (See Unvoiced, Voiced and Nasal Consonants, p. 48.) These two sounds are pronounced with the same mouth position. The difference between them depends on whether or not the voice is involved in the pronunciation. The difference has nothing to do with hardness or softness, and E, I and Y have no effect on how TH is pronounced.

The terms **hard** and **soft** need to be reserved strictly for C and G. Remedial students are often confused about these terms. Until this confusion is straightened out, they do not make much progress either with C or with G or with TH.

Consonant Teams

Modern English has 25 different consonant sounds, whereas the Ancient Latin alphabet which we use has only 21 consonant letters. In order to stretch this alphabet to fit the English language, we use a number of consonant letter teams for the extra consonant sounds. We also use a number of special teams for consonant sounds at the end of root words.

1. Teams for Special English Consonant Sounds

Children and remedial students must be warned that they cannot work out the special sounds of these teams by trying to blend the regular sounds of the two letters which are teamed up to take care of each special sound. Instead they must learn to see each team as a unit—two letters for a single sound. They also need to understand that they need to know these teams just as thoroughly as they know the sounds of single consonant letters, like T or J.

a. CH as in **ch**ur**ch**, s**ch**ool and ma**ch**ine

CH is a team for the special English consonant sound at the beginning and end of **ch**ur**ch**. This is the only way we have to represent this sound at the beginning or end of a native English root word.

CH can also have a K sound, as it does in s**ch**ool. This occurs in the Latin style of spelling. In such words, the CH is a Roman attempt to represent a Greek sound which was foreign to the Latin language. In borrowing words from the Greek, the Romans tried to maintain the Greek flavor by certain special spellings of this kind. In pronouncing this particular Greek sound, the closest the Romans could come was a K sound. These words still retain the K sound for CH in modern English. This has happened partly because so many of these CH's are blended with S, R, or L, as in **sch**edule, **chr**onic and **chl**orine. Since it is impossible for us to pronounce the normal sound of CH with these other consonants, we stick to the Roman sound for these CH's.

CH can also have an SH sound, as it does in machine. CH is the French team for our SH sound. CH has this sound in words which we have borrowed fairly recently from France. These words tend to deal with automobiles, high cuisine, and high fashion. Our retention of the French pronunciation of the CH's reflects the cultural leadership of France in these fields.

The fact that CH can have three different sounds can, of course, cause confusion. Children and remedial students should be taught to use the regular English sound of CH, and try the other possibilities only if the ordinary sound does not make sense.

b. GH as in straight

GH is a team which represented a special Germanic sound in Old English. In Modern English, this sound has entirely disappeared. (See "Silent Consonants," p. 60.)

c. -NG as in long

NG is a team for the special English consonant sound at the end of long. It also occurs at the end of the native English suffix -ing. This is the only way we have to represent this special English consonant sound. Because this sound occurs only at the end of the word, and English speakers are not very sharply aware of final consonant sounds, it can take students a certain amount of time to master -NG.

One source of confusion is that N alone represents this sound in words ending in -nk, as in bank. The regular sound of N is pronounced by laying the tip of the tongue up behind the front teeth and humming. -NG is pronounced by laying the front and back of the throat together and humming. But when we pronounce an N on the way to a K sound, the tongue is drawn back from the regular N position, and automatically takes on an -NG sound. This can pose a problem for children and remedial students unless the teacher helps them understand what is going on in the mouth in saying these words.

d. PH as in **ph**one

PH is a consonant team for the sound of F. Like CH for the K sound, this is a team the Romans used for a Greek sound which they could not quite pronounce. It occurs in words which the Romans borrowed from the Greeks, or in Roman roots recently incorporated into modern technical terms. Because PH seems like such a ridiculous way to spell F, and because the word **phone** is seen on every pay telephone booth, PH is very easy for students to master.

e. SH as in **sh**oe

SH is a team for the special English consonant sound at the beginning of **sh**oe and the end of fi**sh**. This is a sound the Romans did not have. However, the **-ci-**'s, **-ssi-**'s and **-ti-**'s in thousands of Latin words all took on this sound on entering Modern English. Examples are: politi**ci**an, mi**ssi**on and na**ti**on. SH itself is strictly for the beginnings and ends of native English root words. In the Latin style of spelling, SH occurs only in fa**sh**ion and cu**sh**ion.

The SH team is fairly easy for children to learn for reading and spelling, partly because the word **she** is so common. But the Latin words which use other letters for this sound can present a problem when children begin to encounter them in quantity in the later grades.

f. TH as in **th**is and **th**ing

TH is a team for two different native English consonant sounds. It is pronounced by sticking the tongue out slightly, and blowing across it. For TH as in **th**is, the voice is used with this pronunciation. For TH as in **th**ing, the voice is not involved. (See "Unvoiced, Voiced and Nasal Consonants," p. 48.)

Voiced TH occurs at the beginning of the pronouns **thou** and **they**, and all their forms; at the beginning of the demonstrative pronouns, **this**, **that**, **these**, **those**, **there**, **then**, etc.; and at the beginning of the definite article **the**. TH as in **this** is for **pointing** words (what else does demonstrative mean?), while TH as in **thing** is for main-idea words like **thumb**, **thank** and **thin**.

TH is also voiced **between** vowels in native English words like **mother, leather** and ba**the**. It is usually unvoiced at the end of the root, as in pa**th** and mou**th**.

In the Latin style of spelling, TH is always unvoiced, as in **th**eology, e**th**ics and ma**th**ematics. These Latin words contain TH's because the unvoiced TH was a Greek sound. Since this sound did not occur in Latin, the Romans pronounced it as T. However, on entering English, most of these Greek TH's went back to the original TH sound. **Thomas, Thames** and **thyme** are the only ones we pronounce with plain T.

g. WH as in **when** and **wheel**

WH is a team for the native English consonant sound which careful speakers pronounce at the beginning of **wh**en. It does not occur at the ends of words. WH is pronounced the same as W-, except that WH- is unvoiced, whereas W- is voiced. (See "Unvoiced, Voiced and Nasal Consonants," p. 48.)

This sound, however, is rapidly disappearing from Modern English speech. In most regions, it is pronounced the same as plain W-. In these regions only well-educated people use the special WH- sound. Young children can be taught to use it in the correct places, and parents usually want them to learn it, even if this pronunciation does not occur naturally in their own speech.

But the older remedial students have great difficulty with this sound if it is not already a natural part of their speech. If they try to use the correct WH- sound, they soon begin substituting it for **all** the W- sounds, saying such things as, "Tom **wh**as going out **wh**est **wh**ith his dad."

Fortunately, there is no real need to teach remedial students the correct sound of WH. They understand the WH- words perfectly well by sounding them out with plain W- sounds. This does, however, pose a spelling problem. They can master spelling with WH- if you teach them to use it only for question words (the interrogatives), and for words whose meanings are connected with whistling or whining noises. (See WH-, p. 273).

2. Teams for the End of the Word

In English spelling, there are a number of special letter combinations which are used when a consonant sound is the last sound of the **root** word, as follows:

-CK is for K at the end of the root, right after a **short** vowel sound

-DGE is for J at the end of the root, right after a **short** vowel sound

-FF is for F at the end of the root, right after a **short** vowel sound

-LL is for L at the end of the root, right after a **short** vowel sound

-SS is for S at the end of the root, right after a **short** vowel sound

-TCH is for CH at the end of the root, right after a **short** vowel sound

-ZZ is for Z at the end of the root, right after a **short** vowel sound

Examples of the words affected by these doublings are:

back, fu**dge**, sti**ff**, we**ll**, pa**ss**, sco**tch** and ja**zz**.

-K is for K at the end of the root after anything else.
-GE is for J at the end of the root after anything else.
-F is for F at the end of the root after anything else.
-L is for L at the end of the root after anything else.
-SE is for S or Z at the end of the root after anything else.
-CH is for CH at the end of the root after anything else.
-ZE is for Z at the end of the root after anything else.

Examples of words ending in these letters and teams are:

ris**k**, lea**k**, boo**k**; hin**ge**, pa**ge**, gou**ge**; gul**f**, loa**f**, roo**f**; cur**l**, fee**l**, too**l**; ten**se**, plea**se**, hou**se**, rou**se**; ben**ch**, rea**ch**, cou**ch**; bron**ze**, bree**ze**, gau**ze**

This list needs to include more words than the one above in order to show that the single letters and teams in the second list are used after **consonant** sounds, after **long vowel** sounds, and after **special English vowel** sounds, that is, after **anything else** except a short vowel sound.

First-graders learning to read with a phonics-first approach seem to be able to take all these variations in stride. They see words exhibiting these teams and single letters so often that they can read and spell them with little problem.

Remedial students, however, have been so confused about letters and sounds that the teams can be very difficult for them. They need to learn the rules which are given here. A useful mnemonic device is to identify the words that require consonant doublings as "**flask** words." The word **flask** ties up into one neat bundle the letters involved in the most frequently-used doublings: F, L, S, and K.

There are excellent reasons for the use of most of the final consonant doublings. Remedial students can master the teams more easily if these reasons are shared with them. See "The Letter C," p. 89; -FF, p. 131; "The Letter L," p. 170; and "The Letter S," p. 222.

In addition to general problems with these teams, remedial students are often very much confused between the teams CK and CH, because they are vaguely similar in appearance. The rules and reasons for the various consonant teams can help them sort out this confusion, also.

-VE as in bra**ve**, ha**ve**, twel**ve** and nati**ve**

The only other team that we have for a final sound is -VE. This team is used for the sound of V regardless of whether it comes at the end of the root or at the end of a suffix.

This team is another relic of Latin spelling. The Romans never used plain V at the end of the word, so neither do we. Linguists differ in their explanations of this phenomenon. It therefore seems foolish to pass on any of these explanations to children. Just the same, children want to know what the E is doing after a V, especially in words like ha**ve**, twel**ve** and nati**ve**, where the silent E is having no influence on the previous vowel. An effective answer is a joking one. The V, standing up on a sharp point is very tippy, and children enjoy the idea that the E is just there to keep the V from falling over. Remedial students also enjoy this explanation.

Consonant Blends

Blends of consonant sounds are a prominent feature of English speech. We have many places where two consonant **letters** coming together in a word represent a team, as in the combinations CH, SH and TH. (See "Consonant Letter Teams," p. 51.) We also have a number of consonant combinations where one of the letters is silent as in KN- and -MB. (See "Silent Consonants," p. 60.) But all other consonant letter combinations represent consonant **blends**.

These are combinations in which each letter retains its own sound. Consonant blends can occur either at the beginning or the end of a word, as in

> **bl**ack, **pr**oud, **sw**eet, re**st**, pai**nt**, he**lp**, bi**rd**, a**ct**, **spl**ash, wo**rld**

Most of the consonant blends involve two different sounds, but some of them involve three different sounds.

Young children who are learning to read by a phonics-first approach usually have little difficulty in sounding out the consonant blends, either for reading or for spelling. A little bit of modeling by the teacher is usually enough to help them get the idea of how to slip the blended consonant sounds together in an understandable pronunciation.

For remedial students, however, the blends can present a major problem because of confusions which developed in their earlier attempts to read. They tend to pronounce the two consonants of a blend at the beginning of a word too separately. Then an unwanted vowel sound slips in between the two consonant sounds, making the final pronunciation impossible to understand. With blends at the end of the word, they tend to ignore one of the sounds, often coming out with a word quite different from the one they are trying to read. (**Lap** for **lamp**; **men** for **mend**.)

When they have trouble with blends at the beginning of the word, they need a lot of modeling by the teacher, and a good deal of coaching to help them get the blends together. For blends at the end, they need practice in getting through the vowel part of the word, using the first consonant to close their mouths, and whispering the last one. Although there are many more different blends at the ends of words than at the beginning, all of them can be handled by this one strategy.

Blends at the beginning, however, are more troublesome. Among the ABC pages of this book, there are special pages for these blends. They will be found among the pages for B, C, D, F, G, P, Q, S and T.

Silent Consonants

Modern English employs a variety of silent consonants. Some of them take part in letter-interactions, and others are relics of obsolete pronunciations.

1. Letter-Interactions

   a. Internal Consonant Doubling

   When native English suffixes beginning with vowels are added to roots containing a short vowel followed by a single consonant letter, that letter is doubled in order to keep the first vowel short, as in ru**b**/ru**bb**ed, ma**d**/ma**dd**en, bi**g**/bi**gg**er, dru**m**/dru**mm**ing, fu**n**/fu**nn**y, ho**p**/ho**pp**ing, fa**t**/fa**tt**est.

   But in pronouncing these lengthened words, we do not pronounce the extra consonant. It is used only to show that the vowel of the root is short. The extra consonant letter is silent. To see how it sounds when we actually do pronounce a consonant twice, compare the following: dru**mm**ing/drum **m**ajor, ma**dd**en/mad **d**og, fa**tt**est/hat **t**rick. In a phrase, the first of two identical consonant sounds is essential to the meaning of the first word, while the second sound is essential to the meaning of the second word. We must therefore pronounce both in order to be understood. But in words lengthened by suffixes, the last consonant sound of the root is needed only once, while the extra consonant letter is there only to interact with the vowels and keep the first one short.

   When young children or remedial students are first learning to use doubled consonants in spelling, they often convince themselves that both of the doubled consonants are pronounced. This produces excellent spelling for a little while. But when the lessons move on to other matters, and the spotlight is no longer upon these words, the student, hearing only one P in **hopping**, will write only one P, producing **hoping** by mistake. It is best to dispel this confusion immediately, instead of allowing it to become well enough established to cause problems later.

The silent consonants involved in consonant doubling are by far the most frequently-occuring silent consonants in English words. There are a few others, however, which take part in letter-interactions.

b. Silent L

In one-syllbale words containing a single vowel letter followed by one or two consonant letters, the vowel is usually short, as in pan or pant. But when a single A or O is followed by -LL, the short sound of the A is changed to an AW sound, as in **ball**; and the short sound of O is changed to a long O sound, as in **roll**. After A or O, a single L followed by a different consonant has the same effect, as in b**ald**, s**alt** or c**old**, c**olt**. But if the last letter is K or M, the L goes silent, as in talk, calm, and folks. Nevertheless, the L is still interacting with the vowel and changing its sound. In such words, the silent L is the only indicator that the vowel has a special sound.

c. Silent T

We have silent T's in words like castle, fasten and soften. These are words where the root ends in **-st** before the suffix **-le**, or words where the root ends in **-st** or **-ft** before the suffix **-en**.

In many of these words, the root does not exist in Modern English as an independent word. For example, the root of **hustle** is **hust-**, which means nothing to us by itself. Sometimes the root exists as an independent word, like **cast**, but that word seems to have no relation to the **-le** form, **castle**. But whenever the root does exist as an independent word, the T has its normal sound until the **-le** is added, as in nest/nestle. Roots which take **-en** are usually independent words, as in soft/soften, fast/fasten, Christ/christen or haste/hasten.

In the longer forms, even though the T is silent, it is interacting with the vowels to show that the first vowel is short.

2. Obsolete Consonant Sounds

In the following consonant combinations, one letter has its

normal sound, while the other is silent. These are not examples of letter-interactions. Instead, the silent member of each combination is a relic of a sound which was pronounced in earlier times.

a. KN- as in **kn**ife

K is always silent before N at the beginning of a root word. (See KN-, p. 169.) In related German words, the K is still pronounced to this day. Most of these words have meanings referring to shapes like knees or knuckles, or to things done by knees or knuckles.

b. WR- as in **wr**ite

W is always silent before R at the beginning of a root word. (See WR-, p. 276.) All of these words have meanings related to twisting, as in **wring**, **wrestle** or **wry**. Even **writing** is a process of making **twisty** lines.

c. GN as in **gn**at, rei**gn**, and si**gn**

G is silent before N either at the beginning or end of the word. Where the root ends in GN, and native English suffixes are added, the G remains silent. Before Latin suffixes, however, the G takes on its regular sound, and makes the first vowel short, as in **sig**-nal and inter-**reg**-num. (See GN, p. 142.)

d. MB and MN as in la**mb** and autu**mn**

After M, B and N are silent at the end of the root word. But in longer forms, the B or N often has its usual sound, as in cru**mb**/crum-**b**le, conde**mn**/condem-**n**ation. (See MB, MN, p. 178.)

e. GH as in strai**gh**t

Old English employed a German consonant sound which we no longer use. It can be heard at the end of the name of the composer, Johann Sebastian Ba**ch**. In Old English, this sound was represented by the consonant team GH. But on the way into modern English, this sound completely disappeared, and the vowels before it became long, regardless of what sounds they had had earlier. Examples are li**gh**t, ei**gh**t and thou**gh**. The confusions of this change, however, are reflected in the variety of vowel sounds which we now have for OUGH. There was one Old English dialect in which these GH's became F's instead of disappearing entirely. A few survivals of this dialect remain in Modern English, as in lau**gh** and enou**gh**, where the vowels came out with short vowel sounds.

3. Individual Silent Consonants

   a. H as in **h**our, ex**h**ibition, **gh**etto, r**h**eumatism and o**h**

H at the beginning of the syllable usually represents the first sound in **h**at. But in four root words borrowed from the French, H is silent at the beginning. These four words are **h**our, **h**onor, **h**erb and **h**eir. We also have quite a group of other words based on these four words like **hourly**, **dishonesty**, **herbal** and **heiress**, where the H is also silent.

We also have a few silent H's after the prefix **ex-**, as in ex**h**ibit. After other prefixes, however, the same H is pronounced, as in in**h**ibit and pro**h**ibit. There are also a few other words where H is silent because it is inconvenient to pronounce.

H is silent after G at the beginning of the syllable. In two of these words, **gh**etto and spa**gh**etti, the silent H is interacting with the other letters to keep the G from being soft before an E. The remaining words beginning with GH are all native English words expressing the scary aspect of the spirit world. Examples are **gh**ost, **gh**oul and **gh**astly.

After R at the beginning of the word, H is silent, as in R**h**ode Island. These are remnants of Latin spellings for borrowed Greek words. There are very few of these words.

Finally, after a vowel, H is always silent. The words involved are chiefly exclamations or hesitation sounds, like a**h**, e**h**, o**h** and u**h**.

   b. P as in **p**neumonia, **P**salms and **p**terodactyl

P is always silent at the beginning of the word if the consonant after it cannot be blended with the P. These, again are Greek spellings. Consonant blends of this kind were pronounced in Greece, but the Romans could not handle them any better than we can, so the P's have been silent from Roman times on.

4. Scholarly Insertions

Finally, there are a few words in which scholars of the Eighteenth Century inserted silent consonant letters in words where they felt they belonged. This was a time when the history of the English language was just being discovered, and scholars were fascinated by the relationships between English and earlier languages.

Examples of such silent letters are the B in de**b**t, the C in mus-**c**le, and the S in i**s**land. The scholars noticed B's in earlier forms of the word **debt**, and the B which we still pronounce in **debit**, and decided that **debt** really needed a B. For **muscle**, they felt that the C of **muscular** was needed. For the S in **island**, they reached back over many centuries, and lifted the S from the Latin word **insula** (which does, after all, survive in our word **peninsula**). Roughly a dozen such scholarly insertions have become frozen into words, and survive in our modern spelling. All of these words appear as exceptions on the consonant pages for whatever silent consonant they contain.

Homonyms and Spelling Options

One of the chores that teachers face is the task of helping children with homonyms, words which sound exactly alike, but have different meanings and different spellings. Examples are:

sail/sale, here/hear, right/write, road/rode, fur/fir
cent/sent, vane/vain/vein, hall/haul

Children who are being taught with a phonics-first approach can sound these words out easily, and context automatically suggests the correct meaning of whichever one appears in a sentence. But in writing, the homonyms can present a problem.

In general, spelling should be a matter of pronouncing a word and putting down the letters which will guide the reader to pronounce the same thing. But when the word is a member of a homonym pair, the task is not quite this straight-forward. The meaning of the written result will depend not only on the sounds prescribed for the reader to pronounce, but also on which option has been used in representing the sounds.

When children or remedial students first encounter this problem, they can find it difficult. Beginners try to avoid making mistakes, and remedial students are so terrified of mistakes that they will hesitate indefinitely, rather than run any risks.

Teachers need to realize that inexperienced readers have not yet read widely enough to have built up clear mental images of how the different members of a homonym pair should look. She should help the children realize this, too, and encourage them to experiment with the possibilities. The children will soon find that once they see both options down in black and white on the paper, they can tell which one is needed for their immediate purpose. Even remedial students find this to be true.

This problem, of course, extends far beyond the homonyms. **Neat** and **sleep**, for instance are words which have no homonyms. Yet each has only one correct spelling. For these words, also, children should be encouraged to try both spelling options, and wait until they have both down in black and white to decide which one looks better. If they do this consistently, they will soon become so sure of the right spellings that they will no longer have to experiment with the more frequently-used words. But they should still be encouraged to experiment whenever they are not sure of a word, until all of them have been mastered.

What children really need to know thoroughly, as they approach the end of the letter-sound lessons, is exactly what options there are for each sound. It is also helpful for them to have an idea of how heavily the different options are used. By this time, they will have read widely enough to have some impressions of their own about this. But they can be fascinated by the actual facts, which are shown in the ABC pages of this book.

Indeed, a good way to review what has been taught about letter-sounds is to take each speech sound and ask the class to list all the ways it can be spelled. Then have them speculate about how often each one is used, and finally have the teacher get the relevant numbers from the ABC pages, and let the class see how close they came to being right.

The Letter A

In English, the letter A has three basic sounds, long, short and broad.

1. A is short when it is within the syllable, as in

    tap, trap, tramp, chance, trap-ping, chan-cy, con-trap-tion

    In the case of a word beginning with a vowel, A is short if it has a consonant after it in the same syllable, as in

    at, **a**nd, **a**ct, **a**c-tive, **a**t-tic, **a**d-vo-cate

2. A is long, and sounds like the **name** of the letter A —

    a. When it is the last letter in the syllable, as in

    a-corn, b**a**-king, cr**a**-dle, f**a**-tal, v**a**-c**a**-tion, com-bi-n**a**-tion

    (But in the Latin style of spelling, these A's are often short, as in c**a**-bin, or-g**a**-nic, re-**a**-li-ty.)

    b. In the spelling pattern A__E, as in

    b**a**ke, c**a**ne, d**a**re, be-h**a**ve, se-d**a**te, con-gre-g**a**te

    In the letter groups -ANGE and -ASTE, A is also long, as in ch**a**nge and p**a**ste.

    c. In the vowel teams AY and AI, as in

    r**ay**, d**ay**, st**ay**, de-l**ay**, dis-pl**ay**, at the end of the root word, and in

    r**ai**n, ch**ai**r, st**ai**n, p**ai**l, con-t**ai**n, pre-v**ai**l, within the root word

3. Broad A has the same two sounds as short O in h**o**t and d**o**g. (In some regions, these sounds are the same, while in others they are different.)

    a. Broad A has the same sound as the O in h**o**t —

    1) When it is the very last letter in the word, as in f**a** l**a** l**a**

    2) When the short sound is changed by final R, or by R followed by a different consonant sound, as in

    c**a**r, c**a**rt, c**a**r-ton, c**a**r-na-tion

But if the next sound is a vowel, it will capture the R sound, and leave the A unchanged, as in

car-ry, bar-rel, pa-ra-graph, da-ring

3) When the short sound is changed by final LM, as in

calm, palm, psalm

4) When the short sound is changed by a W sound before the A, as in

wash, swab, squat, quan-ti-ty

The broad A sound of WA is changed to a long O sound by final R, or by R followed by a different consonant sound, as in

war, warm, quart, war-den

(Compare the sounds of war and wore.)

b. Broad A has the sound of short O in dog —

1) When the short sound is changed by final LL, or by L followed by a different consonant sound, as in

ball, bald, salt, talk, al-ways, fal-ter, bal-sam

But if the next sound is a vowel, it will capture the L sound, and leave the A unchanged, as in

al-ley, gal-lant, re-a-li-ty, wha-ling

And on the Latin side of English, A often remains short, even before L plus a different consonant, as in talc and cal-ci-um

2) In the vowel teams AW and AU, as in

paw, jaw, hawk, awk-ward, crawl, yawn, aw-ning, at the end of the root word, and before K, L, or N, and in

cause, caught, haul and ap-plaud, within the root word

This sound is usually counted as one of the six special vowel sounds of English. (See "Vowel Sounds and Vowel Letters," page 29.)

Unstressed A

Like the sounds of most English vowels, the sounds of A are

muffled beyond recognition in the syllables which are the most hurried, and are therefore the least stressed. This can happen to any A spelling, as in

fi-n**a**l, dis-t**a**nt, **a**-lone, de-moc-r**a**-cy, pi-r**ate**, o-r**ange**, cer-t**ain**, so-d**a**, dol-l**ar**, up-**ward**, he-r**ald**, res-t**au**-rant

Schwa* is usually used by dictionaries to respell the vowel sounds of these unstressed syllables.

The letter A forms the second member of the vowel teams EA and OA. (See "The Letter E," page 104, and "The Letter O," page 182.)

* In dictionaries, schwa look like this: ə.

✓ spelled ok
○ list

See also:

A__E, p. 73
Foreign A, p. 86

A as in acorn

Exceptions:

		Unstressed	
baby	taking	along	any
bacon	named	away	many
paper	races	across	(short E)
table	later	about	
April	potato	around	water
			papa
			(broad A)

		Unstressed
shaken	agent	located
basin	daring	cinnamon
cable	labor	dependable
famous	volcano	theater
patient	quotation	primary

		Unstressed
alien	oasis	chaotic
blazon	creative	deplorable
matrix	erasure	convalescent
scathing	pollination	supremacy
vagrant	complacency	instability

A is a vowel letter. It is long in a syllable that ends in A. When there is a single consonant letter between vowels, the first vowel is long before the native English suffixes, and certain Latin suffixes. The vowel is often long before Latin suffixes when there is an R- blend between vowels, as in **April**.

1121 words have long A in a stressed syllable, where the vowel sound is clear.

143 words have long A in an unstressed syllable, where the vowel sound is often muffled.

This count excludes words like **taking**, where the native English suffix simply changes the word's form.

See also:

WA, p. 271
Foreign A, p. 86

A as in apple

Exceptions:

what
father
mamma
   (broad A)

bass
chamber
ancient
cambric
cambridge
champagne
   (long A)

forecastle
   (silent A)

Arkansas
   (AS = AW)

		Unstressed
am	asking	admit
and	daddy	woman
can	fatter	giant
had	quacked	finally
dance	standing	important

		Unstressed
ranch	athlete	general
valve	demand	approach
flat	relapse	urban
cattle	volcanic	adventure
rather	reality	defendant

		Unstressed
ban	vanquish	campaign
wrath	transfer	accessible
vat	mortality	bacteriology
flax	dissatisfy	continental
tact	agriculture	severance

A is a vowel letter. It is short in a syllable that ends with a consonant letter. When there are two consonants between vowels, the first vowel is almost always short. In many of the long, Latin words, the first vowel is short even when there is only one consonant between vowels, as in **volcanic**.

2616 words have A before a consonant in a stressed syllable, where the short A sound is clear.

2040 words have A before a consonant in an unstressed syllable, where the vowel sound is often muffled.

A as in fa la la

See also:

AH, p. 74
Short O, p. 187
WA-, p. 271
Foreign A, p. 86

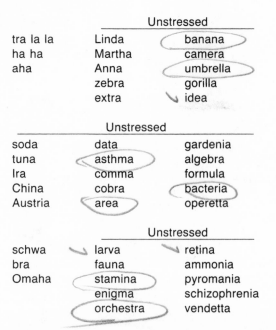

		Unstressed
tra la la	Linda	banana
ha ha	Martha	camera
aha	Anna	umbrella
	zebra	gorilla
	extra	idea

	Unstressed	
soda	data	gardenia
tuna	asthma	algebra
Ira	comma	formula
China	cobra	bacteria
Austria	area	operetta

		Unstressed
schwa	larva	retina
bra	fauna	ammonia
Omaha	stamina	pyromania
	enigma	schizophrenia
	orchestra	vendetta

Exceptions:

the article **a**
(long if stressed,
muffled if
unstressed

father
mamma
water
papa
   (broad A within
   the word)

A is a vowel letter. It is broad when it is the very last letter in the word. Within the word, the same sound is spelled by the letter O, as in **hot**.

Only 9 words have A at the end in a stressed syllable, where the broad A sound is clear.

233 words have A at the end in an unstressed syllable, where the vowel sound is muffled.

See also:

E, p. 110
Foreign A, p. 86

A__E as in cake

Exceptions:

are
  (broad A)

have
comrade
forbade
  (short A)

take	safe	airplane
made	stare	baseball
gave	chase	careful
same	place	became
ate	cage	awake

		Unstressed
grace	bracelet	pirate
rage	salesman	manage
lake	prepare	furnace
ache	replacement	accurate
fare	demonstrate	advantage

		Unstressed
ale	blockade	beverage
strafe	create	desperate
gale	overrate	discourage
phrase	palisade	obstinate
scale	disgraceful	immediate

Vowel-consonant-silent-E is a special long vowel spelling pattern. The silent E makes the A "say its name." The E remains silent when a syllable beginning with a consonant is added to the word.

399 words have A__E in a stressed syllable, where the long A sound is clear.

625 words have A__E in an unstressed syllable, where the vowel sound is often muffled.

These words are not counted under long A, p. 70.

Exceptions:

faery
(long A)

AE as in Aesop

Long E	Short E
Caesar	aesthetic
algae	
encyclopaedia	
archaeology	
alumnae	
paeon	Aeschylus
praetor	Daedalus
propaedeutic	

Michael

AE is a vowel team for long E or short E. These are Greek and Latin spellings.

This is the entire list of words containing AE.

AH as in hurrah

bah	ah
dahlia	sahib
pariah	

AH is a vowel team for broad A.

This is the entire list of words containing AH.

See also:

AY, p. 85
EI, p. 119

AI as in rain

Exceptions:

said
again
against
 (short E)

aisle
 (long I)

plaid
 (short A)

mail	pain	straight
tail	train	fairy
sail	chain	railroad
wait	hair	afraid
maid	stair	explain

Unstressed

gain	contain	mountain
faint	complain	bargain
waist	failure	captain
claim	remain	curtain
praise	hairdresser	retail

Unstressed

braise	proclaim	portrait
bail	affair	chieftain
faith	curtail	villainy
prairie	prevail	clairvoyant
maim	ailment	certainty

AI is a vowel team for long A. It is used within the root instead of AY. Notice how often AI comes before L, N and R. In a few Latin words, the team breaks up, as in mo-sa-ic.

271 words have the team AI in a stressed syllable, where the long A sound is clear.

37 words have the team AI in an unstressed syllable, where the long A sound is often muffled.

These words are not counted under long A, p. 70.

-AL as in canal

See also:

AL-, p. 77
-ALL, p. 78

Exceptions:

withal
(broad A)

	Unstressed	
Al	royal	general
Hal	final	musical
pal	central	hospital
gal	signal	medical
corral	animal	several

	Unstressed	
local	total	renewal
rival	equal	colonial
fatal	metal	actual
normal	ideal	unusual
trial	special	accidental

	Unstressed	
pedal	annual	geographical
dismal	educational	mechanical
brutal	fraternal	transcendental
martial	immaterial	confidential
glacial	remedial	capitalism

When a word ends in A followed by a single L, the A is short. Final AL is a common Latin suffix.

5 words have final AL in a stressed syllable, where the short A sound is clear.

549 words have final AL in an unstressed syllable, where the short A sound is muffled.

These words are also counted under short A, p. 71 and under L, p. 173.

See also:

-AL, p. 76
-ALL, p. 78
-ALLY, p. 79

No exceptions

AL as in also or Alfred

A as in also	Short A
almost	alphabet
always	album
altogether	
already	
although	
Walter	algebra
falsify	contralto
walnut	alcohol
almanac	calcium
almond	altitude
falter	calculate
palsy	malfunction
walrus	albino
alternate	malnutrition
alderman	malpractice

When AL comes before a different consonant, the A may be broad, as in **al**so, or it may be short, It is more likely to be short on the Latin side of the language.

40 words have AL before a different consonant with a broad A sound.

75 words have AL before a different consonant with a short A sound.

These words are also counted under L, p. 173 and those containing short A are also counted under short A, p. 71.

See also:

-AL, p. 76
AL-, p. 77
-ALLY, p. 79

-ALL as in call

all	talk	called
ball	walk	falling
fall	salt	taller
hall	bald	smallest
wall	chalk	hallway
stall	calm	stalling
squall	palm	salty
malt	psalms	exalt
balk	gall	forestall
false	stalk	installment

Unstressed

mall	herald
alms	cobalt
psalmist	windfall
embalm	asphalt

Exceptions:

shall
scalp
valve
talc
salmon
Alps
  (short A)

half
calf
salve
  (short A and
  silent L)*

In these words, the root ends in ALL or in AL plus a different consonant. A in the middle of the syllable is usually short, but the L changes it to broad A, making it sound like the short O of **dog**. Before final K or M, the L goes silent, but it still makes the A broad. Before final M, the broad A sounds like the short O of **hot**. -ALL is a native English letter team.

88 words have A changed by L in a stressed syllable, where the broad A sound is clear.

8 words have A changed by L in an unstressed syllable, where the broad A sound is often muffled.

*In some regions, these words are pronounced with a broad A.

In most of these words the L sounds, and is included in the count for L, p. 173, or LL, p. 176.

See also:

-ALL, p. 78
-OLLY, p. 194
-ARRY, p. 82

ALL- as in rally

Except in words
like:

calling,
taller, etc.

Here a native
English suffix
is added to
words from
p. 78.

		Unstressed
Sally	shallow	really
alley	gallon	finally
valley	palace	usually
gallop	alligator	generally
salad	valentine	balloon

	Unstressed	
balance	actually	realize
value	normally	socialist
salary	idealism	moralize
analysis	morally	realist
metallic	penalize	specialist

	Unstressed	Long A
gallant	virtually	palings
fatality	bimetallism	scaly
italicize	federalist	whaler
allegation	dualism	azalea
hospitality	imperialist	alias

In these words, the L does not make the A broad because the L sound goes off with the next syllable.

166 words have ALL or AL in a stressed syllable before a vowel. In these words, the A sound is clear.

123 words have ALL or AL in an unstressed syllable before a vowel. In these words, the A sound is often muffled.

These words are also counted under short A, long A, and L, pp. 71, 70, and 173.

-ANGE and -ASTE as in change and paste

See also:

-E, p. 110
-E, p. 111

Exceptions:

anger
tangerine
caste
angelic
flange
tangent
  (short A)

strange	ranger	pastry
taste	stranger	engaged
waste	danger	arrange
		angel
baste	wasteful	endanger
haste	changeless	arrangement
tasty	manger	distaste
hasty	basting	interchange
hasten	exchange	
chaste	chasten	interchangeable
grange	estranged	rearrange
mangy	distasteful	foretaste
changeling	archangel	

The final E is silent. It makes the A long, even though there are two consonant letters between the A and the E. The E remains silent when a syllable that begins with a consonant is added. ANGE and ASTE are best considered as special letter groups.

44 words have ANGE or ASTE in a stressed syllable, where the long A sound is clear.

Only one word, **orange**, has ANGE in an unstressed syllable, where the vowel sound is muffled.

These words are not counted under A__E, p. 74, or under silent E, p. 110.

See also:

-ARRY, p. 82
WAR-, p. 272

AR as in car

Exceptions:

scarce
  (long A)

catarrh
  (double R, H)

bizarre
  (double R, E)

		Unstressed
far	large	dollar
jar	starry	sugar
hard	garden	beggar
tar	farmer	coward
part	remark	wizard

		Unstressed
carve	scarlet	custard
barb	harvest	cellar
charge	carpet	eastward
scarred	architect	singular
parsley	department	peculiar

		Unstressed
arsenal	disarmament	vinegar
harmony	carnival	billiards
foolhardy	pharmacy	participate
departure	marvelous	nuclear
charlatan	carbohydrate	standardize

In these words, the R is at the end of the word, or is followed by a different consonant. A in the middle of the syllable is usually short, but the R changes it to a broad A, making it sound like the short O of **hot**. AR is a special letter team.

389 words have A changed by R in a stressed syllable, where the broad A sound is clear.

217 words have A changed by R in an unstressed syllable, where the vowel sound is often muffled.

These words are also counted under R, p. 219.

See also:

-AR, p. 81
-ERRY, p. 122
-IRRI-, p. 165
-ORRY, p. 198
-ALLY, p. 79

-ARR- as in carry

		Unstressed
marry	Harry	arrive
barrel	arrow	arrest
narrow	parent	arithmetic
carrot	wheelbarrow	macaroni
parrot	caramel	

Except in words like:

starry
jarring, etc.,

Here R is doubled before a native English suffix added to words ending in AR.

		Unstressed
tariff	charity	separation
barren	apparent	cigarette
parallel	character	dungarees
garrison	embarrassment	documentary
daring	comparison	summarize

		Unstressed
marathon	honorary	alimentary
parity	planetarium	narration
familiarity	hilarious	dispensary
paramount	visionary	popularize
peculiarity	subsidiary	parenthesis

In these words, the R does not make the A broad because the R sound goes off with the next syllable.

146 words have AR or ARR in a stressed syllable before a vowel letter. In these words the A sound is clear.

26 words have AR or ARR in an unstressed syllable before a vowel letter. In these words the vowel sound is often muffled.

These words are also counted under short A, long A, and R, p. 71, 70, and 219.

See also:

AW, p. 84
Foreign A, p. 86

AU as in sauce

Exceptions:

aunt
laugh
   (short A)

gauge
   (long A)

beauty
   (long U)

sauerkraut
   (OU as in
   shout)

Paul	August	automobile
haul	author	autumn
caught	laundry	daughter
taught	caution	naughty
because	sausage	astronaut
fault	haunted	audio
gauze	jaunty	auditorium
pause	faucet	authentic
launch	saucer	autograph
fraud	applause	cauliflower
clause	pauper	auxiliary
jaunt	exhaust	authorize
vault	jaundice	hydraulic
automatic	inauguration	manslaughter

AU is a letter team for the special English vowel sound heard in **sauce**. It is used within the root instead of AW.

169 words have AU as in **sauce**.

See also:
AU, p. 83

AW as in jaw

No exceptions

saw	laws	seesaw
paw	drawn	awful
crawl	sawing	outlaw
draw	squawk	drawer
straw	yawn	strawberry
shawl	lawn	rawhide
pawn	brawl	lawyer
squawl	sprawl	awkward
dawn	thawing	withdraw
flaw	bylaw	drawback
bawl	bawdy	catawba
brawn	hawser	withdrawal
gawky	sawyer	
	dawdle	

AW is a letter team for the special English vowel sound heard in **paw**. AW is used at the end of the root and before final L, N or K. Before other consonants, AW becomes AU, as in **pause**. AW is a native English spelling.

77 words have AW as in **jaw**.

See Also:

AI, p. 75
EY, p. 126

AY as in play

Exceptions:

says
  (short E)

quay
  (long E)

say	away	birthday
day	today	runway
pay	playing	highway
may	stayed	driveway
gray	daylight	railway
clay	wayfarer	stowaway
bray	mayor	hearsay
nay	daybreak	gangway
stray	prayer	noonday
gay	layman	photoplay

Unstressed

flay	portray	anyway
wayward	mainstay	yesterday
dismay	astray	Saturday
mayhem	payable	always
tramway	causeway	essay

AY is a vowel team for long A. It is used at the end of the root. Within the syllable, AY becomes AI, as in **plain**.

133 words have AY in a stressed syllable, where the long A sound is clear.

10 words have AY in an unstressed syllable, where the long A sound is often muffled.

These words are not counted under long A, p. 70.

In foreign spellings, A is usually broad, as in garage

A E	AY, AU or A within the syllable	A at the end of the syllable
madame	kayak	pajamas
	restaurant	
morale	yacht	bravo
barrage	goulash	llama
mirage	andante	raja
promenade	cayenne	drama
camouflage	chauffeur	safari
sabotage	renaissance	toccata
montage	gauche	pasha
persiflage	mauve	naive
locale	bayou	

These words are English enough to be included in the Hanna listing, but many of their letter sounds reflect their languages of origin.

12 words have A__E. These are French. Some of these A's are short.

4 words have AU. These are French.

3 words have AY. These are French or Eskimo.

10 words have A within the syllable. These are from various languages.

42 words have A at the end of the syllable. These are mainly Italian or Spanish.

See also:

B, p. 88
MB, p. 178

B as in bat

Exceptions:

doubt
debt
subtle
  (silent B)

ball	better	begin
big	bunny	baby
bear	Billy	birthday
tub	rubber	bubble
job	grabbing	table
beak	bashful	barometer
booth	starboard	laboratory
curb	boyish	probable
bulb	oblong	biography
knob	describe	inhabit
berth	biceps	bourgeoisie
ban	bisect	beneficial
subside	absorb	collaborate
bailiff	belated	backgammon
forbade	submerge	subterranean

B is a consonant letter for the first sound in **bat** and the last sound in **tub**.

2339 words have B as in **bat**.

See also:

-LE, p. 175
-RE, p. 220

B as in bright and blue

brown	brushes	brother
break	broken	umbrella
brick	bringing	library
black	blinked	blanket
blow	blazing	problem
branch	braided	brilliant
breath	brimming	celebrate
bruise	bridegroom	broccoli
bleat	blotter	gambling
blind	obliged	blizzard
bleak	bromide	cerebral
brunt	abridge	celebrity
brazen	calibrate	libretto
blarney	blaspheme	bludgeon
sublime	blemish	obligatory

BR- and BL- are consonant blends. The blend sometimes splits up between vowels, as in **problem**. If the blend splits, the B makes the first vowel short. Very often, the BR blend does not split, and the first vowel is long, as in library.

231 words have the blend BR-.

168 words have the blend BL-.

These words are also counted under B, L and R, pp. 87, 173 and 219.

The Letter C

In English, the letter C has two sounds, hard and soft. When it is hard, it sounds like K, and when it is soft, it sounds like S. As can be seen, C has no sound of its own. The only way to tell how a C sounds is to notice the letter that comes right after it.

In the Ancient Roman alphabet, C had only one sound, the K sound. But as modern Italian, Spanish, French and English evolved from Ancient Latin, these K sounds gradually went soft before E, I and Y sounds. For this reason, C is soft before E, I and Y in Modern English. When C is soft, it always sounds like unvoiced S, never like Z, which is the voiced version of S.

1. C is hard before any letter except E, I or Y, as in

> **c**an, **c**op, **c**ut, **c**lip, **c**rab, fa**c**t, ac**c**ent, a**c**me, a**c**ne, ac**q**uire, lila**cs**, un**c**le, a**c**re

Also, C is hard if there is nothing after it, as in musi**c**.

2. C is soft before E, I or Y, as in

> **c**ent, **c**edar, **c**ertain, **c**ity, **c**ider, **c**ircle, **c**ymbal, **c**ypress, dan**c**e, ra**c**e, ra**c**es, ra**c**ed, ra**c**er, ra**c**ing, ra**c**y

It makes no difference what the sound of the E, I or Y happens to be. These letters automatically make C soft when they come right after it.

We have many words which contain both hard and soft C's, as in

> a**cc**ent, **c**ir-**c**le, **c**y**c**le, a**cc**ident, **c**ir**c**umferen**c**e, **c**on**c**ert

When C comes before Latin suffixes containing unstressed I and another vowel, the S sound is distorted to an SH sound, as in

> ra**c**ial, spe**c**ial, cru**c**ial, offi**c**ial, patri**c**ian, atro**c**ious

When we need to spell a K sound before an E, I or Y, we use the letter K, as in

> **k**ept, **k**eep, **k**erchief, **k**it, **k**ite, sha**k**e, sha**k**en, sha**k**er, sha**k**ing, sha**k**y, lea**k**ing, pee**k**ing, loo**k**ing, ban**k**er, as**k**ed

C is the first letter in two consonant teams, CK and CH.

1. CK is used to spell the sound of K at the end of the root, right after a short vowel, as in

     pa**ck**, pe**ck**, pi**ck**, po**ck**, pu**ck**

   These are always words which can take the native English suffixes, **-ed**, **-ing**, **-er**, **-y**, **-en**, etc. If such a word ended in C alone, the C would have to be doubled before the suffix. But since all these suffixes begin with E, I or Y, the vowel of the suffix would make the second C go soft: "pa**cc**ing." To avoid this we would have to give the second C a backbone, and turn it into a K. Another possibility would be to end the word with K alone. Then the longer forms would need double K: "pakking." But then, the first K would violate the rule that K is used only before E, I or Y. It is easier to spell all these words with CK in the first place, and not have to solve these problems afresh every time they arise.

2. CH has three sounds in English.

   a. CH is a letter team for the special English consonant sound at the beginning of **ch**ildren. This sound did not occur in the Latin language. Therefore, the Latin alphabet which we use has no single letter available for representing it. It occurs frequently in English, as in

      chair, **ch**eck, **ch**ill, **ch**op, **ch**unk, coa**ch**, pea**ch**, approa**ch**

      CH is vaguely similar to CK in appearance. As a result, remedial students who have never understood how letters represent speech sounds, often confuse them. Once they gain a clear understanding of the different functions of these two consonant teams, this confusion can gradually be overcome.

      At the end of the root, right after a short vowel, the CH sound is spelled TCH, as in

      ca**tch**, e**tch**, pi**tch**, bo**tch**, clu**tch**

      Like the words ending in CK, these are all words which can take the native English suffixes, **-es**, **-ed**, **-ing**, **-y**, etc. When the suffix is added, the inserted T keeps the first vowel short without introducing any unwanted sound into the word, as in

cat-chy, pit-cher, hat-chet, clut-ches, et-ching

This works because the CH sound is actually a complex sound which is begun by placing the tongue in the same position which produces a T sound.

b. CH sounds like K in words of Greek origin, as in

school, Christmas, chlorine, character, stomach, psychological

These are words which the Romans borrowed from the Greeks. They contained a special Greek sound which the Romans could not pronounce. But in order to maintain the Greek flavor of the words, the Romans respelled the sound CH. Such words sometimes contain other vestiges of Greek spellings, as well, like the silent P and the Y within the word in psychological.

c. CH sounds like SH in words borrowed from the French, as in

machine, parachute, chenille, chef

In French, the sound which we spell SH is regularly spelled CH. We retain the French sounds in these words in order to retain the French flavor. Notice that the I's also have a foreign sound.

C as in cat

See also:

Soft C, p. 93
K, p. 168
Q, p. 214

can	called	bicycle
came	cutting	music
car	coldest	uncle
could	scared	picnic
coat	candy	circus
act	contest	activity
coop	instinct	instinctive
cane	object	objection
coast	traffic	almanac
curl	medical	cosmetic
cod	access	consonant
cam	cobra	coincidence
talc	clinic	counterfeit
peptic	concoct	amplification
metric	extinct	apologetic

Exceptions:

Caesar
facade
   (soft before
   A)

muscle
indict
victual
   (silent C)

There are 48
words which
use K before
A, O or U.
Examples
appear on p. 168

C is a consonant letter which has no sound of its own. Here it is hard, and sounds like K. C is hard whenever it is not followed by E, I or Y.

3915 words have hard C.

See also:

Hard C, p. 92
-CI-, p. 98
-E, p. 111

Exceptions:

soccer
sceptic
   (hard C be-
   fore E)

cello
concerto
   (soft
    C = CH)

crescendo
   (soft
    C = SH)

C as in city

cent	raced	bicycle
mice	dancer	scissors
face	circus	science
prince	pencil	December
once	except	policeman
scene	reduce	ocean
cider	descend	conscious
center	ancient	accident
succeed	social	society
policy	office	official
cede	efficacy	efficient
cyprus	deficit	deficient
jaundice	ascension	associate
exceed	excessive	association
suffice	cellular	appreciation

C is a consonant letter which has no sound of its own. Here it is soft, and sounds like S. C is soft before E, I or Y. Soft C takes on an SH sound before unstressed E or I followed by another vowel, as in **ocean** and **social**.

These are words of Latin origin. Originally all these C's were hard.

1295 words have soft C.

C as in clown and crown

See also:

-LE, p. 175
-RE, p. 220

Exceptions:

kleptomania
(K instead
of C)

cry	cracking	across
cream	creepy	crayon
crawl	crowded	exclaim
class	cleaned	including
cluck	clothes	clever
crew	increase	criminal
crime	cradle	microscope
crouch	describe	description
cliff	declare	declaration
scrap	secret	secretary
croak	ascribe	clergyman
crimp	crevice	ecliptic
crypt	discreet	seclusion
clench	conclave	credulity
cleat	cyclic	nucleus

CL- and CR- are consonant blends. C is hard before L and R.
These blends sometimes split up between vowels, as in **declaration** and **secretary**. If the blend splits, the vowel before it is short.
Otherwise, the vowel before the blend is long, as in **declare** and **secret**.

194 words have the blend CL-.

327 words have the blend CR-.

These words are also counted under C, L and R, and SCR
pp. 92, 173 and 219, and 231.

See also:

CH, p. 96
CH, p. 97
-TCH, p. 247
-TU-, p. 251

Exceptions:

yacht
  (silent CH)

CH as in chicken

child	teaches	chapter
chair	chased	checkers
church	pinching	sandwich
lunch	changing	chocolate
march	children	handkerchief
chunk	challenge	enchantress
churn	chowder	achievement
search	chisel	challenger
torch	approach	attachment
wrench	merchant	treachery
chafe	surcharge	chastity
char	orchard	charitable
chide	chisel	archery
launch	urchin	chargeable
quench	anchovy	enfranchise

CH is a consonant team for the first sound in **chicken** and the last sound in **each**. This is the special English sound of CH.

382 words have CH with its native English sound.

See also:

CH, p. 95
CH, p. 97

CH as in Christmas

Exceptions:

school	chorus	stomach	drachm
	anchor	toothache	schism
	echo		(silent Ch)

Christ	orchid	Christianity
chord	chloride	chemistry
ache	schedule	character
scheme	scholastic	mechanics
chrome	architect	psychology

chasm	epoch	chaotic
chaos	strichnine	technique
ocher	chronology	chameleon
schizoid	alchemy	

In words of Greek origin, CH is a team for the sound of K. Because it represents this simple sound, the E of **ache** can make the A long.

Notice that Greek CH can form the consonant blends CHR-, CHL- and SCH-.

146 words have Greek CH. This includes 15 words with the blend CHR-, 6 words with the blend CHL-, and 12 words with the blend SCH-.

See also:

CH, p. 95
CH, p. 96
SH, p. 235

CH as in Chicago

chef	mustache	parachute
	Chevy	pistachio
	machine	
cache	chiffon	Michigan
chic	chauffeur	Charlotte
chute	champagne	Chevrolet
crochet	ricochet	chivalry
chaperon	chandelier	
gauche	chenille	echelon
schwa	chateau	nonchalance
	chamois	chauvinism
	cliche	

In words borrowed recently from France. CH is a team for the sound we normally spell as SH. Notice how many of the vowels in these words also have foreign sounds.

40 words have French CH.

-CI- as in special

See also:

Soft C, p. 93
-I-, p. 156
-SI-, p. 236
-SSI-, p. 238
-TI-, p. 250
SH, p. 235

No exceptions

ancient		conscience
social		delicious
precious		magician
		suspicion
		musician

glacier	official	commercial
crucial	malicious	politician
racial	efficient	association
spacious	socialist	appreciate
vicious	financial	excruciating

specious	depreciate	emaciated
	clinician	judiciary
	capacious	paramecium
	pernicious	meretricious
	omniscient	efficacious

In these words the soft C has an SH sound. The unstressed I before a vowel changes the S sound of the soft C to an SH sound. These are all words of Latin origin.

121 words have C changed to an SH sound by unstressed I before a vowel.

These words are also counted under soft C, p. 93.

See also:

C, p. 92
C, p. 93
K, p. 168
QU, p. 215

-CK as in duck

Exceptions:

Mac
Doc
Vic
   (no K: slang)

trek
   (no C: foreign)

shellac
chic
bloc
sac
   (no K: foreign
   forms)

blackguard
   (silent CK)

back	blocks	checkers
neck	thicker	blackboard
pick	Jackie	chicken
rock	stockings	bucket
luck	sticky	tickle
check	nickel	hickory
buck	buckle	mackerel
dock	attack	stockholder
wick	wicked	unlucky
wreck	unlock	pickpocket

In Suffixes

knack	deadlock	hammock
thwack	hackney	gimmick
chock	grackle	hummock
wrack	cockney	panicky
wick	lackadaisical	trafficking

CK is a consonant team for the sound of K. It is used at the end of the root, right after a short vowel. This spelling is convenient, since so many of the words can take endings beginning with E, I or Y. We would have to use K in **ducking** even if the root word were spelled "**duc**."

276 have CK at the end of the root.

  18 have CK at the end of the suffix. These are remnants of Middle English spelling.

      These words are also counted under C and K, pp. 92 and 168.

D as in dog

See also:

DGE, p. 102
-ED, p. 117

Exceptions:

add
odd
   (See p. 295)

handkerchief
handsome
   (silent D)

did	ended	around
down	jumped	study
had	called	different
gold	Daddy	second
card	riding	Sunday
damp	decide	orderly
aid	disease	discomfort
dare	student	independent
guide	huddle	radio
blind	advance	forbidden
deuce	adapt	definitive
dirk	decade	condescending
dunce	donor	providence
bard	lurid	advocate
pod	cascade	

D is a consonant letter for the first sound in **dog** and the last sound in **had**.

3864 words have D as in **dog**.

See also:

-LE, p. 175

D as in dreaming and dwarf

drink	dresser	children
draw	drawing	hundred
drive	dropped	drawer
dry	dreamy	dragon
drum	dries	laundry
drill	drama	draftsman
drown	drowsy	dressmaker
drag	squadron	hydrogen
drain	dreadful	cathedral
dwell	drainage	Edward
drab	dreary	drapery
drake	drought	cylindrical
dram	syndrome	dehydrate
drench	eavesdrop	hydraulic
Dwight	dwindle	rhododendron

DR- and DW- are consonant blends. These blends very seldom split up between vowels. When the blend does not split up, the vowel before it is long, as in **hydraulic**.

148 words have the blend DR-.

5 words have the blend DW-.

These words are also counted under D, R and W, pp. 100, 219, and 268.

See also:

G, p. 132
J, p. 167

-DGE as in bridge

Exceptions:

fudge	lodging	midget	judgment
badge	judged	badger	acknowledgment
judge	dodger	hedgehog	fledgling
pledge	smudgy		abridgment
grudge	pledged		(no E after
			the G)

budge	ridgepole	drawbridge
edge	begrudge	misjudge
trudge	budget	sledgehammer
ledge	fidget	dislodge
lodge	gadget	

In Suffixes

sludge	ledger	knowledge
dredge	adjudge	acknowledge
midge	bludgeon	cartridge
nudge	cudgel	partridge

DGE is a consonant team for the sound of J. It is used at the end of the root, right after a short vowel. The silent E is needed to make the G soft. The D serves to insert an extra consonant letter so that the silent E cannot make the vowel long.

55 words have -DGE at the end of the root.

7 words have -DGE at the end of the suffix.

These words are also counted under G, p. 137.
They are not counted under D, p. 100.

See also:

-TU-, p. 251
-I-, p. 156

-DU- as in graduate

| | soldier | education |
| | | gradually |

educate	educator	educational
procedure	modulate	soldiery
gradual	undergraduate	graduation
individual	grandeur	cordial
schedule	pendulum	cordiality

assiduous	sedulous	arduous
credulous	modulous	glandular
deciduous	residual	undulate
incredulous	residuum	verdure
individualism	individuality	fraudulent

In these words, the unstressed I, and the Y- element of the unstressed long U, change the D sound to a J sound. These are all words of Latin origin.

This is the entire list of words in which I and U make D sound like J.

These words are also counted under D, long U, and unstressed I before a vowel, pp. 100, 257, and 156.

The Letter E

In English, the letter E has three basic sounds, long, short and silent.

1. E is short —
   a. When it is within the syllable, as in

   > pet, fled, swept, felt, sense, pet-ting, pen-ding, re-pen-tant

   In the case of a word beginning with a vowel, E is short if it has a consonant after it in the same syllable, as in

   > egg, end, ef-fort, en-ter, es-ti-mate, ex-tra

   b. In the vowel team EA when it is within certain words, as in

   > head, meant, health, plea-sure

   This is the only case of a short vowel sound spelled by a team. Notice how many of these words have other forms where EA is long, as in mean, heal, please.

The short sound of E is changed to a special English vowel sound by final R, or by R followed by a different consonant sound, as in

> her, herd, cer-tain, per-fect, per-ma-nent, de-ter-mine

But if the next sound is a vowel, it will capture the R sound, and leave E unchanged, as in

> ber-ry, her-ring, he-rald, me-rest, pe-ri-od

The short sound of EA is changed to the same special English vowel sound by R followed by a different consonant sound, as in

> heard, learn, hearse, ear-nest

But if the next sound is a vowel, it will capture the R sound, and leave the EA unchanged, as in

> hea-ring, dea-rest, wea-ring, bea-ring

The sound of ER as in her is one of the six special vowel

sounds of English. See "Vowel Sounds and Vowel Letters", page 29.

2. E is long, and sounds like the **name** of the letter E —

   a. When it is the last letter in the syllable, as in

      h**e**, **e**-ven, P**e**-ter, d**e**-cent, **e**-lastic, s**e**-cr**e**-tion, pr**e**-vi-ous

      (But in the Latin style of spelling, these E's are often short, as in sp**e**-cial, s**e**-pa-rate, d**e**-mo-crat.)

   b. In the spelling pattern E__E, as in

      th**ese**, h**ere**, com-p**ete**, ath-l**ete**, in-com-pl**ete**

   c. In the vowel teams EA, EE and IE, as in

      s**ea**, s**ee**, **ea**-ger, ab-sen-t**ee**, at the end of the syllable, and in

      m**ea**t, m**ee**t, re-p**ea**t, dis-cr**ee**t, ch**ie**f, f**ie**ld, within the root.

   d. In the vowel teams IE and EY when they are in suffixes, as in

      mo-v**ie**, can-d**ie**s, can-d**ie**d, al-l**ey**, chim-n**ey**

      (Suffixes with this sound are usually spelled plain **-y**, as in hap-**py**. See "The Letter Y," page 280.)

3. E is silent when it is the very last letter in a word which also contains another vowel letter. Final silent E has the following functions:

   a. After a single vowel letter followed by a single consonant letter, silent E makes the previous vowel long, as in

      t**a**pe, th**e**se, t**i**me, t**y**pe, t**o**ne, t**u**be

   b. Silent E adds length to a very short word, making it look important enough to be a main-idea word, as in

      t**ie**, **ore**, **ewe**, **awe**

   c. After a single S which has another consonant or a vowel team before it, silent E shows that the S belongs to the root, as in

      den**se**, fal**se**, pur**se**, hou**se**, pau**se**, prai**se**

      Here the E shows that the S is not a suffix, as it is in den**s**, fall**s**, purr**s**, how'**s**, paw**s** and pray**s**

d. After a single Z which has another consonant or a vowel team before it, silent E shows that the Z belongs to the root, as in

bronze, gauze, freeze

This does not seem very necessary, but whatever S does, Z does, too.

e. After a V, silent E keeps the V from being the last letter in the word, as in

have, be-have, carve, elves, leave, grieve

No language which employs the letter V permits it to be final in the word. Unfortunately, this leaves English with no satisfactory way to spell the short vowels in **have, live** and **give**, or in the many words ending in the suffix **-ive,** such as na-**tive.**

f. After C or G, silent E makes the C or G soft, as in

face, chance, force, page, change, badge, large, hinge

Many words ending in silent E can take suffixes beginning with consonants. In such words, the E remains silent, as in

statement, basement, toeless, densely, amazement, forgiveness, forceful, largely

Many words ending in silent E can take suffixes beginning with vowels. Then, the E must be dropped before the suffix is added, as in

baker, tied, denser, freezing, giving, forcible, largest, basal

But the E is not dropped if the vowel of the suffix would harden a soft C or G, as in noticeable, chargeable

Unstressed E

Like the sounds of most English vowels, the sounds of E are muffled beyond recognition in the syllables which are the most hurried, and are therefore the least stressed. This happens mainly to sounds spelled by the simple letter E, as in

telephone, competition, funnel, basket, confident, confidence

Schwa* is usually used by dictionaries to respell the vowel sounds of these unstressed syllables.

E in Teams for Other Vowel Sounds

1. EY / EI, as in th**ey**. th**ei**r—
   a. EY spells long A at the end of the root, as in

      pr**ey**, o-b**ey**, con-v**ey**
   b. EI spells long A within the root as in

      eight, w**ei**gh, fr**ei**ght, v**ei**n, r**ei**gn, sur-v**ei**l-lance

2. EW / EU, as in f**ew** and f**eu**d—
   a. EW spells long U at the end of the root or before final N, as in

      d**ew**, gr**ew**, bl**ew**, h**ew**, h**ew**n, cur-f**ew**
   b. EU spells long U within the root as in

      d**eu**ce, **Eu**-rope, f**eu**-dal, pn**eu**-mo-ni-a

---

* In dictionaries, schwa looks like this: ə.

See also:

E__E, p. 113
Silent E, p. 110
Foreign E, p. 128

E as in even

Exceptions:

A few foreign
words.

Unstressed

me	the	belong
she	begin	remember
we	elect	December
be	decide	enough
idea	remain	behind

Unstressed

fever	report	reality
cedar	beholder	geology
secret	belief	elastic
veto	prepare	deliberate
legal	deny	appetite

Unstressed

precinct	event	evaporate
cathedral	destroy	democracy
rebate	belittle	inadequate
evil	deposit	hideous
premium	cinema	molecule

E is a vowel letter. It is long in a syllable that ends in E. When there is a single consonant letter between vowels, the first vowel is long before the native English suffixes, and certain Latin suffixes. The vowel is often long before Latin suffixes when there is an R-blend between vowels, as in **zebra**. E is also long in the prefixes **be-**, **de-**, **e-**, **pre-**, **re-** and **se-**, especially when they are unstressed.

395 words have long E in a stressed syllable, where the vowel sound is clear.

1476 words have long E in an unstressed syllable, where the vowel sound is not always clear.

This count excludes words like **completed**, where the native English suffix simply changes the word's form.

See also:

EA, p. 115
Foreign E, p. 128

E as in exit

Exceptions:

pretty
England
English
   (short I)

		Unstressed
bell	February	lasted
leg	November	garden
men	everyone	children
felt	elephant	longest
egg	forgetting	pocket

		Unstressed
bet	oneself	moment
fence	suggest	insect
bench	sketched	confidence
neck	senate	amusement
press	telescope	turpentine

		Unstressed
dwell	texture	orchestra
vent	rectangle	parallel
condense	desperate	incumbent
infect	execute	installment
confess	identity	concentrate

E is a vowel letter. It is short in a syllable that ends with a consonant letter. When there are two consonants between vowels, the first vowel is almost always short. In many of the long, Latin words, the first vowel is short even when there is only one consonant between vowels, as in **elephant**.

2485 words have E before a consonant in a stressed syllable, where the short E sound is clear.

1918 words have E before a consonant in an unstressed syllable, where the vowel sound is often muffled.

E as in rake

See also:

-ANGE, p. 80
Foreign E, p. 128

			Unstressed
cake	careless	awake	pirate
these	evening	complete	college
like	likely	desire	service
home	homesick	suppose	handsome
cute	useful	excuse	minute

Exceptions:

maybe
recipe
  (long E at the
  end)

			Unstressed
brace	lateness	debate	baggage
scene	merely	extreme	athlete
pride	tireless	decline	native
choke	lonely	compose	purpose
cube	lively	endure	lettuce

			Unstressed
pave	casement	engrave	delicate
theme	hereby	concede	acetylene
rhyme	spiteful	subscribe	examine
globe	polestar	invoke	troublesome
mute	tuneful	induce	furniture

E at the end is silent if there is another vowel in the word. This is the spelling pattern vowel-consonant-silent-E. It shows that the vowel before the consonant is long. Notice that when a suffix beginning with a consonant is added to these words, the silent E remains silent.

1338 words have vowel-consonant-silent-E in an stressed syllable, where the vowel before the consonant has a clear long sound.

1434 words have vowel-consonant-silent-E in an unstressed syllable, where the vowel sound is often muffled. If the vowel is I, it often becomes short.

See also:

Silent E, p. 110
Foreign E, p. 128
-SE, p. 233
-VE, p. 267
-ZE, p. 292
-ANGE, p. 80

Exceptions:

scarce
  (long A)

lens
  (no final E)

E as in dance

chance	curve	raise
since	serve	leave
large	horse	choose
badge	nurse	choice
twelve	sense	house

Unstressed

bulge	increase	entrance
piece	involve	balance
bronze	discharge	attendance
carve	collapse	endurance
pause	convince	tortoise

Unstressed

coerce	espouse	fragrance
conceiving	condense	syringe
revenge	appraise	obedience
response	enlargement	compliance
divorce	defenseless	perseverance

E at the end is silent if there is another vowel letter in the word. Silent E usually makes the vowel before it long. But it cannot do this if there are two consonants between the first vowel and the E, or if the vowel sound is represented by a vowel team. In these words, the E is making a C or G soft, or is part of an -SE, -VE or -ZE team. Notice that when a suffix beginning with a consonant is added to these words, the silent E remains silent.

825   words have two consonants or a vowel team before silent E in a stressed syllable, where the vowel sound before the consonants is clear.

244   words have two consonants or a vowel team before silent E in an unstressed syllable, where the vowel sound of the syllable is often muffled.

These words are also counted under soft C, p. 93; soft G, p. 137; -SE, p. 233; -SE, p. 234; -VE, p. 267; and -ZE, p. 292.

-E as in giraffe

grille		kitchenette
belle		cigarette
steppe	barrette	vaudeville
butte	gazette	comedienne
cayenne	croquette	silhouette
gazelle	roulette	etiquette
bizarre	palette	statuette
fosse	impasse	pipette
chenille	cretonne	coquette
gavotte	finesse	demitasse
rosette	nacelle	mignonette
layette	crevasse	

These are French spellings. The vowel-double-consonant-E at the end usually shows that the last syllable is stressed. Notice the French sounds of the OU's and the CH.

This is the entire list of words with vowel-double-consonant-E. **Palette** is the only one where the last syllable is not stressed.

See also:

Silent E, p. 110
Foreign E, p. 128

Exceptions:

were
  (ERE = ER)
there
where
ere
  (long A)
allege
  (short E)

E__E as in these

here	evening	sincerely
Steve	merely	interfere
Pete	complete	extremely
eve	stampede	precede
scene	convene	athlete
theme	compete	atmosphere
scheme	supreme	centipede
gene	gangrene	hemisphere
sphere	obscene	acetylene
mere	serene	supercede
cede	morpheme	maganese

Vowel-consonant-silent-E is a special long-vowel spelling pattern. The second E makes the first E "say its name." The second E remains silent when a syllable beginning with a consonant is added to the word.

Notice how few words use E__E. Most of our long E words are spelled with the vowel teams EA and EE.

92 words have E__E spelling long E.

These words are not counted under long E, page 108.

See also:

Short EA, p. 115
EAR-, p. 116
EAU, p. 128
also, p. 295
(very short
words)

EA as in meat

each	ears	easy
read	leader	teapot
dear	meaning	season
clean	leaves	reason
sea	pleased	teacher
leaf	beamed	feature
beach	healer	disappear
feast	dream	daydream
flea	steamer	increase
deal	peaked	measles
lea	meager	misdemeanor
reap	squeamish	entreaty
ream	bequeath	unseasonable
sheaf	appease	malfeasance
heave	feasible	upheaval

Exceptions:

beauty
　(long U)

yea
　(long A)

EA is a vowel team for long E. It is used mainly within the root but it can also come at the end. In a few Latin words the team breaks up, as in r**e-a**-lity. Most of our long E sounds are spelled with EA or EE.

EA is also a team for short E. There is no way for the eye to tell which sound is spelled by a given EA. The reader must be prepared to use whichever sound makes sense in the context in which the EA appears.

325　words have EA as in meat.

　These words are not counted under long E, p. 108.

See also:

EA, p. 114
EAR-, p. 116

EA as in bread

Exceptions:

great
break
steak
   (long A)

head	heavy	already
read	ready	treasure
deaf	breakfast	instead
breath	wearing	gingerbread
bear	weather	feather
lead	cleanser	heaven
dread	abreast	treachery
death	healthy	jealousy
meant	bearing	meadow
dealt	pleasant	deadlock
realm	steadfast	cleanliness
heady	zealous	endeavor
masthead	zealot	pleasantry
homestead	leathern	immeasurable
threadbare	forbear	pleasurable

EA is a vowel team for short E. This is the only case of a letter team being used for a short vowel.

EA is also a team for long E. There is no way for the eye to tell which sound is spelled by a given EA. The reader must be prepared to use whichever sound makes sense in the context in which the EA appears. But notice how often these words are related to words in which EA is long (heave/heavy, deal/dealt, mean/meant, please/pleasure).

Students should not be made to learn words like **bear** as exceptions, even though they rhyme with long A words like **care**. The R sound automatically distorts both short E and long A sounds so that these words become rhymes.

156 words have EA as in **bread**.

These words are not counted under short E, p. 109.

See also:

Long EA, p. 114
Short EA, p. 115

EAR- as in learn

Exceptions:

earth	earning	early
earn	learnt	earthquake
heard		earthworm
earl	earthy	earthly
pearl	unheard	rehearsal
search	pearly	searchlight
	research	rehearse
dearth	learnéd	earldom
hearse	unearth	earthenware
yearn	earnest	unearthly
earthen	unearned	unlearnéd

beard

  (long E)

heart
hearth
hearken
  (broad A)

When EA comes before R and a different consonant, the R changes the E sound to the special English vowel sound of ER.

This is the entire list of words that have EAR- before a different consonant.

These words are also counted under R, p. 219.

-ED as in jumped, filled or batted

Sounding like T	Sounding like D	Sounding like ed
picked	robbed	landed
laughed	tugged	traded
reached	dodged	nodded
baked	pulled	knitted
sniffed	named	pasted
dashed	returned	decided
chopped	preferred	discarded
addressed	displeased	completed
advanced	relieved	connected
eloped	settled	departed
menaced	redeployed	countermanded
trafficked	mortified	interrogated
ravished	disallowed	apprehended
prefixed	ennobled	docketed
prefaced	enlightened	billeted

-ED is a suffix added to verbs to show past action. The E is usually silent. It is sounded only after D and T, where a vowel sound is needed to help the listener realize that the suffix is in use. Otherwise, the D is voiced if the ED follows a vowel or a voiced consonant. But if it follows an unvoiced consonant, the D loses its normal voicing, and sounds like T.

Students should be encouraged to spot the root, and say it in such a way as to make it mean that it happened "yesterday." This will yield the correct sound for the -ED.

There is no count for these words, since they are only lengthened forms of root words already counted.

See also:

Foreign E, p. 128
also, p. 295
(very short
words)

EE as in sheep

Exceptions:

been
breeches
(short I)

see	seeing	between
feet	greener	Halloween
green	sweetest	cheerful
street	needed	reindeer
trees	sleepy	sixteen
flee	tepee	housekeeper
beef	cheesecloth	evergreen
sleeve	degree	agreement
tee	tweezers	guarantee
breeze	succeed	sweetheart
breech	decree	nominee
weep	genteel	indiscreet
seethe	redeem	proceeding
reek	beseech	velveteen
spleen	esteem	unseemly

EE is a vowel team for long E. It is used mainly within the root but it can also be at the end. In a few Latin words, the team breaks up, as in pre-emi-nent. In a few words, -EE is a suffix, as in nomin**ee**.

Most of our long E sounds are spelled with EE or EA.

307 words have EE as in **sheep**.

These words are not counted under long E, p. 108.

See also:

EY, p. 126

EI as in their

Exceptions:

conceive
deceive
perceive
receive
ceiling
   (long E after
   C)

either
neither
seize
leisure
weir
weird
   (long E)

heifer
   (short E)

Geiger
height
sleight
feisty
stein
seismograph
poltergeist
kaleidoscope
   (long I)

their	theirs	reindeer
eight	eighteen	neighbor
weigh	eighty	neighborhood
weight		
neigh		

		Unstressed
veil	heirloom	foreign
heir	freighter	sovereign
reign	heiress	forfeit
freight	heavyweight	counterfeit
beige		
sleigh	heinous	
skein	surveillance	
sheik	inveigle	

EI is a letter team for long A. It is used within the root instead of EY. Notice how many of these words end in silent GH, or in GN spelling N. In a very few Latin words, the team breaks up, as in **re-in**-force.

Most people seem to be confused by the old rhyme about I before E. It may be better to learn that EI within the word spells long A, that IE within the word spells long E, and that the CEI's are special. Rhyme or no rhyme, there are still many exceptions.

44 words have EI in a stressed root syllable, where the long A sound is clear.

9 words have EI in an unstressed syllable, where the long A sound is often muffled.

EO and OE are very unusual

Long E	Short E
people	Leonard
townspeople	leopard

Long E	Short E	Long O
phoenix	jeopardy	yeoman
subpoena	jeopardize	yeomanry
phoebe		
amoeba		
onomatopoeia		

EO and OE can be vowel teams, as shown above.

In words like **pigeon** and **gorgeous**, EO is not a vowel team. The E only serves to make the G soft.

Ordinarily, E and O belong to different syllables, as in g**e-o**g-ra-phy, cour-t**e-o**us and p**o-e**t.

This is the entire list of words in which EO and OE within the root are vowel teams.

See also:

-ERRY, p. 122
-IR, p. 164
-UR, p. 265

ER as in her

Exceptions:

err
  (see p. 122)

foyer
  (ER = long A)

sergeant
  (ER = AR)

concerto
  (short E)

Unstressed

mother	after	another
father	better	October
farmer	flower	everything
paper	number	different
under	eastern	government

Unstressed

clerk	person	perhaps
herd	perfect	perform
nerve	service	overhead
jerk	refer	permission
certain	university	interview

Unstressed

serf	submerge	intercede
berth	nervousness	underestimate
fern	alternative	reservation
assert	terminal	overburden
perjury	conversion	supervise

ER is a letter team for the special English vowel sound heard in **her**. E within the syllable is usually short. But R at the end of the word, or R before a different consonant, changes the short E to this special sound. -ER is very common as a suffix.

329 words have ER in a stressed syllable at the end of the word, or before a different consonant. In these words, the special vowel sound is clear.

1737 words have ER in an unstressed syllable at the end of the word, or within the word, as in **every**. In many of the words with internal -ER, the vowel sound is entirely lost, as in **interested**.

This count excludes many words with added **-er**, like **greener**. It includes only words like **baker**, with meanings distinct enough to warrant a separate entry in the dictionary. The words counted here are also counted under R, p. 219.

See also:

-ER, p. 121
-ARRY, p. 82
-IRRI-, p. 165
-ORRY, p. 198

ERR- as in berry

berry	ferry	blueberry
merry	very	American
cherry	sheriff	terrible
error	kerosene	prosperity
merit	inherit	territory
herald	hysterics	ceremony
heroism	sterilize	stationery
peril	periscope	period
therapy	spherical	incoherent
experiment	numerical	bacteria

In these words, the R does not change the E to a special vowel sound, because the R sound goes off with the next syllable.

129 words have ER or ERR in a syllable where the unchanged E sound is clear.

In words where ER is unstressed before a vowel, as in **different**, the E sound is usually changed by the R, unless it is lost entirely as in **temperature.**

These words are also counted under long and short E, pp.108 and 109, and under R, p. 219.

See also:

-E, p. 111
-S, p. 228
-ED, p. 117
Foreign E, p. 128

-ES as in boxes

dresses	faces	oranges
catches	teaches	sandwiches
washes	bushes	finishes
bridges	cages	villages
fixes	blazes	promises
cases	licenses	furnaces
prances	expenses	actresses
gashes	reflexes	annexes
plunges	arranges	drawbridges
dozes	displeases	advertises
lasses	devices	depresses
hoaxes	bonuses	enterprises
binges	transfixes	hypnotizes
lenses	alleges	cartridges
quinces	justices	duchesses

These words have the suffix **-es** added to them. This is a special form of the suffix **-s**. The **-es** form is used when a word ends in the sounds of S, Z, CH, SH, or J. The muffled E sound of **-es** helps the listener realize that the suffix **-s** is in use.

In some of these words, like **face**, the E is silent in the root, but sounds when **-s** is added. In others, like **dress**, the root has no silent E, and the **-es** form of **-s** must be added.

There is no count for these words, since they are only lengthened forms of words already counted.

EU as in feud

See also:

EW, p. 125
Foreign E, p. 128

No exceptions

Eugene	Europe	
sleuth	feudal	rheumatism
deuce	neutral	maneuver

		Unstressed
neutron	eulogy	grandeur
eunuch	pseudonym	pneumonia
pseudo	therapeutic	neurotic
		lieutenant

EU is a vowel team for long U. It is used within the root instead of EW. In a few Latin words, the team breaks up, as in pe-tro-le-um. EU is sometimes a Greek spelling, sometimes a French spelling.

27 words have the team EU in a stressed syllable, where the long U sound is clear.

12 words have the team EU in an unstressed syllable, where the long U sound is not always clear. However, even when most of the long U sound is lost, we maintain the Y-sound with which long U begins, as we do in **grandeur**. This is what tends to make the D of **grandeur** sound like J.

See also:

EU, p. 124

EW as in few

Exceptions:

sew
   (long O)

EW within the
   root:

lewd
newt

chew	grew	jewel
flew	screw	newspaper
drew	threw	nephew
knew	new	review
blew	mew	Jewish
brew	corkscrew	brewery
crew	dewdrop	jewelry
dew	skewer	renewal
pew	renew	reviewer
stew	sewer	newfangled
shrew	askew	curfew
hewn	anew	mildew
strew	steward	sinewy
strewn	pewter	viewpoint

EW is a vowel team for long U. It is used at the end of the root and before final N. Before other consonants, EW becomes EU, as in **feud**. EW is a native English spelling.

It is usually true that a long vowel "says its name." But the name of long U begins with a Y-sound which is often lost, because it is so difficult to pronounce after certain consonants, especially L and R. For example, the Y-part of the long U sound is clearly heard in **few**, but it is lost in **flew** and **grew**.

64 words have EW for long U.

EY as in they

See also:

AY, p. 85
EI, p. 119
EY, p. 127

whey	obey	
hey	greyhound	
prey	convey	conveyer
survey	heyday	surveyor
	surveying	disobey
bey	purvey	conveyance
	eyrie	purveyor
		abeyance

Exceptions:

key
  (long E)

eye
geyser
  (long I)

EY is a vowel team for long A. It is used at the end of the root.
Within the syllable, EY becomes EI, as in **their**.

This is the entire list of words containing EY for long A.

See also:

EY, p. 126
-Y, p. 285

No exceptions

EY as in money

turkey	monkey	honeybee
chimney	honey	donkey
valley	alley	
barley	hockey	attorney
cockney	jersey	baloney
jockey	volley	parsley
galley	journey	honeysuckle
abbey	trolley	palfrey
blarney	pulley	journeyman
kidney	parley	

EY is a vowel team. In these words, the EY is a suffix. As a suffix, EY sounds like the -Y of **puppy**.

43 words have EY as a suffix.

In foreign spellings E varies, as in ballet and Socrates

French	Greek	Other
cafe	acme	
bouquet		
encore		
rendezvous		
entree	acne	mesa
fete	beta	posse
crochet	diabetes	andante
plateau	apostrophe	ukulele
chauffeur	anemone	adobe
negligee	epitome	alcalde
entrepreneur	hyperbole	tsetse
clientele	phoebe	
bureaucracy	bases	
	indices	

These words are English enough to be included in the Hanna listing, but many of their letter sounds reflect their languages of origin. In these words, the E at the end sounds, except in **fete** and **clientele**. In the Greek words, there is also a long E sound in the **-es** suffixes.

75 words have foreign sounds for E, ES, ET or **EZ** at the end, or for the teams EE, EU or EAU.

See also:
FF, p. 131
GH, p. 141
PH, p. 213

Exceptions:
of
  (F = V)

F as in fan

fun	funny	himself
five	filling	before
fall	feeder	father
leaf	faces	afternoon
knife	offer	different
gift	forgive	difficult
fair	define	definite
fuse	prefer	preference
left	forecast	professor
craft	safeguard	fiftieth
fern	falsify	modification
brief	clarify	amplification
feat	terrific	felony
chafe	preface	magnificent
fend	fortnight	fertilize

F is a consonant letter for the first sound in **fan** and the last sound in **leaf**.

1907 words have F as in **fan**.

See also:

PH, p. 213
-LE, p. 175

F as in frog and fly

free	freezing	Friday
friend	fresher	frighten
from	floppy	afraid
floor	flutter	flower
flat	flashing	snowflakes
frown	fraction	frequently
freight	refrain	refreshments
flood	frontier	conflicting
flax	flavor	confronted
fleet	reflect	refrigerate
frail	frugal	inflation
frock	fragrant	inflammable
fret	defray	flexible
fluke	inflict	fraternize
flange	fluid	fraudulent

FR- and FL- are consonant blends. These blends very seldom split up between vowels. When the blend does not split up, the vowel before the blend is long, as in **refrain** and **reflect**.

143 words have the blend FR-.

171 words have the blend FL-.

These words are also counted under F, L and R, pp. 129, 173, and 219.

See also:

-LE, p. 175

Exceptions:

if
of
chef
clef
motif
  (final F)

giraffe
  (added E)

-FF as in sniff

off	huffing	cuff
fluff	stiffest	staff
muff	stuffing	sheriff
bluff	buff	rebuff
gruff	scoff	plaintiff
scuff	cliff	tariff
chaff	bailiff	midriff
ruff	distaff	pontiff
whiff	mastiff	
skiff		

FF is a letter team for sound of F at the end of the word. It is used right after a short vowel. There does not seem to be any justification for this doubling, unless it was adapted to avoid confusion with the suffix **-s**, at a time when S at the end of the word was written ∫ and F was written ⨍.

39 words contain FF at the end of the word. These words are also counted once each under F, p. 129.

The Letter G

In English, the letter G has two sounds, hard and soft. When it is hard, it spells the first sound of **go**. When it is soft, it sounds like J. The way to tell how a G sounds is to notice the letter that comes right after it.

In the Ancient Roman alphabet, G had only one sound, the sound it has in **go**. But as modern Italian, Spanish, French and English evolved from Ancient Latin, these hard G sounds gradually went soft before E, I and Y sounds. For this reason, G is normally soft before E, I and Y in Modern English.

1. G is hard before any letter except E, I or Y, as in

    game, **g**o, **g**un, **g**lass, **g**rass, do**g**fish, fra**g**ment, si**g**nal, ba**g**pipe, fla**g**ship, pi**g**tail, do**g**wood, zi**g**zag, ea**g**le, o**g**re.

    Also, G is hard when it has nothing after it, as in

    ba**g**, be**g**, bi**g**, bo**g**, bu**g**

2. G is normally soft before E, I, and Y, as in

    germ, **g**iant, **g**ym, **g**inger, hin**g**e, pa**g**e, pa**g**es, pa**g**ed, pa**g**ing, ca**g**y

    It makes no difference what the sound of the E, I, or Y happens to be. These letters usually make G soft when they come right after it.

    Hard and soft G work like hard and soft C. But there is one important difference. When we need a hard C sound before E, I or Y, we have the letter K available to solve the problem. But the only letter we have for the hard G sound is G. There is a small group of very common words in which G is hard even though the next letter is E or I, as in

    get, **g**ive, **g**irl, be**g**in

    Furthermore, we have no satisfactory solution for the problem of how to show a hard G sound before the native English suffixes, **-ed**, **-ing**, **-y**, etc. Instead of solving this problem, we ignore it, and simply take doubled G before these suffixes as being hard, as in

    hu**gg**ed, hu**gg**ing, di**gg**er, ba**gg**y, do**gg**ie, nu**gg**et

The French and Spanish also have this problem of how to keep G hard before E, I or Y. They have a routine solution for the problem. They insert a silent U between the G and the E, I, or Y. This device appears in some of our words, too, as in

guest, **gui**de, **guy**, pla**gue**, lea**gue**, **gui**llotine

Most of these words are borrowed from French.

The Italians, who also have this problem, solve it by inserting silent H between the G and the E, I or Y, as in **ghe**tto and spa**ghe**tti.

Finally, we never use J when the J sound is the last sound in the word. Instead, we use G with silent E to make it soft, as in

pa**ge**, hu**ge**, lar**ge**, for**ge**, plun**ge**, hin**ge**, bul**ge**

In **page** and **huge**, the final silent E is doing two jobs, making the G soft, and also making the vowel long. In the other sample words, the first consonant after the vowel determines the vowel sound, while the E confines itself to making the G soft.

But when we want a short vowel sound immediately before final GE, we must insert an extra consonant letter to keep the silent E from affecting the vowel. The letter we insert is D, as in

ba**dge**, e**dge**, bri**dge**, lo**dge**, ju**dge**

D makes phonetic sense for this purpose because the J sound is a complex sound which is begun by placing the tongue in the normal position for D.

A J sound at the end causes one additional problem in English, in the words that rhyme with **change**. By all the logic of the English spelling system, the N in **change** should make the vowel short, just like the N's in **hinge** and **plunge**. But this is a problem that has no good solution. Using a letter team for the long A sound ought to do the trick. But the only letter teams we have for long A within the root are AI and EI. Spelling **change** with one of these would make it look like "chainge," or "cheinge." Either of these solutions makes the word look as though it had the suffix **-ing** buried within it. This is too confusing to be practical. Therefore, we have to be satisfied with the letter group ANGE for these words. There is quite a group of words where **-ang-** indicates long A, both in one-syllable words and in longer forms, as in

range, strange, **danger**, **angel**, changing, m**angy**

Letter Teams Containing G

G is a member of the consonant teams NG, GH and GN.

1. NG is a consonant team for the last sound in **long**. This sound did not occur as a final sound in the Latin language. Therefore, the Latin alphabet which we use has no single letter available for representing it. We use NG at the end of the root, as in

ha**ng**, le**ng**-then, si**ng**, so**ng**, su**ng**

And in the suffix **-ing**, as in baki**ng**.

When suffixes are added to verbs ending in NG, the team retains its normal sound, as in

ha**ng**ed, ha**ng**er, ha**ng**ing, si**ng**ing, si**ng**er, lo**ng**ing

But when suffixes are added to adjectives ending in NG, the G takes on the hard G sound, as in

lon**g**er, stron**g**est, youn**g**er

Where the basic word includes a suffix, the G may be hard or soft, as in

fin**g**er, an**g**le, sin**g**le, bun**g**le, **g**in**g**er, tan**g**erine, an**g**el

2. The team GH stands for a sound which was common in Old English but does not exist in Modern English. It did not exist in Latin either, and therefore the Latin alphabet which we use had no single letter available for representing it. When Modern English was first being written, the team represented a sound like the German CH in **Bach**. But with the disappearance of this sound, the GH team has become silent in most words, as in

li**gh**t, strai**gh**t, cau**gh**t, throu**gh**, thou**gh**, fou**gh**t

There were some sections of England where these words were pronounced with an F sound for the GH team. A few of our Modern English words still have this sound for GH, as in

lau**gh**, cou**gh**, enou**gh**

At the beginning of the syllable, GH sounds like hard G, as in

ghost, **gh**ast-ly, **gh**et-to, spa-**gh**et-ti

3. In the consonant team GN, the G is silent at the beginning or the end of the root, as in

gnat, si**gn**, rei**gn**, forei**gn**, assi**gn**, beni**gn**

But if Latin suffixes are added to these words, the team splits up, and both letters have their normal sounds, as in

si**g-n**al, re-si**g-n**a-tion, be-ni**g-n**ant

See also:

Soft G, p. 137

G as in goat

Exceptions:

egg
  (see p. 295)

exaggerate
  (first G silent)

diaphragm
phlegm
paradigm
seraglio
  (silent G)

game	getting	garden
girl	given	again
gun	biggest	hungry
dog	shaggy	wagon
bag	going	together
gay	gadget	bugle
gears	gossip	signature
gift	eager	vagabond
goal	leggings	engagement
gulf	ragged	regardless
goad	cargo	inorganic
brig	gibbon	boondoggle
gird	triangle	propaganda
girth	lagoon	allegory
gaunt	goulash	litigation

G is a consonant letter for the first sound in **goat** and the last sound in **dog**. This is the hard sound of G. G is hard whenever it is not followed by E, I or Y.

We also use this sound in some very common words like **get** and **give**, where the next letter is E or I. Since we have no other letter for hard G, we must use G for these words.

1367 words have hard G. This count includes 43 words where G is hard before E and I.

See also:

Hard G, p. 136
-DGE, p. 102
J, p. 167

G as in giant

Exceptions:

43 common
words like **get**
and **girl**

40 words like
tiger whose
hard G is hard
before a native
English suffix,
and many like
begging, where
hard G is
doubled before
a native English
suffix.

margarine
algae
gaol
   (soft before
   A)

cage	largest	gypsy
change	stranger	orange
large	stages	general
gym	message	village
age	cottage	geography
gem	ranger	passenger
germs	forging	gentleman
gyp	baggage	hydrogen
sponge	ginger	tragedy
huge	suggest	regional
genes	genius	eugenics
gist	genus	progeny
gibe	cogent	terminology
merge	ingest	longitude
bilge	strategic	tautological

G is a consonant letter. Before E, I or Y, it is soft and sounds like J. When a J sound is at the end of the word, it is always spelled with G and silent E.

727 words have soft G.

See also:

GU-, p. 143
-LE, p. 175
-RE, p. 220

G as in green, gloves, and penguin

gray	grassy	grandmother
ground	growing	grasshopper
grade	growled	angry
glass	glider	geography
glad	glitter	ugly
groom	graceful	gratitude
graft	griddle	aggressive
grease	grocer	immigrant
glue	gloomy	glamorous
gloat	language	distinguish
grief	angler	glossary
grange	anguish	negligent
glade	gracious	degradation
glimpse	gravity	topography
grime	glucose	regression

GR- and GL- are consonant blends. G is hard before R and L. These blends sometimes split up between vowels. If the blend splits, the vowel before it is short, as in **progress**. Otherwise, the vowel before the blend is long, as in **program**.

GU- is also a consonant blend. In this blend the G is hard, and the U represents the sound of W.

291 words have the blend GR-.

 83 words have the blend GL-.

 17 words have the blend GU- sounding like GW-.

> These words are also counted under hard G, L, R and U as a consonant, pp. 136, 173, 219, and 260.

See also:

GH-, p. 140
-GH, p. 141
IGH, p. 162
OUGH, p. 203

GH as in straight

light	caught	through
might	taught	although
fight	bought	frighten
right	thought	neighbor
sight	eight	daughter
naughty	eighty	thoughtless
weight	eighteen	lightning
freight	weightless	neighborhood
neigh	freighter	overweight
blight	delight	knighthood
sleigh	inveigh	manslaughter
weighty	benighted	haughty
sprightly	onslaught	

GH is a consonant team for an Old English sound which has now been lost. In most words, GH is now silent.

165 words have silent GH.

See also:

GH, p. 139
-GH, p. 141

GH as in ghost

ghetto
spaghetti

aghast   ghoul   burgher
ghastly   ghostly   burgh

sorghum

GH is a consonant team. At the beginning of the word or syllable, it is a team for hard G.

This is the entire list of words that have GH sounding like hard G.

See also:

GH, p. 139
GH, p. 140

Exceptions:

ugh
  (GH = G)

GH as in laugh

rough   enough   cough
tough   laughter

laughable   roughen

slough (uff)

GH is a consonant team. At the end of the word, it is sometimes a team for the sound of F.

This is the entire list of words having GH with the sound of F.

See also:
-IND, p. 163

GN as in sign

gnome	reign	foreign
gnaw	gnat	design
	assign	

resign	resign	assignment
align	campaign	sovereign
gnarled	champagne	foreigner
arraign	cognac	poignant
		alignment

deign	malign	consignment
feign	benign	sovereignty
unfeigned	impugn	mignonette
gnu	ensign	poignancy
gnash		arraignment

GN is a consonant team for the sound of N. Occasionally, it represents a sound like a blend of N and Y-, as in **poignant**.

When GN is followed by a Latin suffix, the team often breaks up, and the G becomes hard as in si**g-n**al, ma-li**g-n**ant.

This is the entire list of words that have GN sounding like N.

These words are also counted under N, p. 179.

See also:

Hard G, p. 136
Soft G, p. 137
G blends, p. 138
-UE, p. 263

GU as in guest

Exceptions:

guard
guarantee
  (GU with silent
  U before A)

guess	league	
guild	guilty	guillotine
guide	fatigue	catalogue
vague	guitar	synagogue
guy		
rogue	guilder	analogue
fugue	guileless	demagogue
vogue	guernsey	pedagogue
guile	intrigue	beleaguer

GU can be a consonant team for hard G. When the next letter is E, I or Y, the U serves to prevent the E or I from making the G soft.

36 words have GU as a team for hard G.

These words are also counted under hard G, p. 136.

In French words, GE has a special sound

garage

rouge   gendarme   camouflage
beige   regime   sabotage
             barrage   lingerie
             massage   bourgeoisie
             mirage

cortege   persiflage
montage   negligee
prestige

In French, G is soft before E, I or Y, just as it is in English. But it has a special sound which is respelled ZH in English dictionaries.

These words are English enough to be included in the Hanna listing, but many of their letter sounds reflect their French origin.

This is the entire list of English words that have soft G with a French sound.

The Letter H

In English, the letter H has one basic sound, the first sound in **help**. It has this sound when it is the first letter in the word or syllable, as in

hat, hit, hole, dollhouse, childhood

In a small group of words borrowed from French, H is silent at the beginning of the syllable, as in

hour, heir, ho-nor, dis-ho-nest

There are also a few Latin words where H goes silent at the beginning of a syllable because it is inconvenient to pronounce the H sound in that position, as in

ex-haust, ex-hi-bit, pro-hi-bi-tion, ve-hi-cle

Notice, however, that the H does sound in related words where it is more easily pronounced, as in pro-hi-bit and ve-hi-cu-lar.

H almost never occurs alone after a vowel in English, although it does occur in

oh, ah, hah, eh, uh

Notice that these are all approximations of different types of inarticulate grunts.

Consonant Teams Containing H

H is the second letter in the consonant teams CH, GH, PH, RH, SH, TH and WH. All of these are teams for sounds which did not exist in the Latin language. Therefore, the Latin alphabet which we use has no single letters available for representing them.

1. CH has three sounds in English, as in

chicken, school and chef, (See "The Letter C," p. 89.)

2. GH has three sounds in English, as in

straight, laugh and ghost (See "The Letter G," p. 132.)

3. PH sounds like F in English, as in

phone and graph (See "The Letter P," p. 209.)

4. RH sounds like R in English, as in

rhyme, rhythm and Rhodes (See "The Letter R," p. 216.)

5. SH has one sound in English, as in

    ship, ca**sh**, lea**sh** (See "The Letter S," p. 222.)

6. TH has two sounds in English, as in

    this and **th**ing (See "The Letter T," p. 241.)

7. WH has one sound in English, as in

    what, **wh**eel, **wh**eat (See "The Letter W," p. 268.)

Notice that in all these teams, the H is the second letter of the team. This observation can be helpful to remedial students whose reversal tendencies cause them to place the H before the other letter ("hse" for **she**).

See also:

Silent H, p. 148

H as in hat

he	helped	history
house	horses	hundred
here	hiding	himself
have	handy	hungry
head	hottest	hello
half	higher	handsomely
hinge	hobby	however
harm	habit	horizon
heal	behave	adhesive
hymn	rehearse	inherit
hag	hireling	abhorrence
hale	harlot	prehensile
hart	enhance	harbinger
hue	hoarfrost	maharaja

H is a consonant letter for the first sound in **hat**. It has this sound only when it is the first letter in the syllable. When H is not the first letter in the syllable, it is a member of one of the letter teams, CH, GH, RH, PH, SH, TH or WH.

The sound of H, as in **hat**, does not occur as a final sound in English.

796 words have H as in **hat**.

See also:

H, p. 147

H as in hour

oh	honest	shepherd
hurrah	graham	fishhook
ah	John	
eh		
heir	forehead	silhouette
honor	gingham	philharmonic
hourly	dishonest	vehicle
exhaust	heiress	exhibition
	vehement	annihilate
herb	demijohn	honorific
herbage	nihilism	exhilarate
		exhortation

H is a consonant letter. In these words it is silent. The words beginning with silent H are borrowed from French. Many of the other words have related forms where the H sounds as in **herd**, **prohibit**, **vehicular** and **harmony**.

45 words have silent H.

The Letter I

In English, the letter I has three basic sounds, long I, short I and long E. We also use the letter Y for these three sounds. In general, we use I when the letter is within the word, and Y when it is at the end. If Y is within the word, it indicates a Greek origin; and if I is at the end, it is a foreign spelling (as in **ski**).

1. I / Y is short when it is within the syllable, as in

> bit, mist, print, quilt, bit-ten, print-ed, pre-dic-tion, gym, sym-bol

In the case of a word beginning with a vowel, I is short if it has a consonant after it in the same syllable, as in

> it, imp, ig-loo, in-te-rest, im-pres-sion

The short sound of I / Y is changed to the special English vowel sound of ER by final R, or by R followed by a different conso-nant sound, as in

> sir, third, sir-loin, cir-cum-stance, m**yrrh**

But if the next sound is a vowel, it will capture the R sound, and leave the I sound unchanged, as in

> mir-ror, ir-ri-gate, spi-rit, ti-ring, sy-rup, ty-rant

2. I / Y is long and sounds like the **name** of the letter I —

a. When it is the last letter in the syllable, as in

> I, bi-ting, i-de-a, de-ci-ded, ty-rant

(But in the Latin style of spelling, these I / Y's are very often short, as in cli-nic, mi-ne-ral, de-ci-sion, phy-sics.)

b. In the spelling pattern I__E, as in

> b**ite**, f**ive**, t**ire**, de-c**ide**, spe-cia-l**ize**, t**ype**, a-na-l**yze**

c. In the vowel team IGH, as in h**igh**, n**igh**t, r**igh**t

d. In the letter groups -IND, -ILD and -IGN, when they are at the end of the root, as in

> f**ind**, k**ind**, w**ild**, ch**ild**, s**ign**, al**ign**

But in longer forms of these words, the I often goes short, as in

kin-dred, wil-der-ness, chil-dren, sig-nal, ma-lig-nant

Notice that when the I goes short, the G of -IGN sounds.

e. When it is spelled -Y or -IE at the end of a root word, as in

by, cry, fly, sky, re-ply, de-ny, sa-tis-fy, tie, pie

And when IE is substituted for the -Y of the root, as in

flies, cried, re-plies, de-nied, sa-tis-fied

f. When I / Y before another vowel is in a root syllable, as in

li-on, ri-ot, sci-ence, tri-al, bi-o-lo-gy, pi-o-neer, re-li-a-ble, ap-pli-ance, cy-a-nide

And when I before another vowel is in the stressed syllable of a complex suffix, as in

va-ri-**e**-**ty**, so-ci-**e**-**tal**, psy-chi-**a**-**trist**

3. I and Y represent a long E sound—

a. When Y or IE are suffixes, and in the suffix **ly**, as in

can-d**y**, hap-p**y**, his-to-r**y**, li-bra-r**y**, a-bi-li-t**y**, quick-**ly**, slow-**ly**, fun-da-men-tal-**ly**

b. When I / Y is before another vowel in a suffix, as in

hap-pi-**er**, ra-di-**o**, pe-ri-**od**, fu-ri-**ous**, me-di-**um**, va-ri-**ous**, em-bry-**o**

This type of I corresponds very closely to the suffix -Y of such words as hap-py and fu-ry. But it often sounds more like the consonant Y of can-yon, as in

mil-lion, cham-pion, a-lien, com-pa-nion

In a great many words, this Y-sound of a suffix containing I before a vowel distorts the sound of the consonant which the I captures from the previous syllable. It can turn S or T sounds into SH sounds, and Z sounds into ZH sounds, as in

mis-**sion**, com-pul-**sion**, ra-**cial**, na-**tion**, par-**tial**, vi-**sion**, oc-ca-**sion**, con-fu-**sion**, gla-**zier**

For the behavior of suffixes beginning with I before a vowel, see pages 322 to 325, under "The Latin Style of Spelling," in Appendix B.

c. In the vowel team -IE- when it is within the root word, as in

chief, field, piece, fierce

d. In foreign spellings. In languages other than English, I usually represents the sound of our long E. In borrowed words, we often imitate the foreign pronunciation, and the foreign sound of the I's can persist for a long time after the word becomes fully English, as in

ski, antique, machine, police, concertina

Unstressed I / Y

Unlike the sounds of other English vowel letters, the sounds of I / Y are fairly distinct even in unstressed syllables. When the next letter is a consonant the I / Y remains detectably long or short, depending on how it would sound if it were stressed, as in

i-de-a-lism, li-bra-ri-an, ta-king, in-ci-den-tal-ly, pro-hi-bi-tion, psy-cho-lo-gy, cryp-to-gra-phy

As was outlined above, when Y, and I before a vowel, are unstressed because they are in suffixes, they have a distinct long E sound. Some linguists (and many dictionaries) identify this as a short I sound. But using a long E sound for these I / Y's seems to be the most useful approach for beginners and remedial students who are attempting to sound out a word that looks unfamiliar. In any case, the difference in sound between unstressed long E and unstressed short I is nearly undetectable to the layman, and the student reader is most certainly a layman.

I / Y in Teams for Other Vowels

I / Y is the second member of the vowel teams AI / AY, EI / EY, OI / OY and UI. (See "The Letter A," p. 67; "The Letter E." p. 104; "The Letter O," p. 182; and "The Letter U," p. 253.)

See also:

-I, p. 154
Foreign I, p. 166
Long Y, p. 286

I as in ivy

Exceptions:

business
(silent I)

		Unstressed
rider	tiger	direction
biting	spider	idea
shiny	siren	biography
whiter	bicycle	rhinoceros
timer	surprising	

		Unstressed
twilight	title	librarian
spiral	irony	biology
slimy	primary	ideal
cider	diary	gigantic
driver	society	identity

		Unstressed
bison	likable	admiral
guidance	revival	vibration
pilot	reprisal	itinerary
stipend	refinery	diameter
tribal	advisable	ironic

I is a vowel letter. It is long in a syllable that ends in I. When there is a single consonant letter between vowels, the first vowel is long before the native English suffixes, and certain Latin suffixes. The vowel is often long in Latin words when there is an R-blend between vowels, as in **microscope**.

386 words have long I in a stressed syllable, where the vowel sound is clear.

143 words have long I in an unstressed syllable, where the vowel sound is sometimes muffled.

This count excludes words like **biting**, where the native English suffix simply changes the word's form.

See also:

-IND, p. 163
Foreign I, p. 166
Short Y, p. 287

I as in Indian

Exceptions:

climb
pint
ninth
  (long I)

island
isle
viscount
  (long I and
  silent S)

indict
  (long I and
  silent C)

		Unstressed
it	digger	running
big	missed	music
this	tricky	credit
him	didn't	cabin
string	city	magic

		Unstressed
limp	fifty	disgusted
fib	spinach	installment
nip	permission	improvement
mix	assistant	ownership
pitch	condition	quantity

		Unstressed
ill	manilla	sceptic
sprint	submissive	diploma
silt	signature	insurance
timber	religion	astonish
quibble	manipulate	tuberculosis

I is a vowel letter. I is short in a syllable that ends with a consonant letter. When there are two consonants between vowels, the first vowel is almost always short. In many of the long, Latin words, the first vowel is short even when there is only one consonant between vowels, as in **manipulate**.

2434 words have I before a consonant in a stressed syllable, where the vowel sound is clear.

3934 words have I before a consonant in an unstressed syllable. In spite of being unstressed, the short I sound remains fairly clear.

See also:

Long -Y, p. 284
Suffix -Y, p. 285

I as in Rabbi or ski

I	ski	macaroni
hi	taxi	spaghetti
hi-fi	zombi	
yogi	confetti	alibi
anti	broccoli	alkali
chili	khaki	Rabbi
alumni	cadi	safari
fungi	nisei	timpani
	mufti	maharani

At the end of the word, I may be long or it may have a long E sound. In English, I is at the end of the word only in foreign spellings, slang forms, and in the pronoun I.

This is the entire list of words with I at the end.

The words where the I is long are also counted under I, p. 152.

See also:

Long I, p. 152
-IED, p. 161

-I- as in lion

crier	science	diary
driest	diamond	violin
liar	giant	violet
flier	quiet	
dial	society	diagram
client	variety	diameter
riot	violence	biology
trial	reliable	biography
diet	triangle	appliance
bias	denial	compliance
ion	defiance	priority
brier	propriety	psychiatrist
pious	pliable	ultraviolet
liable	violate	viaduct

When I comes before another vowel, it does not usually form a team with the second vowel. Instead, the I is at the end of one syllable, and the other vowel begins its own syllable. If the I is in the root, as in **reliable**, or if it is in a stressed syllable, as in **variety**, it is long.

124 words have I sounding like long I before another vowel.

These words are also counted under long I, p. 152.

See also:

-IED, p. 161
Suffix -Y, p. 285
-CI-, p. 98
-SI-, p. 236
-SSI-, p. 238
-TI-, p. 250

-I- as in radio

funnier	Indian	question
happiest	curious	television
tinier	soldier	nation
prettiest	million	motion
copier	period	vacation
furious	social	abbreviate
various	partial	appreciate
medium	region	education
librarian	conscience	condition
patriot	official	musician
dubious	dominion	visionary
passion	aquarium	partiality
radium	gardenia	recipient
memorial	devious	initiation
sodium	hernia	collegiate

When I comes before another vowel, it does not usually form a team with the second vowel. Instead, the I is at the end of one syllable, and the other vowel begins its own syllable. If the I is part of a suffix, it is unstressed, and sounds like -Y in funny.

Unstressed I before a vowel is very common on the Latin side of English. (See "Suffixes like **-ial**," pp. 323, 324.) In many such words the vowel sound of the I is lost in the effect that its unstressed long E sound has on the preceding consonant.

1719 words have unstressed I before a vowel.

See also:

Silent -E, p. 110
Foreign I, p. 166
Y_E, p. 288

I—E as in bike

Exceptions:

give
live
  (short I)

		Unstressed
like	sidewalk	notice
fire	awhile	promise
ice	decide	engine
ride	bonfire	favorite
white	meantime	imagine

		Unstressed
slice	lifelike	reconcile
dime	subscribe	advertise
bride	rhinestone	apprentice
dive	divide	relative
wire	retirement	medicine

		Unstressed
stride	justice	adjective
chime	native	conservative
prime	motive	organize
vise	protective	juvenile
guide	creative	hypocrite

Vowel-consonant-silent-E is a special long vowel spelling pattern. The silent E makes the I "say its name." The E remains silent when a syllable beginning with a consonant is added to the word.

394 words have I_E in a stressed syllable, where the long I sound is clear.

484 words have I_E in an unstressed syllable. In these words, the I is often short in spite of the silent E.

These words are not counted under long I, p. 152, or under short I, p. 153.

-IE as in pie

See also:

-IE, p. 159
-IE-, p. 160
-IED, p. 161
Long -Y, p. 284
  also, p. 295

No exceptions

lie	untie
tie	necktie
die	

belie
magpie

fie
hie
vie

IE is a vowel team. When IE is at the end of the root, it is stressed and sounds like long I.

This is the entire list of words which have the team IE at the end of the root.

These words are not counted under long I, p. 152.

See also:

Long -IE, p. 158
-IE-, p. 160
IED, p. 161
Suffix -Y, p. 285

-IE as in movie

No exceptions

brownie	laddie	birdie
collie	lassie	genie
prairie	caddie	menagerie
coolie	eerie	reverie
		calorie
		lingerie
eyrie		coterie
		bourgeoisie

IE is a vowel team. In these words, IE is a suffix. It sounds like the suffix -Y in **funny**.

This is the entire list of words which have the suffix -IE.

-IE- as in chief

See also:

EI, p. 119
Suffix -IE, p. 159
Long -IE, p. 158

field	fielder	believe
thief	pieces	relief
priest		masterpiece
shield		
niece		

Exceptions:

friend
  (short E)

sieve
  (short I)

grief	achieve	achievement
weird	windshield	disbelief
fierce	hygiene	besieger
yield	frontier	chandelier
tier	cashier	

		Unstressed
brief	grievance	chesterfield
fiend	priesthood	mischievous
wield	reprieve	handkerchief
shriek	cavalier	
pierce	centerpiece	

When IE is within the root of the word, it is a letter team for long E. Notice how many of these words end in LD, F or VE. IE also has this sound in a few **-ier** suffixes, as in front**ier**.

71 words have IE in a stressed syllable, where the long E sound is clear.

 6 words have IE within a root in an unstressed syllable, where the vowel sound is often muffled.

These words are not counted under long E, p. 108.

See also:

Long -IE, p. 158
Suffix -IE, p. 159
Long -Y, p. 284
Suffix -Y, p. 285

-IED and -IES as in tried and hurries

cried	replies	cities
dried	supplied	candied
fries	multiplied	movies
pies	satisfied	families
lies	butterflies	histories
dies	certified	hobbies
tried	dignified	varied
relied	occupies	envied
denies	qualifies	libraries
applied	prophesied	realities
pried	salaried	similarities
modifies	academies	extremities
crucified	casualties	bibliographies
liquefied	emergencies	conspiracies
petrified	prophecies	intermediaries

If a word ends in Y, we change the Y to I before adding the suffix **-ed**. Before adding the suffix **-s**, we change the Y to I and add E before the S. If the word ends in -IE, like **tie** or bird**ie**, we simply add D or S.

The endings -IED and -IES have the same vowel sound that -Y or -IE has in the original word.

There is no count for these words, since they are only lengthened forms of words already counted.

See also:
Silent GH, p. 139

IGH as in light

No exceptions

right	brightness	delight
bright	lightning	frightened
might	tightly	tonight
sight	fighter	flashlight
knight	sunlight	nightgown
flight	spotlight	overnight
high	eyesight	nightingale
slight	birthright	copyright
sigh	playwright	highland
	midnight	highwayman
blight	insight	unrighteous
plight	fortnight	wheelwright
thigh	alight	
nigh	outright	
	sprightly	

IGH is a vowel team for long I. This is a remnant of old German and Old English spelling.

88 words have IGH.

These words are not counted under long I, p. 152. They are counted under GH, p. 139.

See also:

GN, p. 142
Short I, p. 153

-IND as in find

Exceptions:

wind (blowing)
build
guild
gild
rescind
   (short I)

kind	kindest	behind
mind	minded	blindfold
child	children	childhood
wild	wilder	wilderness
sign	signing	signal
bind	remind	assignment
blind	unwind	resignation
grind	design	designer
rind	resign	alignment
mild		kindliness
unbind	consignment	womankind
align	designation	mildew
malign	malignant	ensign
	unmindful	

When IND, ILD and IGN are at the end of the word, the I is long. The I remains long when a native English suffix is added. But in longer forms, the I often goes short.

51 words have -IND, -ILD or -IGN at the end of the root with a long I sound.

These words are not counted under long I, p. 152. They are counted under D, GN, L and N, pp. 100, 142, 173, and 179. Those with short I are counted under short I, p. 153.

IR as in girl

See also:

-ER, p. 121
-IRRI-, p. 165
-UR, p. 265
-YR, p. 289

sir	dirty	circle
bird	stirring	circus
chirp	whirling	squirrel
first	chirping	birthday
skirt	birdie	thirteen
birch	squirming	virtuous
birth	mirthful	circulate
firm	circuit	circumstance
twirl	thirsty	confirmation
flirt	sirloin	circumference
fir	girdle	firmament
firth	affirm	affirmative
mirth	skirmish	virtuous
smirk	virgin	virtual
girder	circlet	circumvent

Exceptions:

souvenir
fakir
  (long E)

birr
whirr
  (double R)

IR is a letter team for the special English vowel sound of ER.
I within the syllable is usually short. But R at the end of the word,
or R before a different consonant, changes the short I to this
special sound.

114 words have IR at the end of the word or before
    a different consonant.

These words are also counted under R, p. 219.

See also:

-IR, p. 164

IRR- as in mirror

Exceptions:

squirrel
(IR as in girl)

Words like
stirring
(where R is
doubled be-
fore a native
English suffix
is added.)

sirup
chirrup
stirrup

spirit	irregular	irrigate
miracle	irrelevant	irritation
spiritual	conspiracy	irresponsible
mirage	delirious	irresistible
	dirigible	irrational

dispirited	irritant	tiring
empirical	irradiate	siren
satirical	irresolute	direct
virile	irrespective	spiral
		irony

In these words, the R does not change the I to a special vowel sound, because the R sound goes off with the next syllable.

53 words have IR or IRR before a vowel letter.

These words are also counted under long I and short I, pp. 152, and 153, and under R, p. 219.

In foreign spellings, I varies, as in machine and lingerie.

I__E	I within the syllable	I at the end of the syllable
policeman		ski
automobile		mosquito
magazine		piano
gasoline		
submarine		
sardine	souvenir	yogi
antique	meringue	trio
fatigue		liter
chlorine		lira
		cuisine
pique	motif	nisei
naive	debris	cuirass
artiste	petit	diva
pristine	fakir	merino
benzine		liana

Words of this kind are English enough to be included in the Hanna listing, but many of their letter sounds reflect their languages or origin.

90 words have I with a foreign sound. The sound is almost always the same as our long E sound.

See also:

Soft G, p. 137
-DGE, p. 102
-DU-, p. 103

J as in jeep

Jean	Johnny	Judy
Jane	jumping	jacket
Jack	jokes	January
job	judged	jolly
just	joining	enjoy
jar	object	injection
jot	subject	journalism
joy	rejoice	objective
jig	adjust	majesty
jab	project	trajectory
jest	adjourn	jeopardize
jamb	sojourn	subjunctive
jilt	conjure	jurisprudence
joist	jetsam	prejudice
jowl	adjudge	adjudicate

J is a consonant letter for the first sound in **jeep**. We never use J as the last letter in the word. Instead, we use -GE or -DGE.

235 words have J as in **jeep**. In 60 of these, the next letter is E or I, even though the usual letter for this sound before E and I is soft G.

See also:

Hard C, p. 92
Hard CH, p. 96
-CK, p. 99
QU, p. 214
-X, p. 277

K as in keep

king	walked	kitchen
keep	kitten	Thanksgiving
kite	drinking	handkerchief
ask	shaky	kangaroo
make	lucky	breakfast
tuck	skillful	needlework
key	kindly	cantankerous
speak	lukewarm	remarkable
stake	pitchfork	basketball
skull	crinkle	pickpocket
kelp	fakir	alkaloid
kiln	akin	skeletal
musk	bodkin	frankincense
dank	evoke	kleptomania
shrike	bethink	obelisk

Exceptions:

disc
arc
franc
zinc
talc
bloc
chic
sac
　(all final C in
　the root.)

K is a consonant letter for the first sound in **keep** and the last sound in **speak**. In English spelling, K is used only before E, I or Y, where C will not work to show the K sound.

Root words ending in a K sound must be spelled with K because most of them take the native English suffixes beginning with E, I and Y.

904 words have K as in **keep**. Of these, 40 have A, O, U or L after the K. These are all borrowed from other languages.

See also:

GN, p. 142
N, p. 179

KN as in knee

know	knocker	knowledge
knew	knife	knighthood
knot	kneeling	
knight	knitting	
knead	knapsack	unknown
knob	knothole	acknowledge
knives	knuckle	
knack	penknife	
knoll	knavish	foreknowledge
knave	knurled	knickerbocker

KN- is a native English letter team for the sound of N. It occurs only at the beginning of the root. At one time, these K's were pronounced.

Notice how many of these words have meanings connected with shapes like **knees** or **knuckles**, or with actions performed by **knuckles**.

37 words have KN as in knee.

These words are also counted under N, p. 179.

The Letter L

L is a consonant letter for the first sound in **look**. The sound of L in American English is a very sophisticated sound and, as a result, the letter L is especially difficult for reading students.

When one says that our L has a sophisticated sound, one means that it is quite a lot more difficult to pronounce than the spontaneous L sound that occurs in the babbling of infants. Children take a long time to master the trick of saying L in the adult American way. Most of them are still pronouncing L in a babyish way during the first year of school. It is very hard for them to combine the L sound with other consonant sounds, as in **bl**ack and **cl**ock. As a result, they become especially confused about such words when they have to learn them as whole words in word-memorization classrooms.

The spontaneous L sound of infant babbling is a voiced consonant which is pronounced quite far forward in the mouth. The adult L of American English is pronounced farther back in the mouth, and is much more heavily voiced than the infant L. Before the vowel sound, L behaves like any other consonant. Compare **hot**, **not** and **lot**. The L blends with the O sound in the same way as the H or the N. But we voice an L sound after the vowel especially heavily, so much so that the voice remains almost as unrestricted while the L is being pronounced as it is during the vowel sound, as in **tell**, **tile** and **tail**. This can confuse remedial spelling students very seriously.

L after the vowel is even harder for children to pronounce than L before the vowel. If they are not getting careful work in phonics, they become confused about these words, also, when they begin trying to read. In fact, L can cause so much confusion that children soon begin to build up a block against reading these words. Then, at the first glimpse of a word containing L, they begin to guess wildly, which causes more trouble, which causes even wilder guessing, and so on. By the time such children become remedial students the problem can be severe.

As far as speech goes, most people eventually master the American L, and can handle it after long vowel sounds, and after short E, I and U sounds (as in **help, hill, hulk**), without any distortion of the vowel sounds. But the short sounds of A and O are **normally** distorted when L follows them in the same syllable (as in **call** and **cold**; see below). This, of course, only increases the confusion of children who are having trouble with reading.

The letter L is used in the following ways.

1. L before the vowel.

   a. L is the first letter in the syllable in words like

      last, let, look, loud, tab-let, quick-ly, care-less

   b. L is the last member of a consonant blend in words like

      black, **cl**ean, **chl**orine, **fl**ag, **gl**ad, **pl**an, **sl**ip, **spl**ash

   c. **-le** is a native English suffix, as in lit-**tle**. Although the L is before the E, we pronounce this suffix the way we pronounce the suffix **-el**, as in tun-**nel**. Because of this pronunciation, **-le** behaves like a suffix beginning with a vowel. It captures the final consonant sound from the root syllable of the word, and runs off with it. (See "Syllables and Stress, English Suffixes," page 304.) For this reason, consonant doubling is used to show a short vowel sound before this suffix, as in

      ap-ple, ta-ble, bub-ble, bu-gle

2. L after the vowel. (See " 'Long' and 'Short', p. 31."

   a. L after long vowel sounds, and special English vowel sounds that behave like long vowels. Examples are

      pail, feel, tile, coal, rule, boil, howl, cool

      In these words, the glide at the end of the long vowel sound closes the mouth before the L is pronounced. The result is often much like a two-syllable word. Students must be warned to give the vowel sound its full length before adding the L sound. After identifying the word, the student can then repeat the word with a more normal pronunciation.

   b. L after short E, I and U. Examples are

      tell, help, jelly, elder; fill, milk, pillow, filter; dull, bulk, sullen, sulky

      Notice that if the L sound is at the end of the root word,

we use LL to spell it. Most final doublings of this kind serve a specific purpose. There does not seem to be such a justification for -LL, however.

c. LL, or L and a different consonant after A or O. Examples are

hall, halt, hal-ter, fal-ter; roll, hold, hol-ster, sol-dier

Here we have A and O within the syllable, where vowels are normally short. But the L sound in these syllables changes the A so that it sounds like AW in cr**awl**, and it changes the O sound from short to long. This happens regularly on the native English side of our language. But on the Latin side of English, A and O can be short before L followed by a different consonant sound, as in

talc, calcium, alphabet, solve, revolver

d. AL and OL before a vowel sound. Examples are

ral-ly, bal-lad, tal-low, gal-lop, al-ley, cal-lous. hol-ly, fol-low, dol-lar, trol-ley, pol-len, pa-ling, po-ling

Here, the suffix captures the L sound and runs off with it, leaving the first vowel unchanged. Students must be warned that these ALL's and OLL's do not sound as they would at the end of words like **call** and **roll**.

3. Silent L.

L is silent before final K and M sounds after A and O, as in

talk, calm, folk, Holmes

Here, although the L has no sound of its own, it is needed to warn the reader of the changed sounds of the A's and O's.

Exceptions:

colonel
  (L = R)

L as in leaf

look	helper	leather
please	sleeping	yellow
milk	lived	careful
feel	felt	himself
girl	children	telephone
clip	alarm	equally
trail	loyal	politics
pile	chloride	apologize
bleat	gallant	colorful
howl	include	revolver
vale	calcium	fluoridate
phlegm	evolve	turbulence
plight	allay	similarly
gulch	bellows	telemetry
sleigh	helmsman	astrology

L is a consonant letter for the first sound in **leaf** and the last sound in **feel**. It is the second member of the consonant blends BL-, CL-, CHL-, FL-, GL-, PL-, PHL- and SL-.

When L comes at the end after a long vowel sound it is often pronounced almost like an extra syllable, as in **pile**. The reader must be careful to give the vowel its full length before sounding the L.

6326 words have L as in **leaf**.

L as in walk

See also:

ALL, p. 78
OLD, p. 193

talk	talker	sidewalk
chalk	walking	
	walked	
balk	calm	folklore
stalk	palm	talkative
folk	psalm	kinsfolk
yolk	chalky	almond
balm	almshouse	gentlefolk
qualm		
alms		

Exceptions:

half
calf
could
would
should
   (silent L before
   F or D

almost
almighty
polka
Balkan
alkali
palmate
ophthalmology
   (L sounding
   before K or M
   after A or O)

L is a consonant letter. Here it is silent. In these words, A and O have their sounds changed by the L, even though the L loses its own sound. Notice that the letter after the L is always K or M.

When words ending in LK and LM contain E, I or U, the vowel is short, and the L sounds.

31 words have silent L before K or M.

These words are also counted under -ALL, OLD, K and M, pp. 78, 193, 168 and 177.

See also:

Silent -T-, p. 245

-LE as in table

apple	able	trouble
little	needle	candle
tickle	title	bicycle
bottle	maple	possible
bubble	eagle	bumblebee
scribbler	probable	acceptable
measles	encircle	reasonable
startling	horrible	honeysuckle
trickled	vehicle	responsible
giggly	redouble	settlement
gable	arable	admissible
swaddle	culpable	inaudible
pestle	crucible	redoubtable
dawdle	debacle	comestible
cobbler	mistletoe	impregnable

-LE is one of the native English suffixes. It is pronounced like the suffix **-el** as in **tunnel**. This pronounciation makes **-le** behave like a suffix beginning with a vowel. It captures the last consonant of the root and runs off with it. As a result, two consonants before **-le** are needed to show a short vowel before the suffix, as in **little**. A single consonant before **-le** shows a long vowel in the first syllable, as in **table**. When a suffix beginning with a vowel is added to these words, the final E must be dropped.

630 words have the suffix **-le**.

These words are also counted under L, p. 173.

-LL as in bell

See also:

-AL, p. 76
ALL, p. 78
OLD, p. 193

call	smaller	windmill
fell	telling	waterfall
will	hilly	baseball
roll	rolled	bluebell
full	pulling	downhill
stall	skillful	foretell
cell	install	fulfill
dull	spillway	illness
drill	spellbound	millstone
dwell	foothill	chlorophyll
cull	pall	instill
dell	null	appall
gill	quell	enthrall
knell	rill	crestfallen
mull	boll	atoll

Exceptions:

belle
gazelle
grille
vaudeville
chenille
nacelle
  (silent E)

kiln (silent N)

el
mil
nil
  (single L at the
  end of the root)

-LL is a consonant team for the sound of L at the end of the root. We use -LL at the end after a short vowel. We also use -LL at the end after A or O changed by L.

152 words have -LL at the end.

These words are also counted once each under L, p. 173.

See also:

L, p. 173
-MB, p. 178

M as in man

Exceptions:

mnemonics
   (MN = N)

comptroller
   (MP = N)

me	milk	many
map	smaller	morning
am	jumped	mother
came	making	become
March	seemed	important
mist	hammock	amazement
clamp	admit	margarine
chrome	major	magnetic
prism	metal	socialism
palm	camel	ambulance
maim	mandate	admonish
pomp	monarch	phenomenon
smite	alchemy	sublimate
mall	dictum	medallion
mar	syndrome	impetuous

M is a consonant letter for the first sound in **man** and the last sound in **drum**.

3698 words have M as in **man**.

See also:
GN, p. 142

-MB and -MN as in lamb and condemn

climb	climber	honeycomb
comb	combing	autumn
thumb	bomber	
bomb	crumbs	
dumb		

limb	plumber	column
tomb	plumbing	solemn
hymn	tombstone	succumb
damn	benumb	
jamb	dumbbell	

-MB and -MN are consonant teams for the sound of M.

Notice that in these longer forms, the B or the N sounds:

crumble	damnable
thimble	condemnation
clamber	autumnal
hymnal	columnist

28 words have -MB at the end of the word.

7 words have -MN at the end of the word.

These words are also counted under M, p. 177.

See also:

GN, p. 142
KN, p. 169
MN, p. 178
PN-, p. 211

Exceptions:

Ann
inn
  (see p. 295)

Anne
  cretonne
  (-NNE)

N as in nest

night	needed	anyway
no	noisy	airplane
mean	sending	number
snow	planned	chicken
stand	rainy	interested
nail	inning	unfinished
noun	connect	tradition
bound	flannel	astonishment
thorn	silken	anonymous
near	nasty	disturbance
feint	infer	pecuniary
nape	naive	genealogy
naught	nitric	transgression
niche	colon	vigilance
glen	ermine	notarize

N is a consonant letter for the first sound in **nest** and the last sound in **mean**.

7927 words have N as in **nest**.

NG as in long

See also:

NK, p. 181
-ANGE, p. 80

Exceptions:

tongue
harangue
meringue
(silent UE)

ginger
dingy
stingy
(soft G)

ring	singing	something
thing	crying	morning
sang	going	during
king	stepping	singsong
string	feeling	ding-dong
clang	youngster	ringleader
lung	prolong	kingfisher
sling	lodgings	lengthwise
strength	stronghold	amongst
wring	bowling	alongside
tungsten	sarong	prepossesing
lading	beetling	unassuming
	changeling	unremitting

-NG is a letter team for the special English consonant sound at the end of **long**. This sound does not occur at the beginning of the word. In words with Latin suffixes, like **tangent**, and words ending in **-nge**, like **hinge**, the G is soft.

When suffixes are added to verbs ending in -NG the team remains a team, as in ha**ng**er and lo**ng**ing. When suffixes are added to adjectives or other non-verb roots the team breaks up, and the G has a hard G sound as in lo**ng**est and fi**ng**er.

370 words have the team NG at the end of the word or syllable. This count does not include words with the suffix -ing unless they have a special meaning, as in **bedding**.

See also:

NG, p. 180

-NK as in bank

pink	pinker	Thanksgiving
think	thinking	uncle
thank	thanked	
drink	drinking	
drank	spanking	
blank	anger	frankfurter
chunk	conquer	indistinct
franc	function	fingernail
lynx	language	congressman
zinc	single	entangle
dank	bethink	propinquity
	languor	singularity
	inkling	compunction
	juncture	dysfunction
	ingot	sacrosanct

-NK is a consonant blend that comes at the end of the word. Before K sounds or hard G sounds, N takes on an NG sound.

355 words have N sounding like NG.

These words are also counted under N, p. 179; and under C, G, K, Q or X, pp. 92, 136, 168, 214 or 277.

The Letter O

In English, the letter O has three basic sounds, long O, short O, and short U.

1. O is short when it is within the syllable, as in

> hot, stop, pond, hot-ter, fon-dle, con-cert, a-dop-ted and in

> dog, long, dog-gie, sof-ter, cost-ly, di-a-logue

In some regions, the short O's in the set of examples beginning with **dog** sound different from the short O's in the set of examples beginning with **hot**. In these regions, O as in **hot** sounds like the broad A of AR, while O as in **dog** sounds like the broad A of ALL. In other regions, all the short O's and broad A's sound alike. Novices should learn only the sound that O has in **hot** in their own speech, and be warned to be a little flexible in any word where that sound seems a bit off-color to them.

In the case of a word beginning with a vowel, O is short if it has a consonant after it in the same syllable, as in

> on, off, of-fice, ob-sta-cle, oc-to-pus, op-tion-al

2. O is long and sounds like the **name** of the letter O —

a. When it is the last letter in the syllable, as in

> go, ho-ping, o-pen, to-tal, mo-tion, ex-plo-sion

(But in the Latin style of spelling, these O's are often short, as in pro-duct, to-nic, as-tro-no-my.)

b. In the spelling pattern O__E, as in

> hope, tone, pole, more, re-mote, ex-plode

c. In the vowel teams OA, OE and OW, as in

> toe, grow, blow, at the end of the root, yellow, window, when OW is a suffix, and boat, groan, coal, load, roar, within the root

d. When the short sound of O is changed by final R, by final LL, or by R or L before a different consonant sound as in

or, **for**, **sort**, **fork**, **sor**-d**id**, **for**-tune, con-**tor**-tion, r**oll**, **old**, **cold**, **jolt**, **folk**, h**ol**-ster, s**ol**-dier, re-v**ol**-ting

But if the next sound after the R or L is a vowel, it will capture the R or L sound, and leave the O unchanged, as in

s**or**-ry, b**or**-row, h**or**-rid, f**o**-rest, b**o**-ring, em-p**o**-rium, h**ol**-ly, f**ol**-low, s**o**-lid, t**o**-le-rate, h**o**-ly, de-f**o**-li-ate

And on the Latin side of English, the O sometimes remains short even before L plus a different consonant, as in s**ol**ve, re-v**ol**-ver, v**ol**-ca-no.

To many people, the O of OR does not seem truly long. But it is as close to long O as we can come when the next sound is R, as witness the fact that **for** rhymes with **more**, **store**, **chore**, etc. In any case, using the long O sound for OR words seems to be the most useful approach for novice readers attempting to decode a word which looks unfamiliar.

3. O frequently has a short U sound when the spelling would normally suggest either a short O or a long O sound, as in

s**on**, t**on**, fr**on**t, m**on**th, m**o**-ther, c**om**-pa-ny, **o**-ven, c**o**-lor, h**o**-ney, sh**o**-vel, dis-c**o**-ver, c**ome**, s**ome**, n**one**, d**one**, l**ove**, gl**ove**, d**oes**

This seems to occur mainly before M, N. TH and V, but we also have many cases of O's which are truly long or short before these letters, as in h**ome**, p**on**d, b**one**, cl**o**th, cl**o**-thing, **o**-ver, dr**ove**. Students should be prepared to try a short U sound whenever an indicated long or short O sound fails to make sense.

Unstressed O

Like the sounds of most English vowels, the sounds of O are muffled beyond recognition in the syllables which are the most hurried, and are therefore the least stressed. This happens mainly to the sounds spelled by the simple letter O, as in

p**o**-ta-to, dem-**o**-crat, in-s**o**-lent, **o**c-cur, c**om**-bine, and to OR as a suffix, as in

> doc-**tor**, sai-**lor**, di-rec-**tor**, **ge-ne-ra-tor**, de-no-mi-na-**tor**

Schwa* is usually used by dictionaries to respell the vowel sounds of these unstressed syllables.

O in Teams for Special English Vowel Sounds.

1. OY / OI, as in b**oy**, b**oi**l
   a. OY is used at the end of the root as in

   > t**oy**, j**oy**, an-n**oy**, em-pl**oy**, de-str**oy**, **oy**-ster, l**oy**-al

   b. OI is used within the root as in

   > t**oi**l, c**oi**n, p**oi**nt, h**oi**st, m**oi**s-ture, an-n**oi**nt, sir-l**oi**n

2. OO as in t**oo** and t**oo**k.
   a. OO is long both at the end of the root, and within the root, as in

   > m**oo**, f**oo**d, t**oo**l, r**oo**m, sp**oo**n, l**oo**p, p**oo**r, b**oo**t, bal-l**oo**n, pa-p**oo**se

   b. OO is short within the root especially before K, as in

   > l**oo**k, c**oo**k, sh**oo**k, br**oo**k, g**oo**d, f**oo**t, for-s**oo**k

   There is no way to predict whether an OO will be long or short. However, novices need only learn the long sound, since this will bring them close enough to the correct sound to get the meaning even when the OO turns out to be short.

3. OW / OU as in **how** and **house**.
   a. OW spells this sound at the end of the syllable, before final L and N, and sometimes before final D, as in

   > c**ow**, pr**ow**, t**ow**-er, t**ow**-el, c**ow**-ard, al-l**ow**, h**ow**l, d**ow**n, br**ow**n, cr**ow**d, p**ow**-der

   OW also spells long O, as shown above. There is no way to predict which sound an OW will spell. Novices must be prepared to try both sounds to see which one makes sense.

* In dictionaries, schwa looks like this: ə·

b.OU spells the vowel sound of **how** and ho**u**se within the word, as in

> lo**u**d, p**ou**nd, c**ou**nt, s**ou**r, p**ou**t, a-r**ou**se, pro-n**ou**nce

OU also spells a variety of other vowel sounds within the word, as in

> f**ou**r, s**ou**l, th**ou**gh; j**ou**r-nal, c**ou**-rage; y**ou**ng, fa-m**ou**s, e-n**ou**gh; s**ou**p, y**ou**th, thr**ou**gh; b**ou**ght, f**ou**ght

Much has been made of the great variety of sounds that OU can have. But in practice, this variety is not of much importance to students. They should learn only the sound of OU in ho**u**se, and let the context lead them to the correct variation whenever a different sound occurs.

The vowel sounds of **boy, too, took** and **how** are all special vowel sounds in English. See "Vowel Sounds and Vowel Letters," page 29.

O as in open

See also:

O, p. 187
O, p. 188

Exceptions:

to
do
who
two
(long OO)

		Unstressed
no	rosy	also
so	ago	zero
going	hoping	hero
broken	over	policeman
pony	nowhere	automobile

		Unstressed
program	woven	tomato
story	joker	violin
hello	social	society
holy	notion	aristocrat
total	local	professional

		Unstressed
lo	motive	kilowatt
noble	global	introduce
locate	notary	opinion
robot	overburden	production
trophy	mobilize	history

O is a vowel letter. It is long in a syllable that ends in O. When there is a single consonant letter between vowels, the first vowel is long before the native English suffixes, and certain Latin suffixes. The vowel is often long in Latin words when there is an R-blend between vowels, as in **program**.

580 words have long O in a stressed syllable, where the vowel sound is clear.

1088 words have long O in an unstressed syllable, where the vowel sound is often muffled.

This count excludes words like **hoping**, where the native English suffix simply changes the word's form.

See also:

O, p. 86
-OLD, p. 193
WO-, p. 274

O as in octopus or often

Exceptions:

oh
don't
won't
only
most
post
host
ghost
both
sloth
wholly
comb
gross
chaperon
cognac
ohm
  (long O)

tomb
womb
  (long OO)

iron
  (silent O)

		Unstressed
hot	stopping	wagon
dog	hottest	lemon
fox	softer	carrot
not	floppy	million
off	along	addition
		Unstressed
slot	sorrow	freedom
lost	coffee	ballot
cloth	respond	confess
boss	hospital	collect
dodge	geography	decision
		Unstressed
flog	chronic	official
pod	operate	idiot
bronze	democracy	objective
toss	alcohol	commander
grog	moderate	personnel

O is a vowel letter. It is short in a syllable that ends with a consonant letter. When there are two consonants between vowels, the first vowel is almost always short. In many of the long Latin words, the first vowel is short even when there is only one consonant between vowels, as in **operate**.

If you notice that you or your students use different sounds for the short O's in **hot** and **dog**, see "The Letter O," p. 182.

1531 words have O before a consonant in a stressed syllable, where the short O sound is clear.

1710 words have O before a consonant in an unstressed syllable, where the vowel sound is often muffled.

O as in oven

See also:

Long O, p. 186
Short O, p. 187
O__E, p. 189

come	nothing	above
some	money	something
won	monkey	mother
does	become	brother
love	among	color
ton	monthly	covering
sponge	comfort	accompany
tongue	sonny	government
shove	wonder	colorful
gloves	shovel	discovery
monk	undone	covenant
dove	affront	covetous
	stomach	twelvemonth
	twopence	discoloration

Exceptions:

one
once
   (The O has the
   short U sound,
   but with an un-
   written W
   sound before
   it.)

O is the least reliable vowel letter in English. In all these words the spellings indicate either a long O or a short O sound. But these words have the third sound of O, which is short U. The reader must be prepared to try a short U sound whenever the normal O sound does not make sense.

139 words have O with a short U sound in a stressed syllable where the spelling indicates that the O should be either long or short.

These words are not counted under long O, p. 186, short O, p. 187, or O__E, p. 189.

See also:

Silent E, p. 110
Long O, p. 186
Foreign O, p. 208

O__E as in rope

Exceptions:

gone
forehead
pomegranate
   (short O)

move
lose
whose
prove
   (long OO)

home	hoped	alone
more	clothes	before
nose	broke	suppose
stone	rode	tadpole
those	wrote	
whole	compose	purpose
bone	spokesman	envelope
throne	hopeless	foresee
vote	enclose	foretell
sore	microscope	telephone
chore	impose	antelope
cope	ignore	carnivore
grove	threescore	casserole
stoke	invoke	bellicose
yoke	diagnose	

Vowel-consonant-silent-E is a special long vowel spelling pattern. The silent E makes the O "say its name." The E remains silent when a syllable beginning with a consonant is added to the word.

424 words have O__E for long O.

Purpose is the only word where the long O sound of O__E is severely muffled.

These words are not counted under long O, p. 186.

OA as in boat

Exceptions:

broad
  (OA = AW)

cocoa
  (final OA)

road	soapy	blackboard
coat	roaring	motorboat
coal	toaster	rowboat
goat	coated	oatmeal
board	foamy	railroad
throat	bloated	boardinghouse
roast	moaning	petticoat
coarse	loathing	reproachful
soar	approach	coachman
hoax	unload	toadstool
boar	encroach	uproarious
toad	inroad	hoarfrost
shoal	scapegoat	
poach	coastal	

OA is a vowel team for long O. It is used within the root. OA is a native English spelling. In a few Latin words, the team breaks up, as in co-a-gu-late.

132 words have OA within the root.

These words are not counted under long O, p. 186.

See also:

EO, p. 120
also, p. 295

OE as in toe

Exceptions:

does
  (short U)

shoe
canoe
  (long OO)

hoe	toes	tiptoe
	goes	
doe	foeman	mistletoe
foe	oboe	
woe	woeful	
throes	roebuck	
roe	aloes	

OE is a vowel team for Long O at the end of the root.

This is the entire list of words with -OE.

These words are not counted under long O, p. 186.

See also:

OY, p. 207
Foreign O, p. 208

OI as in point

Exceptions:

choir
 (long I)

noise	noisy	
boil	pointer	
join	joining	
choice		

voice	appoint	tortoise
oil	avoid	porpoise
coin	rejoice	typhoid
joint	poison	
spoil	disappoint	

hoist	ointment	paranoid
broil	moisture	asteroid
loin	embroider	sirloin
toil	sequoia	exploitation
poise	reconnoiter	

OI is a letter team for the special English vowel sound heard in **boil**. It is used within the root instead of OY. In a few Latin words the team breaks up, as in he-r**o**-ic.

109 words have the team OI as in **point**.

Tortoise and **porpoise** are the only words where the OI sound is severely muffled.

See also:

-OLLY, p. 194
-ORRY, p. 198

-OLD as in cold

Exceptions:

wolf
(short OO)

doll
golf
loll
solve
involve
dolphin
volcano
solder
doldrums
solstice
(short O)

control
patrol
(single
final L)

gold	told	tollbooth
hold	sold	goldfish
colt	folded	soldier
roll	golden	
scold	rolling	
bold	holster	polka
jolt	folklore	revolt
polls	moldboard	smolder
folk	molten	upholstery
yolk	threefold	voltage
bolt	bolster	gentlefolk
knoll	freehold	manifold
scroll	behold	embolden
stroll	enroll	

In these words the root ends in -OLL or in OL plus a different consonant. O in the middle of the syllable is usually short, but the L changes it to long O. Before final K, the L goes silent, but it still makes the O long.

84 words have O changed by L.

These words are not counted under long O, p. 186. Those in which the L sounds are also counted under L, p. 173 or -LL, p. 176. Those in which L is silent are also counted under silent L, p. 174.

See also:

-OLD, p. 193

OLL- as in holly

		Unstressed
jolly	solid	collect
dolly	polish	collapse
hollow	holiday	collide
follow	lollipop	
dollar		

folly	politics	biologist
pollen	colony	abolish
column	polygon	volunteer
volume	molecule	
olive	collar	

		Long O
stolid	ideology	oleomargarine
soluble	theology	polar
tolerant	archaeologist	folio
pollination	zoology	resoled
corollary	cryptology	poling

In these words, the L goes off with the next syllable. As a result, the O is short except where the L is single and the suffix makes the O long.

165 words have OL or OLL in a stressed syllable before a vowel letter. In these words the O sound is clear.

19 words have OL or OLL in an unstressed syllable, where the vowel sound is often muffled, as in **corollary**.

These words are also counted under long and short O, pp. 186 and 187.

See also:

OO, p. 196

Exceptions:

brooch
   (long O)

OO as in moon

zoo	soonest	balloon
boo	roomy	rooster
broom	choosing	moonlight
food	blooming	afternoon
school	foolish	kangaroo
loop	moody	foolhardy
pool	booster	waterproof
loose	drooping	gloominess
proof	bamboo	baboon
stoop	bridegroom	boomerang
boon	lagoon	foodstuffs
loom	basoon	soothsayer
festoon	aloof	gooseberry
cocoon	heirloom	anteroom
reproof	offshoot	freebooter

OO is a letter team for the special English vowel sound heard in **moon**. This is the long sound of OO. It is used both within the root and at the end.

OO also has the short sound heard in **book**. There is no way for the eye to tell which sound is spelled by a given OO. The reader must be prepared to use whichever sound makes sense in the context in which the OO appears.

187 words have long OO.

OO as in book

See also:

OO, p. 195

Exceptions:

door
floor
  (long O)

blood
flood
  (short U)

look	cooking	cooky
hook	took	football
foot	stood	goodness
poor	wooden	childhood
good	hooded	neighborhood
brook	crooked	bookkeeper
crook	foothold	barefooted
nook	hoodwink	pocketbook
shook	woolen	brotherhood
soot	cookbook	understood
moor	betook	hardhihood
rook	partook	livelihood
	falsehood	underwood

OO is a letter team for the special English vowel sound heard in **book**. This is the short sound of OO. Like other short vowel sounds, it occurs within the root. Notice how many of these words have K at the end.

OO also has the long sound heard in **moon**. There is no way for the eye to tell which sound is spelled by a given OO. The reader must be prepared to use whichever sound makes sense in the context in which the OO appears.

116 words have short OO.

See also:

-ORRY, p. 198
WOR-, p. 275

OR as in fork

Exceptions:

attorney
  (OR = UR)
horde
  (silent E)

		Unstressed
or	torn	color
for	stormy	forget
corn	shorter	doctor
porch	forty	actor
horse	morning	razor

		Unstressed
nor	northward	tabor
born	reform	junior
force	record	record
pork	important	projector
chord	fortify	comfortable

		Unstressed
morn	abhor	escalator
fiord	abortion	calculator
stork	portable	incubator
torque	formula	counselor
dormant	distortion	prosecutor

In these words, the R is at the end, or is followed by a different consonant. O in the middle of the syllable is usually short, but the R changes it to long O. (Notice that **for** rhymes with O__E words like **more** and **store**. This is as long as an O can be before an R sound. Only or, nor and for have OR at the end of a one-syllable word.)

352 words have O changed by R in a stressed syllable, where the vowel sound is clear.

366 words have OR in an unstressed syllable. In most of these OR is a suffix, as in doct**or**.

These words are not counted under long O, p. 186. They are counted under R, p. 219.

See also:

Short O, p. 187
-OR, p. 197
-ARRY, p. 82
-ERRY, p. 122
-IRRI-, p. 165
-OLLY, p. 194

ORR- as in sorry

sorry	story	tomorrow
forest		porridge
borrow		orange

moral	minority	correspond
sorrow	superiority	horrible
torrent	authority	authority
horror	horizontal	priority
foreign	historical	boring

Exceptions:

thorough
(OR = UR)

		Unstressed
coral	correlate	history
coroner	corrugated	original
orator	incorrigible	correctional
forage	orifice	corrosive
	horrify	corrupted

In these words, the R does not make the O long, because the R sound goes off with the next syllable. As a result, the O is short unless the R is single and the suffix requires a long vowel before it.

88 words have OR or ORR in a stressed syllable before a vowel letter. In these words, the O sound is clear.

13 words have OR or ORR in an unstressed syllable before a vowel, where the O sound is often muffled.

These words are also counted under long O, short O and R, pp. 186, 187, and 219.

See also:

OU, pp. 200
  to 202.
OUGH, p. 203
OUR-, p. 204
OW, p. 205

OU as in shout

Exceptions:

could
should
would
  (short OO)

you
thou
(OU at the end
  of the root)

round	found	about
ground	houses	outside
our	mouthful	mountain
ouch	cloudy	without
mouse	louder	thousand
noun	doubtful	boundary
foul	southwest	accountant
flour	proudly	counterfeit
couch	amount	outstanding
hour	profound	announcement
bout	astound	countermand
snout	scoundrel	counterpart
clout	bounty	fountainhead
grouch	devour	encounter
pouch	dugout	outrageous

OU is a letter team for the special English vowel sound heard in **shout**. It is used within the word instead of OW.

Although only five exceptions are shown here, OU is our most variable spelling. It can also stand for five other vowel sounds. See the references to other pages.

279 words have OU as in **shout**.

See also:

OU, p. 199
OUGH, p. 203
OW, p. 206

OU as in four

fourth		fourteen
pour		shoulder
course		although
court	boulder	resource
dough	courthouse	soulless
mourn	fourscore	downpour
soul	poultry	resourceful
		cantaloupe
gourd	poultice	pompadour
mould	concourse	courtier
	discourse	thorough

In these words, OU represents the long O sound. Notice how many of them have R or L after the OU.

37 words have OU spelling long O.

These words are not counted under long O, p. 186, or under OU, p. 199.

See also:

OU, p. 199
OUGH, p. 203
Foreign O, p. 208

OU as in soup

Exceptions:

buoy
buoyant
buoyancy
   (UO, not OU)

you	your	boulevard
youth	group	through
ghoul	cougar	acoustics
wound	coupon	souvenir
rouge	goulash	camouflage
tour	routine	
sou	tourism	courier
coup	gourmet	contour
troupe	bouquet	bourgeois
		carrousel
		caribou

In these words OU represents the long OO sound. This is the normal sound of OU in French, and many of these words are borrowed from French.

37 words have OU spelling the long OO sound.

These words are not counted under OU, p. 199.

See also:

OU, p. 199
OUGH, p. 203

OU as in young

touch	younger	country
tough	touching	enough
rough		trouble
		famous

youngster	couplet	countryside
double	gorgeous	southerner
couple	jealous	tremendous
cousin	joyous	envious
nervous	luscious	ridiculous

couplet	raucous	southerly
zealous	bilious	curvaceous
callous	heinous	strenuous
pious	dubious	superstitious

In these words, OU represents the short U sound.

26 words have OU spelling short U in a stressed syllable.

350 words have OU spelling short U in an unstressed syllable. Aside from **doubloon**, all of these are words like **famous**, with the suffix **-ous**.

These words are not counted under short U, p. 258 or OU, p. 199.

See also:
OU, pp. 199
to 202.

OUGH is a wild letter team

though	brought	although
through	fought	doughnut
cough	thought	thoughtful
ought	rough	enough
bought	tough	toughen
dough	borough	thoroughbred
drought	furlough	thoroughfare
bough	thorough	roughen
sought	thoughtless	afterthought
	forethought	throughout
nought	doughty	overwrought
wrought	besought	thoroughgoing
slough (ow)	bethought	
slough (uff)		

OUGH is a letter team that represents many different sounds. Students should not attempt to learn anything specific about the sound of OUGH. Instead, they should be advised to sound the consonants of the word before them accurately, and allow the context to suggest the appropriate vowel sound.

This is the entire list of words containing OUGH.

Where appropriate, these words are also counted on pages 200, 201 and 202 for OU, and pages 140 and 141 for GH.

See also:
OU, pp. 199

OUR- as in journey

courage

flourish	encourage
journal	adjournment
nourish	discourage
glamour	undernourish
adjourn	journeyman
	courteous

In these words OU is changed by R to the special English vowel sound of ER. They are all French words, but they have been English longer than the French borrowings listed on page 208.

49 words have OU changed by R.

These words are also counted under R, p. 219.

See also:

OU, p. 199
OW, p. 206

OW as in cow

how	bowing	downwards
now	growling	cowboy
down	crown	flower
brown	brownie	eyebrow
owl	clown	towel
plow	allow	gunpowder
howl	shower	towering
frown	vowel	horsepower
crowd	chowder	downpour
drown	township	downstream
fowl	renown	cowardly
gown	cower	dowager
prowl	trowel	endowment
scowl	dowry	howitzer
vow	browser	cauliflower

OW is a letter team for the special English vowel sound heard in **cow**. OW is used at the end of the root, and before final L, N or D. Before other consonants, OW becomes OU, as in **couch**. OW is mainly a native English spelling.

OW is also a team for long O. There is no way for the eye to tell which sound is spelled by a given OW. The reader must be prepared to use whichever sound makes sense in the context in which the OW appears.

122 words have OW as in **cow**.

See also:

OU, p. 200
OW, p. 205

OW as in snow

know	known	yellow	
blow	grown	arrow	
slow	thrown	window	
show	snowed	Halloween	
low	throwing	follow	
flow	bowling	pillow	
own	below	fellowship	
bowl	crowbar	shadowy	
tow	stowaway	arrowhead	
bow	overthrow	widower	
stow	bellow	barrow	
disown	gallows	bungalow	
bestow	sparrow	foreshadow	
escrow	narrow	unhallowed	
	elbow	sorrowful	

Exceptions:

knowledge
(short O)

OW is a vowel team for long O. OW is used for long O at the end of the root or before final L or N. Most of the words ending in N are past forms of verbs ending in OW. OW is mainly a native English spelling.

OW is also a team for the special vowel sound heard in **cow**. There is no way for the eye to tell which sound is spelled by a given OW. The reader must be prepared to use whichever sound makes sense in the context in which the OW appears.

74 words have OW spelling long O in a stressed syllable, where the vowel sound is clear.

56 words have OW as a suffix with a long O sound.

These words are not counted under long O, p. 186.

See also:

OI, p. 192

OY as in boy

Exceptions:

coyote
(long I)

bouy
(OO, -Y)

OY within the
syllable:

gargoyle

toy	toys	cowboy
joy	toying	enjoy
		royal
annoy	alloy	annoyance
destroy	boycott	employment
loyal	convoy	destroyer
employ	voyage	disloyal
		royalty
coy	viceroy	boysenberry
deploy	foyer	flamboyant
Troy	oyster	corduroy
		clairvoyant

OY is a letter team for the special English vowel sound heard in **boy**. It is used at the end of the root. Within the root, OY becomes OI, as in **boil**.

52 words have OY as in boy.

In foreign words, O combines with other letters in unusual ways.

— OI —

boudoir	memoir	chamois
bourgeois	repertoire	connoisseur
bourgeoisie	reservoir	

The first 6 words here have the normal French sound of OI, which is like our WA in **wasp**.

— OU —

The normal French sound of OU is like our long OO. See page 201, where many French words appear.

— O plus a final consonant —

apropos	depot

The final consonant is silent in these French words.

— O__E —

apostrophe	anemone	hyperbole
catastrophe	epitome	synecdoche

In these Greek words, the O is in one syllable and the E in another.

Words of this kind are English enough to be included in the Hanna listing, but much of their phonics harks back to their languages of origin.

These words and the 37 words counted on page 201 account for all the foreign O sounds in English.

The Letter P

In English, the letter P has one basic sound, the first sound in **pack**.

1. On the English side of the language, P behaves like any ordinary consonant, as in

    pan, **pl**an, **pr**ice, s**p**it, s**pl**it, s**pr**ing, ta**p**, ta**p**e, tar**p**, hel**p**, cris**p**, ta**pp**ing, ta**p**ing, ha**pp**y, a**pp**le, ma**p**le

2. On the Latin side of English, there are two types of special P's.

    P is the first member of the consonant team PH, which always has the sound of F, as in

    phone, s**ph**ere, gra**ph**, **ph**otogra**ph**, al**ph**abet, **ph**ysical, dol**ph**in, tro**ph**y

    This team was used by the Romans to represent a Greek sound which they could only approximate with an F sound. But in order to retain the Greek flavor of borrowed words containing it, they used the PH team. Notice the Y within the word in **physical**. This is another remnant of Greek spelling.

    The Greeks were also able to pronounce the consonant blends PS, PN and PT at the beginnings of words. When the Romans borrowed such words, the P's went silent because the Romans could not pronounce them. They have remained silent ever since, as in

    Psalms, **p**sychology, **p**seudonym, **p**neumonia, **p**tomaine

    Notice again the Y's within the word, CH sounding like K, and EU for long U, which are other remnants of Greek spelling.

    Students should be informed that silent P exists, and advised that when they see a P in an unpronounceable position, they should skip the P and start sounding out with the next letter.

P as in pig

See also:

PH, p. 213
Silent P, p. 211

Exceptions:

cupboard
raspberry
receipt
corps
clapboard
coup
comptroller
(silent P)

park	picked	paper
put	stopping	important
keep	kept	open
jump	sleeper	happy
spend	soapy	asleep
pace	passage	turpentine
pep	report	speculate
depth	impulse	perpetual
spill	accept	interrupt
swamp	polka	suspicious
pact	eclipse	despondent
plight	appraise	optional
spawn	capsule	incipient
lapse	stipend	perpendicular
strop	repulse	typographical

P is a consonant letter for the first sound in **pig** and the last sound in **drop**.

3573 words have P as in **pig.**

P as in psychology

Psalms

psalm	psychic	pneumatic
		pneumonia
		psychiatrist
	pseudo	pneumococcus
	psyche	pterodactyl
	ptomaine	psychical
		parapsychology
		pseudonym

P is silent at the beginning of the word before N, S or T. These are Greek spellings. Notice the examples of Y within the word, EU, and CH sounding like K.

23 words have silent P at the beginning.

These words are also counted under N, S and T, pp. 179, 226, and 244.

See also:

-LE, p. 175

P as in pretty and please

plant	planting	airplane
plus	pressed	April
proud	playing	plenty
price	printer	present
spring	splashing	program
praise	improve	completion
prowl	complain	represent
pleat	supply	diploma
splint	splendid	probable
sprout	outspread	waterproof
plague	plaza	predatory
plea	plural	reprimand
spleen	premise	impromptu
prey	diplomat	replica
prime	sprocket	predestined

PR- and PL- are consonant blends. These blends sometimes split up between vowels as in **represent** and **diplomat**. If the blend splits, the vowel before it is short. Otherwise, the vowel before it is long as in **April** and **reply**. SPR- and SPL- are triple blends.

526 words have the blend PR-.

222 words have the blend PL-.

24 words have the blend SPR-.

12 words have the blend SPL-.

These words are also counted under P, p. 210, and under L, R and S, pp. 173, 219, and 226.

See also:

F, p. 129

No exceptions

PH as in photograph

humph	nephew	elephant
phone		telephone
		geography
		alphabet
		telegraph
phrase	photon	emphatic
phase	dolphin	symphony
graph	hyphen	phobia
nymph	prophet	hemisphere
sphinx	physician	paragraph
phlegm	physics	sophistry
lymph	phosgene	amphibian
phial	naphtha	philosophical
	seraph	phraseology
	zephyr	

PH is a letter team for the sound of F. This is a Greek spelling. Notice the examples of Y within the word. Once in a while, P and H belong to different root words, and retain their normal sounds, as in **loophole**.

239 words have the team PH.

See also:

WA, p. 271
WAR, p. 272
QU, p. 215

QU as in queen

quick	quickly	quiet
quite	squeaky	squirrel
quack	squeezing	question
squeeze	quacked	earthquake
squeak	quarter	

quit	quarrel	equipment
quartz	equal	quality
quail	require	adequate
squad	liquid	consequently
square	conquest	quotation

qualms	tranquil	quantify
quire	quantum	loquacious
squab	quasi	querulous

QU- is the way we spell the consonant blend CW-. The blend sometimes splits up, as in **liquid**. If the blend splits, the vowel before it is short. Otherwise, the vowel before it is long, as in **equal**.

This is the Latin style of spelling this blend. It has replaced all the CW-'s of Old English.

220 words have the blend QU-.

In foreign words, QU sounds like K

	bouquet	mosquito
clique	conquer	mannequin
mosque	lacquer	etiquette
antique	liquor	picturesque
marquee	croquet	oblique
burlesque	turquoise	technique
quay	coquette	coquetry
brusque	marquise	exchequer
torque	baroque	statuesque
casque	critique	
pique	piquant	

These are French spellings. Words of this kind are English enough to be included in the Hanna listing, but many of their letter sounds reflect their French origin. The French use QU for the same purpose we use the letter K, to spell a hard C sound before E, I or Y. Notice that the UE's at the ends of these words are silent. Notice also that in **conquest** the QU- has taken on the normal English pronunciation.

40 words have QU sounding like K.

The Letter R

R is a consonant letter for the first sound in **rabbit**. The sound of R in American English is a very sophisticated sound, and as a result, the letter R is especially difficult for reading students.

When one says that our R has a sophisticated sound, one means that it is quite a lot more difficult to pronounce than the spontaneous R sound that occurs in the babbling of infants. Children take a long time to master the trick of saying R in the adult American way. Most of them are still pronouncing R in a babyish way during the first year of school. It is very hard for them to combine the R sound with other consonant sounds, as in **br**ick and **gr**ass. As a result, they become especially confused about such words when they have to learn them as whole words in word-memorization classrooms.

The spontaneous R sound of infant babbling is a voiced consonant which is pronounced quite far forward in the mouth. The adult R of American English is pronounced farther back in the mouth, and is much more heavily voiced than the infant R. Before a vowel sound, R behaves like any other consonant. Compare **hat**, **mat**, and **rat**. The R blends with the A sound in the same way as the H or M. But we voice an R sound after the vowel especially heavily, so much so that the voice remains almost as unrestricted while the R is being pronounced as it is during the vowel sound, as in **our**, **more** and **sure**. This can confuse remedial spelling students very seriously.

R after the vowel is even harder for children to pronounce than R before the vowel, so they become confused about these words, also, when they begin trying to read, unless they are having very careful phonics instruction. In fact, R can cause so much confusion that children soon begin to build up a block against reading these words. Then, at the first glimpse of a word containing R, they begin to guess wildly, which causes more trouble, which causes even wilder guessing, and so on. By the time such children become remedial students, the problem can be severe.

As far as speech goes, most people eventually master the American R, and can handle it after the long vowel sounds without very much distortion of the vowels. But all the short vowel sounds are normally distorted when R follows them in the same syllable (as in **car**, **for**, **her**, **sir**, **fur**; see below). This, of course, only increases the confusion of children who are having trouble with reading.

The letter R is used in the following ways.

1. R Before the Vowel

    a. R is the first letter in the syllable in words like

    red, ride, room, round, re-mind, e-rase, un-ru-ly

    b. R is the last member of a consonant blend in words like

    brick, **cr**eep, **dr**op, **fr**ight, **gr**ass, **pr**int, **scr**atch, **shr**ed, **spr**ing, **str**eet, **thr**ee, **tr**ace

2. R After the Vowel. (See " 'Long' and 'Short', " page 31.)

    a. R after long vowel sounds, and special vowel sounds that behave like long vowels. Examples are

    pair, **fear**, **tire**, **core**, **pure**, **sour**, **poor**

    In these words, the long vowel sound closes the mouth before the R is pronounced. The result is often much like a two-syllable word. Students must be warned to give the vowel sound its full length before adding the R sound. The words containing long O do not seem so much like two-syllable words as the others do. But even these are most successfully decoded by students who give the O its full length before sounding the R. After identifying the word, the student can then repeat the word with a more normal pronunciation.

    b. R or R and a different consonant sound after a vowel within the syllable. Examples are

    car, **cart**, **carton**; **her**, **term**, **person**; **sir**, **bird**, **circle**; **for**, **fort**, **fortune**; **fur**, **turn**, **purpose**

    Vowels within the syllable are normally short. But the R sound in these syllables changes each vowel sound in a special way. It changes the A sound to the sound of short O as in **hot**. It changes the O sound from short to long (compare the sounds of **for** and **more**). And it changes short E,

I and U to the special English vowel sound ER. The sound of EA is also changed to this sound by R and a different consonant sound, as in **learn** and **early**.

c. R between vowel sounds. When the next sound after R is a vowel sound, the R sound goes off with the next syllable, leaving the vowel sound unchanged, as in

car-ry, car-rot, nar-row; ber-ry, her-ring, er-ror; mir-ror, ir-ritate; sor-ry, bor-row, hor-rible; da-ring, cohe-rent, ti-ring, sto-ry, pu-rest

Only the short sound of U continues to be affected by the R when the next sound is a vowel, as in **hurry**. Remedial students are often baffled by the unchanged sounds of vowels before -RR- and -R-.

3. R is a member of two consonant teams, WR and RH.

a. WR is a native English spelling for the sound of R at the beginning of the word, as in

write, **wr**ist, **wr**ench, **wr**ap, **wr**estle, **wr**inkle

Notice that all these words have meanings connected with the idea of twisting. At one time these W's were pronounced.

b. RH is a Latin team for the sound of R. It occurs in a very few words the Romans borrowed from the Greeks, as in

rhyme, **rh**ythm, **rh**rumatism, **Rh**odes

Notice the Y's within the word, which are also remnants of Greek spelling.

See also:

-AR, p. 81
-ER, p. 121
-IR, p. 164
-OR, p. 197
-UR, p. 265

Exceptions:

iron
  (i-ern)

forecastle
worsted
  (silent R)

R as in rabbit

run	rainy	wonderful
hair	carry	remember
tree	driven	interesting
girl	brightest	important
street	warmer	strawberry
rake	carton	remainder
rich	reduce	tradition
fort	relic	prevention
dwarf	courthouse	preference
crouch	protect	translation
rook	furrow	derivative
fray	ruffian	incorrigible
chord	frenzy	obstetrician
herb	berserk	decipher
dire	beaker	interception

R is a consonant letter for the first sound in **rabbit** and the last sound in **hair**.

R changes the sounds of all the short vowels when it follows them at the end of the word, or before a different consonant, as in **car**, **jerk**, **thirty**, **fork**, **fur**.

When R follows a long vowel, it is often pronounced almost like an extra syllable, as in **fire**. The reader must be careful to give the vowel sound its full length before sounding the R.

R is the second member of the consonant blends BR-, CR-, CHR-, DR-, FR-, GR-, PR-, PHR-, SHR-, TR- and THR-.

9388 words have R as in **rabbit**.

-RE as in ogre

See also:
-LE, p. 175

Exception:

padre
  (-RE = R, E)

acre

acreage
massacre
mediocre

lucre
timbre

-RE after a consonant sounds like the suffix -ER. This is the French version of this suffix.

This is the entire list of words with -RE in American English. The British use -RE more than we do, as in **theatre**.

No exceptions

RH as in rhythm

rhyme   rhinoceros

myrrh   rhomboid   rhapsody
Rhode   rhubarb   rhetoric
  (Island)   rhythmic   rheumatism
        rhinestone   rhythmical

        catarrh   rhododendron
        rhizome   rheostat
                rhetorical
                rheumatic

RH is a team for the sound of R. This is a Greek spelling. Notice the examples of Y and EU within the word.

This is the entire list of words with RH.

The Letter S

S is a consonant letter for the first sound in **sail**. This is its basic sound, and it is unvoiced. However, S is often voiced, and then it sounds like Z. (See Unvoiced, Voiced and Nasal consonants, p. 48.)

1. Unvoiced S

   a. S is always unvoiced at the beginning of the word, as in

      sat, **s**ame, **s**ell, **s**eal, **s**it, **s**ight, **s**op, **s**oap, **s**uch, **s**uit, **s**aw, **s**ound, **s**oil, **s**oot, **s**oon, **s**ir

   b. S is unvoiced when it is the first member of a consonant blend, as in

      scar, **s**chool, **s**kim, **s**lip, **s**moke, **s**nake, **s**pin, **s**plit, **s**pring, **s**queak, **s**tick, **s**treet, **s**wing, de**sk**, cri**sp**, mu**st**

   c. S can be unvoiced between vowels, as in

      ca**s**e, ba**s**in, be**s**ides, i**s**otope, do**s**age, u**s**age, hou**s**e, goo**s**e

   d. S is unvoiced when it is spelled SS between vowels, as in

      a**ss**ault, e**ss**ence, mi**ss**ile, po**ss**ible, ru**ss**et, ta**ss**el

2. Voiced S.

   a. S between vowels is often voiced, having a Z sound as in

      rai**s**in, ea**s**y, ri**s**e, ri**s**en, no**s**e, ro**s**in, mu**s**ic, pau**s**e, hou**s**ing, noi**s**y, bo**s**om

   b. S is voiced when it is the first member of the final consonant blend -SM, as in

      cha**sm**, pri**sm**, bapti**sm**, communi**sm**

3. S as a Native English Suffix

   A single S is the most actively used of all the native English suffixes. It forms the plural of nouns, and the third person singluar of the present tense of verbs (as in: two home run**s**; he run**s**, she run**s**, it run**s**). Regardless of whether it is added to a noun or a verb, the sound of this suffix is determined by the voicing of the sound immediately before it.

a. The suffix -**s** is unvoiced after unvoiced consonants, as in

cu**ffs**, loo**ks**, to**ps**, hi**ts**, ra**kes**, ty**pes**, no**tes**

b. The suffix -**s** is voiced—

1) After vowel sounds, as in

da**ys**, be**es**, ti**es**, sho**ws**, ne**ws**, la**ws**, co**ws**, bo**ys**, bo**os**

2) After voiced consonants, as in

ru**bs**, hea**ds**, ta**gs**, ta**les**, hu**ms**, pa**ns**, sta**rs**, di**ves**, lea**ves**

3) When E is inserted before the S so that the added S can be heard distinctly after S, Z, CH and SH sounds, as in

pa**sses**, bu**zzes**, ca**tches**, coa**ches**, ru**shes**, lea**shes**

These differences in the sounds of the suffix -**s** do not usually cause problems. Since context usually leads the reader to expect the suffix in its normal place, we tend to give the S its correct sound spontaneously, just as we do in speech.

But students do sometimes have trouble with this suffix when it takes the form of -**es**, as it does in the third group above. This difficulty arises because the students have learned to leave the E silent in forms like ri**des**, ho**mes**, la**nes**, and ga**tes**, where the S can be heard perfectly well without any extra help. But many words ending in S, Z and J sounds end with silent E's which must be sounded when the suffix is added, as in

ca**ses**, ri**ses**, ga**zes**, pa**ges**, bri**dges**

Students must be helped to see why the E sounds in some words and not in others before they can begin to overcome this problem.

4. S as the Last Sound in the Root.

Since a single S at the end of the word is a suffix, this spelling is not available to represent the sound of S when the root word ends with an S sound. We have four solutions for different aspects of this problem.

a. Right after a short vowel sound in the root, we use -SS to represent a final unvoiced S sound, as in

mass, mess, miss, moss, muss

We also use -SS at the end of the native English suffixes -**less**, -**ness**, -**ress** and -**ess**, as in

need**less**, help**less**, lame**ness**, sad**ness**, act**ress**, princ**ess**

The -SS in these words shows that the S itself is not the entire suffix as it is in—

needle**s**, prince**s**, acre**s**

b. Right after a short vowel sound in the root, we use -ZZ to represent a final voiced S sound, as in

ja**zz**, fi**zz**, bu**zz**

c. After long vowel teams, special vowel teams, and consonants in the root, we use SE to represent a final S sound, as in

crea**se**, gee**se**, goo**se**, hou**se**, el**se**, fal**se**, sen**se**, lap**se**, glimp**se**, spar**se**, hor**se**, nur**se**

prai**se**, plea**se**, chee**se**, crui**se**, cau**se**, noi**se**, choo**se**, rou**se**, clean**se**

Notice that in the first group of examples the S is unvoiced, and in the second group it is voiced. In a few cases, the voiced S sound is represented by -ZE instead of -SE, as in

mai**ze**, free**ze**, gau**ze**, boo**ze**, bron**ze**

The -SE and -ZE spellings enable the eye to distinguish between such pairs as

laps/lapse, dens/dense, pleas/please, frees/freeze, boos/booze

d. When the root word ends in a KS blend, we use -X to represent the entire blend, as in

ta**x**, se**x**, fi**x**, bo**x**, coa**x**

The -X spelling enables the eye to distinguish between such pairs as

tacks/tax, cokes/coax

5. S in Latin suffixes

   Single S does occur, however, at the ends of the Latin suffixes **-ous, -as, -is, -os** and **-us**. In these suffixes, the S is unvoiced, as in

   > fam**ous**, tremend**ous**, canv**as**, bas**is**, tonsillit**is**, cosm**os**, foc**us**, cact**us**, apparat**us**, bacill**us**

6. S before Latin suffixes containing unstressed I before another vowel, or before unstressed long U.

   a. If the S has a vowel, or an R before it, the voiced S sound is distorted to a ZH sound, as in

      > occa**si**on, amne**si**a, vi**si**on, explo**si**on, confu**si**on, ver**si**on plea**su**re, lei**su**re, enclo**su**re, u**su**al, vi**su**al

   b. If the S is doubled, or has a different consonant before it, the unvoiced S sound is distorted to an SH sound, as in

      > pa**ssi**on, se**ssi**on, mi**ssi**on, concu**ssi**on, compul**si**on, ten**si**on, ti**ss**ue, pre**ss**ure, cen**s**ure

Letter Teams Containing S

1. S is the first member of the consonant team, SH, which represents the first sound in **ship** and the last sound in **fish**. Although this sound occurs frequently in our Modern English pronunciation of Latin words like **passion, tension, pressure, nation** and **special**, it did not exist in Ancient Latin. Therefore, the Latin alphabet which we use has no single letter to represent it. The SH sound is a Germanic sound, which occurs frequently at the beginnings or ends of native English roots. These are the words for which the team SH is used, as in

   > **sh**ape, **sh**ed, **sh**ut, **sh**ow, **sh**rug, ma**sh**, me**sh**, lea**sh**, fi**sh**, ru**sh**, mar**sh**

2. S is the second member of the consonant team PS-. (See "The Letter P," page 209.)

See also:

-S-, p. 227

S as in sun

Exceptions:

island
aisle
viscount
demesne
  (silent S)

see	saying	seven
saw	seemed	baseball
six	singer	lesson
ask	darkest	possible
nest	rested	yesterday
search	essay	colossal
sift	consult	emphasis
wasp	nestle	diagnose
brisk	distance	humorous
roast	focus	serious
sage	abscond	transfigure
serf	sinuous	anthropologist
bask	distasteful	inconsistency
asp	monastic	obesity
grist	desiccate	surveillance

S is a consonant letter for the first sound in **sun** and the last sound in **focus**. In these words, the S is unvoiced.

5219 words have S as in **sun**. This count does not include words with the suffix -S, unless they have a special meaning, as in **mumps**.

See also:

S, p. 226
-SE, p. 234
Z, p. 290

S as in music

Exceptions:

scissors
dessert
dissolve
possess
brassiere
hussar
hussy
  (SS between
  vowels = Z)

nose	houses	business
those	closing	president
these	noisy	visitor
choose	user	otherwise
rise	risen	thousand
fuse	expose	compromise
pose	abuse	easily
wise	result	advertise
lose	husband	enthusiasm
spasm	baptism	magnetism
muse	tourism	paraphrase
chasm	mosaic	pleasantry
prism	physique	romanticism
	crimson	euphemism
	resolve	pantheism

In these words, S is voiced and sounds like Z. S is often voiced between vowels, or between a vowel and an M or a B. It usually takes doubled S to show an unvoiced S sound between vowels, as in **vessel**, but a single S can also be unvoiced between vowels, as in **basin**.

580 words have voiced S between vowels. These words are not included in the count for unvoiced S, p. 226.

See also:

-ES, p. 123

S as a suffix

(2) goats	(she) is	(2) sunflowers
(4) bears	(he) has	(4) afternoons
(7) boys	(it) was	(she) discovers
(he) goes	hers	scissors
(it) works	its	sometimes
upwards	physics	whereabouts
perhaps	footlights	amidships
assets	salesman	unawares
skies	series	frontiersman
shelves	soapsuds	athletics
crimps	hirelings	demagogues
pods	adjourns	adjudicates
brigs	crucibles	medallions
glades	cosmos	tonsilitis
bias	curious	apparatus

Exceptions:

as
us
yes
this
bus
gas
lens
plus
biceps
triceps
forceps
   (-S not a suffix)

A single S at the end of the word is usually a native English suffix. It may also be part of one of the Latin suffixes, **-as**, **-is**, **-os**, **-us** or **-ous** as in **bias**, **tonsilitis**, **cosmos**, **apparatus** and **curious**.

As a native English suffix, **-s** is voiced after a vowel or a voiced consonant; it is unvoiced after an unvoiced consonant. At the end of a Latin suffix, S is unvoiced.

No count is needed for these words. Those with Latin suffixes are counted under unvoiced S, p. 226. The native English suffixes are not included in the Hanna list because they change the word's form, but not its basic meaning.

See also:

SC-, p. 232

S as in stop

stand	scared	story
stone	spelling	instead
store	starter	station
spend	skating	spider
school	spicy	scarecrow
space	escape	telescope
skill	schedule	circumstance
sphere	discard	desperate
stem	respond	hemisphere
scarf	monster	especial
scow	abscond	despicable
scud	despise	barrister
spume	bespeak	ostensible
staid	solstice	schizophrenia
sphinx	scapegoat	conspiratorial

These are all consonant blends of unvoiced S with an unvoiced consonant at the beginning of the syllable. SK, SP and ST can also be blends at the end of the syllable. These blends often split up between vowels. If the blend splits, the vowel before it is short, as in **desperate**. Otherwise, the vowel before the blend is long, as in **microscope.**

148 words have the blend SC-.

60 words have the blend SK.

266 words have the blend SP.

721 words have the blend ST.

12 words have the blend SCH-.

20 words have the blend SPH-.

These words are also counted under S, p. 226, and under C, K, P, T, CH and PH, pp. 92, 168, 210, 244, 96 and 213.

Exceptions:

answer
sword
boatswain
coxswain
(silent W)

S as in sled

slow	sliding	asleep
smoke	smaller	snowball
snake	snowed	slipper
swim	sweetest	sweetheart
sleigh	sweeper	rattlesnake
slam	slogan	slanderous
smart	smuggle	smorgasboard
snip	snapshot	slavery
smudge	coleslaw	manslaughter
swamp	switchboard	persuade
suede	slothful	swastika
sluice	smitten	talisman
snide	greensward	persuasive
swathe	slaked	
swale	assuage	

These are all consonant blends of an unvoiced S with a voiced consonant at the beginning of the syllable. These blends do not often split up between vowels. SM can also be a blend at the end of the word, but then the S is voiced as in **prism**. The blend SW- is spelled SU- in words of Latin origin.

100 words have the blend SL-.

 35 words have the blend SM-.

 12 words have the blend SN-.

 53 words have the blend SW-.

  7 words have the blend SU-.

These words are also counted under S, p. 226, and under L, M, N, W and U, pp. 173, 177, 179, 270 and 260.

S as in splash

spring	stronger	squirrel
straight	scratching	sprinkler
scream	squeezed	scrapbook
squeak	stranger	strawberry
string	spreading	
scrub	describe	abstraction
split	construct	scrupulous
stray	splendid	strategy
stripe	streetcar	inscription
squirm	disclaim	demonstrate
sprig	prescribe	sclerosis
script	offspring	scrutinize
splice	strident	strategic
squid	squeamish	strontium
strive	abstract	instrumental

These are all blends of unvoiced S with two other letter sounds. They are triple blends. These blends do not often split up between vowels.

   4 words have the blend SCL-.

  73 words have the blend SCR-.

  17 words have the blend SPL-.

  27 words have the blend SPR-.

  29 words have the blend SQU-.

 218 words have the blend STR-.

These words are also counted under S, p. 226, under L, p. 173 and R, p. 219, and under C, P, QU- and T, pp. 92 210, 214 and 244, and under the component blends like SP- and PR-.

See also:

C, p. 93

SC as in scissors

science
scientist
scientific

scene	descend	disciple
scent	obscene	miscellaneous
scythe	scepter	fluorescent
	crescent	adolescent
	luscious	fascinate
	rescind	ascetic
	scion	proscenium
	nascent	scintillate
	miscible	
	ascertain	

Exceptions:

sceptic
  (C = K)
muscle
corpuscle
  (silent C
  before l)

discern
  (SC = z)

Before E, I or Y, the consonant blend SC- has a soft C, so that the blend sounds like a plain S-. In Ancient Latin, where all C's were hard, these blends sounded like SK-. Like other blends, this one can split up between vowels. If it splits, the vowel before it is short, as in **crescent**. Otherwise, the vowel before the blend is long, as in **descend**.

75 words contain the blend SC- sounding like unvoiced S.

These words are also counted under S, p. 226 and under C, p. 93.

See also:

-SE, p. 234
-SS, p. 237

-SE as in house

Exceptions:

biceps
triceps
forceps
  (no E at
  the end)

horse	horses	horseback
else	nursed	lighthouse
course	worse	playhouse
mouse	geese	
goose		
coarse	collapse	endorsement
grease	increase	horsepower
sense	expense	summerhouse
loose	falsehood	universe
pulse	immense	housekeeper
copse	diverse	recompense
corpse	perverse	intersperse
lapse	concourse	frankincense
crease	disburse	disbursement
glimpse	tortoise	remorseful

In these words, the root ends in an unvoiced S sound after a consonant or a vowel team. The silent E shows that the S is not being added as a suffix. This enables the eye to distinquish between (one) **lapse** and (two) **laps**, **diverse** and (3) **divers**.

143 words have roots ending in unvoiced -SE.

These words are also counted under S, p. 226 and -E, p. 111.

See also:

-SE, p. 233
-SS, p. 237
-ZE, p. 292

-SE as in cheese

Exceptions:

lens
(no E at
the end)

please	houses	because
noise	caused	
raise		
choose		
tease		

bruise	applause	mayonnaise
praise	arouse	praiseworthy
ease	disease	
pause		

braise	espouse	polonaise
cruise	causeway	gooseberry
browse	appraise	
clause	turquoise	
cleanse		

In these words, the root ends in a voiced S sound after a vowel team. The silent E shows that the S is not being added as a suffix. This helps the eye to distinquish between **please** and (two) **pleas**, **praise** and (he) **prays**, **pause** and (4) paws. In many of these words, there is double insurance against confusion, because the word ending -SE contains a vowel team for the middle of a root, while the one with added -S has a vowel team for the end of a root.

43 words have roots ending voiced -SE.

These words are also counted under -S-, p. 227 and -E, p. 111.

See also:

-CI-, p. 98
CH, p. 97
-SSI-, p. 238
-SU-, p. 239
-TI-, p. 250

Exceptions:

fashion
cushion
   (SH in Latin
   spellings)

SH as in ship

she	shoes	English
show	dishes	finish
shall	wished	shadow
fish	washing	sunshine
should	shorter	yellowish
shade	ashore	foreshorten
shin	shovel	shareholder
shred	ashamed	shrubbery
march	hardship	battleship
leash	threshold	refreshments
shad	banish	partnership
shank	shoddy	worshipful
shrewd	shrinkage	accomplishment
mesh	flourish	establishment

SH is a consonant team for the special English consonant sound at the beginning of **ship** and the end of **fish**. Notice that SH sometimes forms a blend with R as in **shred**. Once in a while, S and H belong to different roots, and retain their normal sounds, as in **grasshopper**.

We use SH for this sound only at the beginning and end in native English roots, and in the suffix **-ish**. When the SH sound occurs before Latin suffixes, it is spelled -CI-, -SCI-, -SI-, -SSI- or -TI-, as in special, conscience, tension, passion or nation; or else it is spelled -S- or -SS- before unstressed long U, as in censure or tissue.

406 Words have SH as in **ship**, of these, 21 have the blend SHR-, and are also counted under R, p. 219.

See also:

-S-, p. 227
-SSI-, p. 238
-I-, p. 156
-ZU-, p. 293

-SI- as in television

vision
division

fusion

decision
confusion
invasion
excursion
explosion

lesion
version

adhesion
allusion
implosion
abrasion
ambrosia

In these words, S has the special consonant sound which is respelled as ZH in dictionaries. S between vowels is often voiced. Here, the unstressed I before a vowel changes the voiced S sound to ZH. The S can have a ZH sound even when the vowel before it is an ER vowel sound, as in **version** and **excursion**. These are all words of Latin origin.

59 words have S changed to ZH by unstressed I before a vowel.

These words are not counted under -S-, p. 227.

See also:

-S, p. 228
-SE, p. 233

SS as in glass

Exceptions:

us
yes
this
bus
gas
pus
plus
thus
  (single S)

crevasse
finesse
fosse
impasse
demitasse
  (-SSE)

bass (voice)
  (long A)

gross
  (long O)

grass	classes	across
dress	dressing	address
miss	crossed	goodness
guess	grassy	careless
pass	kisses	princess
bless	assess	congress
boss	blissful	actress
fuss	confess	business
less	dressmaker	consciousness
toss	assessment	embarrass
lass	abyss	dispossess
cress	cesspool	distressful
stress	caress	harassment
truss	obsessed	
chess	carcass	

-SS is a consonant team for unvoiced S at the end of the root after a short vowel. In these words, the root, or the last syllable, ends in an S sound. The -SS shows that the S is not being added as a suffix. This enables the eye to distinguish between **his** (him's) and (one) **hiss**, (one) **princess** and (two) **princes**, (two) **needles** and **needless**.

280 words have SS at the end of the word.

These words are also counted once each under S, p. 226.

See also:

-SI-, p. 236
-SU-, p. 239
-I-, p. 156

-SSI- as in procession

expression

passion	succession
mission	profession
session	dimension
mansion	controversial
pension	confession
fission	accession
commission	extension
secession	emulsion
digression	dissension

In these words the SS has an SH sound. SS between vowels is unvoiced. Here, the unstressed I before a vowel changes the unvoiced S sound to an SH sound. In some of these words, there is one S after a different consonant. The I changes these S's in the same way. These are all words of Latin origin.

105 words have SS, or a consonant followed by S, changed to an SH sound by unstressed I before a vowel.

These words are not counted under S, p. 226.

See also:

-SI-, p. 236
-SSI-, p. 238
Long U, p. 257

-SU- as in treasure

sure	surely	usually
insure	issue	enclosure
assure	pressure	visual
	tissue	insurance
	leisure	exposure
	measure	casual
surety	tonsure	usurious
	closure	sensuous
	fissure	embrasure
	sumac	erasure
	censure	cynosure

In these words, SS between vowels has an SH sound. So do S at the beginning of the word, and S after a different consonant. Single S between vowels normally has a Z sound, but here it has the special consonant sound which is respelled ZH in dictionaries. The Y- element from the long U sound causes these changes in the S sounds.

63 words have the sound of S or SS changed by long U.

These S's and SS's are not counted under S, p. 226 or under -S-, p. 227.

S at the end of French words is silent, as in rendezvous

corps	chassis	
	chamois	apropos
	debris	
	bourgeois	

Words of this kind are English enough to be included in the Hanna listing, but many of their letter sounds reflect their French origin.

This is the entire list of words ending in silent S.

The Letter T

In English the letter T has one basic sound, the first sound in **top**. T usually behaves like any ordinary consonant letter, as in

time, train, stain, strain, mat, mate, fast, lift, felt, kept, tempt, cart, last, matting, mating, cotton, title, little

Letter Teams Containing T

1. T is the first member of the consonant team TH. This team may be either voiced, as in **this**, or unvoiced, as in **thing**. The Latin language did not contain either of these sounds. Therefore, the Latin alphabet which we use has no single letter for either of these sounds.

   a. TH is voiced—

      1) At the beginning of the pointing words, as in

         the, that, these, there, then, they, them, thy

      2) Between vowels in native English words as in

         mother, feather, either, clothes, bathe, loathe, teething, mouthing

   b. TH is unvoiced—

      1) At the beginnings of nouns, verbs and adjectives, as in

         thief, thumb, thank, thump, thick, thin

      2) When it is the first member of the consonant blend THR, as in

         through, three, thrifty, thread

      3) At the end of the word, as in

         path, death, health, moth, wreath, oath, youth, south, north, cloth, bath, loath, teeth, mouth, fifth, twentieth

      4) In all positions on the Latin side of English. Even though the Romans could not pronounce TH, they used this team to preserve the Greek flavor of borrowed words in which the Greeks used the unvoiced TH sound. On

entering English, these **TH**'s reverted to the ancient Greek **TH** sound, as in

thorax, theory, therapy, author, ethics, cathedral, sympathy, orthodox, my**th**

Notice the Y's within the word. These, too, are remnants of Greek spellings.

3. TCH is a team for the special English consonant sound of CH. It is used to spell this sound right after a short vowel in the root, as in

ca**tch**, e**tch**, di**tch**, no**tch**, clu**tch**

These are words which can take the native English suffixes, **-ed, -ing, -er, -es, -y, -en**, etc. When the suffix captures the CH sound and runs off with it, we tend to use a T sound to close our mouths at the end of the first syllable, as in ca**t-ch**er, e**t-ch**ing or di**t-ch**es. This is natural, because CH has a complex sound, which begins with the mouth in the normal position for T. For this reason, the team TCH makes phonetic sense in words of this kind.

Distortions of the T sound—

1. T before suffixes containing unstressed I before another vowel. The unstressed I distorts the T to an SH sound, as in

na**ti**on, mo**ti**on, condi**ti**on par**ti**al, pa**ti**ence, quo**ti**ent, nego**ti**ate

2. T before unstressed long U. The Y- portion of the unstressed long U distorts the T to a CH sound, as in

na**tu**re, pic**tu**re, furni**tu**re, for**tu**ne, ac**tu**al, cen**tu**ry, punc**tu**ate, vir**tu**e, vir**tu**ous

3. Silent T. T is silent in **-stle, -sten** and **-ften**, as in

cas**t**le, nes**t**le, wres**t**le, fas**t**en, has**t**en, lis**t**en, mois**t**en, of**t**en, sof**t**en

Notice that when the suffix is dropped, the T often sounds, as in

nest, wrest, haste, moist, oft, soft

Even **fasten** means "to make **fast**."

T is the second member of the consontant team PT. (See "the Letter P," page 209.)

T as in top

Exceptions:

mitt
putt
watt
butt
boycott
(double T)
boatswain
Christmas
chestnut
mortgage
(silent T)

take	getting	party
tell	hunted	mountain
not	taken	government
want	later	outside
just	brightest	bucket
tame	splutter	consistent
stow	waistcoat	priority
blunt	private	tolerant
dealt	rusty	handicraft
fact	fifteen	undoubted
taut	ornate	treacherous
tier	cobalt	notorious
blurt	hydrant	inadequate
mute	altar	benevolent
chaste	torrent	alienate

T is a consonant letter for the first sound in **top** and the last sound in **hat**.

7345 words have T as in **top**.

T as in castle

often
Christmas
listen
whistle
fasten

hasten	nestle	christening
hustle	wrestler	epistle
jostle	chestnut	mistletoe
soften	mortgage	thistledown
chasten	forecastle	
hostler	boatswain	
pestle	apostle	
gristle		
moisten		

In these words, the T is silent. Most of the words have T between S and the suffixes **-le** or **-en**. Notice that in related words like **Christ**, **nest**, **fast** and **soft**, the T sounds.

39 words have silent T.

See also:

-LE, p. 175

T as in twin and trains

Exceptions:

two
   (silent W)

tree	tried	travel
trip	tricky	trouble
truck	stretching	strawberry
street	trader	twenty
twice	twelve	between
treat	treason	astronomy
trout	strengthen	strategy
trail	translate	transistor
strike	extreme	contribute
twinkle	twilight	twentieth
trait	distraught	obstruction
truss	abstract	centrifugal
tripe	transom	tranquility
trek	transcribe	protractor
twinge	symmetry	arbitrator

TR- and TW- are consonant blends. These blends do not often split up between vowels. The vowel before the blend is long, as in **retract** and **between**. STR- is a triple blend.

Notice how many of the words with TW- blends have meanings connected with the number two, or with on-and-off sights or sounds (**twinkle**).

492 words have the blend TR-.
 32 words have the blend TW-.
218 words have the blend STR-.

These words are also counted under T, p. 244 and under R, S and W, pp. 219, 226 and 270.

See also:

CH, p. 95

TCH as in pitch.

Exceptions:

which
much
such
rich
attach
detach
bachelor
duchess
lecherous
(T omitted)

ditch
catch
watch
witch

watched
catcher
matches
scratching

hopscotch
kitchen
hatchet
watchdog

blotch
clutch
hatch
stitch
sketch

bewitch
butcher
dispatch
patchwork
satchel

switchboard
stretcher
witchcraft
kitchennette

hutch
notch
crutch

ratchet
etching
wretched

crotchety
witchery

-TCH is a letter team for the special English consonant sound of CH. We use -TCH to show this sound right after a short vowel in the root.

CH represents a complex consonant sound, which begins with a T sound. When suffixes like **-er**, **-es**, or **-ing** are added to words ending in a CH sound, the T sound tends to attach itself to the first syllable, while ordinary CH begins the second syllable. Thus, the -TCH spelling makes phonetic sense.

63 words have -TCH after a short vowel in the root.

These words are also counted under CH, p. 95. They are not counted under T, p. 244.

See also:

TH, p. 249

TH as in this and that

the	these	although
there	those	themselves
then	theirs	either
they	clothes	together
than	with	otherwise
thee	northern	nevertheless
thou	farther	trustworthy
thy	breathing	feathery
bathe	heathen	motherhood
smooth	brethren	fathomless
thence	withal	
thus	therefrom	
blithe	forthwith	
lithe	hither	
swathe	thither	

TH is a letter team for the special English consonant sound at the beginning of **this** and in the middle of **mother**. In these words, TH is voiced. Voiced TH is used at the beginning of the pointing words. It also occurs between vowels in native English words. The word **with** can end with voiced TH if the next word begins with a vowel or a voiced consonant.

150 words have voiced TH.

See also:

TH, p. 248

Exceptions:

Thomas
thyme
Thames
   (TH = T)

TH as in thing

thimble	thinking	birthday
three	thanked	nothing
throw	seventh	thirty
thumb	threw	Thursday
mouth	thickest	thousand
thorn	thunder	mathematics
oath	thirsty	authority
thread	throughout	anthology
north	healthy	thermostat
month	athlete	sympathy
thatch	thorax	ethnology
lath	thymus	monolithic
thwart	zenith	authentic
throes	naphtha	psychopathic
thresh	ether	diphthong

TH is a letter team for the special English consonant sound at the beginning of **thing** and the end of **north**. In these words, TH is unvoiced. Unvoiced TH is used at the beginning of nouns, verbs and adjectives. It also occurs between vowels in the Greek words, which come to us through Latin. After the reader goes beyond children's materials, all the TH's in unfamiliar words will be unvoiced TH's.

Once in a while, T and H belong to different roots, and retain their normal sounds, as in **pothole**.

Unvoiced TH blends with R and W, as in **three** and **thwart**.

468 words have unvoiced TH. Of these, 50 have R blends, and are also counted under R, p. 219. Three of them have W blends, and are counted under W, p. 270.

TI as in nation

See also:

-CI, p. 98
-SSI-, p. 238
-I-, p. 156

Exceptions:

equation
  (TI = ZH)

	station	question
	motion	education
	action	direction
	caution	addition

section	national	constitution
option	vacation	circumstantial
patience	condition	recognition
partial	completion	intentional
initial	migration	suggestion

bestial	cognition	differential
quotient	negotiate	impartiality
diction	deduction	notification
ratio	apportion	proclamation
function	probation	dietitian

In these words, T has an SH sound. The unstressed I before a vowel causes this change in the T sound. These are all words of Latin origin.

866 words have T changed to an SH sound by unstressed I before a vowel. Of these, 624 are **-tion** words.

These words are not counted under T, p. 244.

See also:

-DU-, p. 103
-SU-, p. 239
Long U, p. 257

TU as in picture

Exceptions:

victual
   (silent U)

	nature	natural
	capture	statue
	future	furniture
	fortune	temperature
	posture	adventure
culture	actual	agriculture
gesture	fortunate	spiritual
feature	eventual	punctuation
moisture	signature	literature
virtue	mutual	situation
stature	botulism	ineffectual
creature	ritual	estuary
denture	habitual	infatuated
vulture	saturated	architecture
texture	fluctuate	picturesque

In these words, T has a CH sound. The Y- element of the unstressed long U causes this change in the T sound. These are all words of Latin origin.

173 words have T changed to a CH sound by unstressed long U.

These words are not counted under T, p. 244.

In French words final T is silent, but a final silent E makes it sound

-T	-TE	-TTE
beret	route	cigarette
bouquet	suite	kitchenette
buffet	fete	gazette
ballet	forte	roulette
croquet	petite	croquette
qourmet	elite	barrette
ricochet	garrote	gavotte
sobriquet	artiste	pipette
depot	baptiste	butte
petit	debutante	statuette
debut	marquerite	silhouette
		mignonette
		rosette
		layette
		palette
		etiquette

Notice the French sounds of many of the vowels like I, E and OU, and of the consonant team CH. Although these words are English enough to be included in the Hanna listing, many of their letter sounds reflect their French origin.

This is the entire list of words that have T affected by the French style of spelling.

The Letter U

In English, the letter U has three basic sounds, long, short and the vowel sound of **put**.

1. U is short when it is within the syllable, as in

   but, fun, drum, bulk, just, dump, mut-ter, bun-dle,
   sub-ject, pro-nun-ci-a-tion

   In the case of a word beginning with a vowel, U is short if it has a consonant after it in the same syllable, as in

   up, **u**n-der, **u**n-like

   The short sound of U is changed to the special English vowel sound of ER by final R, or by R followed by another consonant, as in

   f**ur**, t**ur**n, b**ur**st, t**ur**-k**e**y, p**ur**-ple, **ur**-gent, h**ur**-ry

   But if the next letter is a vowel, it will capture the R and leave the U unchanged, as in

   pu-rest, fu-ry, se-cu-ri-ty

2. U is long, and sounds like the **name** of the Letter U—

   a. When it is the last letter in the syllable, as in

   u-nit, fu-el, tu-ning, stu-dent, hu-mor, con-fu-sion
   flu, ru-mor, bru-tish, flu-ent, in-tru-sion, lu-bri-cate

   The long sound of a vowel is exemplified by the name of the vowel letter. The name of U begins with a consonant Y sound. It could be respelled **yoo**. The Y- part of the long U sound is the only thing that makes it different from the long sound of OO, as in f**oo**d. The Y- part of the long U sound is quite striking in the words in the group beginning with **unit**, above. But it is completely absent in the examples in the group beginning with **flu**, because it is impossible to pronounce a Y- sound after the American pronunciations of L or R. The student should learn to use the full letter-name for long U, and then be prepared to drop the Y- part of it when convenient. However, it is the Y- sound which distorts the S of **s**ure and in-**s**ure, turning it into an SH sound.

(In the Latin style of spelling, U at the end of the syllable is sometimes short, as in stu-dy, pu-nish, ju-gu-lar. But even in the Latin style, U is normally long if there is only one consonant between the U and the next vowel, as in student, accumulate, illuminate.)

b. In the spelling pattern U__E, as in

use, **cute**, **tube**, **duke**, for-**tune**, com-**pute,** in-**sure,** rule, crude, flute, in-trude

The first line of examples contains words in which the Y-part of the long U sound can be heard, and the second line contains words where it is suppressed by R or L.

c. In the vowel teams UE and UI, as in

d**ue**, h**ue**, bl**ue**, tr**ue**, con-str**ue**, at the end of the root and in

s**ui**t, j**ui**ce, n**ui**-sance, fr**ui**t, br**ui**se, within the root

In each set of examples, the first line contains words where the Y- part of the long U sound can be heard, and the second line contains words where it is suppressed by R or L.

d. The long sound of U is also represented by the teams EW and EU, as in

ewe, **few**, **mew**, **pew**, **chew**, grew, flew, blew at the end of the root

f**eu**dal, d**eu**ce, n**eu**tral rh**eu**matism, within the root.

In each set of examples, the first line contains words where the Y- part of the long U sound can be heard, while the second line contains words where it is suppressed by L or R. (See EU and EW, pp. 124 and 125.)

3. In a few words, U within the word spells the special vowel sound of short OO. (**Put** rhymes with **foot**.) Examples are —

p**u**t, p**u**ll, f**u**ll, b**u**ll, p**u**sh, b**u**l-let, b**u**sh-el, b**u**l-wark

Unstressed U

1. When short U is unstressed, it is just as severely muffled

as are unstressed A, E, and O, as in fi-na**l**, chan-n**e**l, and pis-t**o**l. But the ordinary sound of short U is so much like schwa that loss of stress does not seem to change short U as radical-ly as it changes the other vowel sounds. Short U is unstressed in

un-til, cen-s**u**s, me-di-**u**m, s**u**b-scrip-tion, cir-c**u**m-stance

2. When long U is unstressed most of its sound is muffled beyond recognition. But the Y- part of the long U sound is almost never lost, even in the syllables that are the most hurried, and are therefore the least stressed, as in

po-p**u**-la-tion, oc-c**u**-py, mo-n**u**-ment, in-so-l**u**-ble, re-g**u**-late, fai-l**u**re, vo-l**u**me, fi-g**u**re, te-n**u**re

The Y- part of the long U sound is so persistent that it distorts D, S, T and Z sounds when they are captured from roots by syllables containing long U's. D's take on J sounds, S's take on SH sounds, T's take on CH sounds, and Z sounds take on ZH sounds, as in

e-**du**-ca-tion, ver-**dure**; is-**sue**, pres-**sure**; con-gra-**tu**-late, na-**ture**; u-**su**-al, mea-**sure**, a-**zure**

U in Teams for Other Vowel Sounds

U forms the second member of the vowel teams AU, EU and OU. See "The Letter A," page 67; "The Letter E," page 104; and "The Letter O," page 182.

U as a Consonant

The letter U sometimes behaves like the consonant W. U sounds like the consonant W—

1. In the consonant blend QU, as in

quake, **qu**een, **qu**ick, **qu**o-ta-tion, con-**qu**est

(But after Q, U is occasionally silent, in words borrowed from the French, as in an-ti**que**, pla**que**, con-**qu**er.)

2. When it occasionally forms a blend with other consonant letters, especially G and S, as in

lan-**gu**age, an-**gu**ish, per-**su**ade, as-**su**age, **pu**eb-lo

These are words of Latin origin.

Silent U

U does not form a consonant blend with G when the next letter is E, I or Y. Instead, the U is silent, and serves to keep the G hard before these vowels, as in

guess, guide, guil-lo-tine, guy

See also:

UE, p. 262
-DU-, p. 103
-SU-, p. 239
-TU-, p. 251
OO, p. 195

Exceptions:

busy
  (short I)

bury
  (short E)

victual
  (silent U)

U as in uniform

		Unstressed
during	bluish	natural
music	human	united
Lulu	stupid	century
sugar	tulip	usually
truly	ruler	education

		Unstressed
unit	cruel	supreme
humor	ruin	actually
tuna	fury	influence
bugle	confusion	formula
student	curious	graduation

		Unstressed
fluid	cucumber	volume
plural	lubricate	visual
cubic	insurance	calculate
mural	accumulate	adventurous
duty	endurance	document

U is a vowel letter. It is long in a syllable that ends in U. When there is a single consonant between vowels, the first vowel is long. This is true for most of the U's even in the Latin words.

It is usually true that a long vowel "says its name." But the name of U begins with a consonant Y- sound which is often lost, because it is so difficult to pronounce after certain consonants, especially L and R. The Y- part of long U is clearly heard in **unit** and **music**, but it is lost in **truly**.

438   words have long U in a stressed syllable, where the vowel sound is clear.

521   words have long U in an unstressed syllable, where the Y-part of the long U sound is often all that can be heard as in **volume**.

This count excludes words like **using**, where the native English suffix simply changes the word's form.

See also:

U, p. 257

U as in up

Exceptions:

Ruth
truth
Duluth
impugn
(long U)

us	cutting	hungry
duck	lucky	study
fun	funny	number
jump	runner	under
judge	hunted	hundred

Unstressed

punch	begrudge	supposed
bluff	bucket	subscribe
thump	chuckle	unhealthy
crutch	subway	cactus
pulse	upkeep	product

Unstressed

blunt	summary	uphold
gust	consumption	apparatus
cull	butler	unstable
tuft	destructive	stadium
hunch	punishable	frustration

U is a vowel letter. U is short in a syllable that ends with a consonant letter. When there are two consonants between vowels, the first vowel is almost always short. In a few of the Latin words, U is short even when there is only one consonant between vowels, as in **punish**.

1027 words have U before a consonant in a stressed syllable, where the short U sound is clear.

518 words have U before a consonant in an unstressed syllable. In spite of being unstressed, the vowel sound remains fairly clear.

See also:

OO, p. 196
U, p. 258

U as in put

push	putting	awful
full	fuller	beautiful
pull	pulled	careful
bush	pussy	bulldozer
bull	pushing	bullet
bullion	pudding	ambush
bully	pulley	fulfill
bushel	pulpit	forgetful
butcher	output	powerful
cuckoo	cushion	scornful
bullock	artful	unmindful
bulwark	truthful	worshipful
fulsome	vengeful	disdainful
pullet	wistful	remoresful
	tactful	pitiful

In these words, U is within the syllable, so that it appears as though it should be short. But here the U has its third sound, which is the same as short OO. (**Put** rhymes with **foot**.) Notice that most of these words have the syllables **bull**, **pull**, **full** or **bush**.

37 words have U with its third sound in a stressed syllable, where the vowel sound is clear.

113 words have U with its third sound in an unstressed syllable. Most of these are words like **careful**, with the suffix **-ful**.

See also:

G Blends, p. 138
GU, p. 143
QU-, p. 214
S Blends, p. 230

U as in language

quilt	squash	quarter
		penquin
quiz	quiver	acquainted
suite	persuade	linguistic
suave	anquish	distinguish
pueblo	cuisine	extinguish
		LaGuardia
quell	assuage	equity
sanguine	dissuade	consanguinity
guano	languid	

There are only a few words where U forms a team with the vowel letter which comes after it. In the words on this page, U has the consonant sound of W. This is a Latin or Spanish spelling.

248 words have U with a consonant sound. Of these, 220 involve the consonant blend QU-.

See also:

-E, p. 110
-UE, p. 262
-DU-, p. 103
-SU-, p. 239
-TU-, p. 251

U__E as in tube

Exceptions:

butte
(double T be-
tween U and
E)

		Unstressed
sure	cubes	nature
use	useful	minute
rule	costume	picture
cute	excuse	future
tune	absolutely	adventure

		Unstressed
flute	insure	measure
cure	exclude	pressure
duke	abuse	enclosure
pure	secure	contribute
huge	amusement	furniture

		Unstressed
dude	assume	volume
fume	commute	refuge
nude	lukewarm	schedule
tube	mature	misfortune
	obscure	agriculture

Vowel-consonant-silent E is a special long vowel spelling pattern. The E makes the U "say its name." The E remains silent when a syllable beginning with a consonant is added to the word. In many of these words the Y- part of the long U sound is prominent, as in **cube**. In many others it is lost, as in **rule**. (See long U, p. 257.)

153 words have U__E in a stressed syllable, where the long U sound is clear.

179 words have U__E in an unstressed syllable. In these syllables the vowel sound is often muffled, and the consonant captured from the root is often changed in sound by the Y-part of the long U.

These words are not counted under long U, p. 257.

-UE as in glue

See also:

U__E, p. 261
-UE, p. 263
also, p. 295

No exceptions

blue	dues	bluebird
true	statue	blueberry
Sue		avenue
		value
		argue
clue	untrue	barbecue
cue	rescue	continue
sue	pursue	revenue
	issue	tissue
		virtue
flue	accrue	bluebottle
rue	construe	gruesome
hue	fondue	
	subdue	

UE is a vowel team for long U. It is used at the end of the root.
The Y- part of the long U sound is lost in many of these words.
(See long U, p. 257.)

44 words have -UE sounding like long U.

These words are not counted under long U, p. 257.

See also:

-UE, p. 262
GU-, p. 143
QU-, p. 215

-UE as in tongue

league

morgue	colleague	catalogue
plague	intrigue	synagogue
vague	harangue	dialogue
plaque	unique	
clique	opaque	

brogue	grotesque	analogue
fugue	critique	pedagogue
vogue		picturesque

Except in the word **argue**, UE is silent at the end of the word after G or Q. These are French spellings. Since the U is silent, the silent E can make the first vowel long, but the vowel often has a French sound, instead.

43 words have silent UE at the end.

UI as in fruit

juice	juicy	suitcase
suit		
cruise	cruiser	suitable
bruise	fruitful	unsuitable
	pursuit	nuisance
	lawsuit	
sluice	suitor	

UI is a vowel team for long U within the root. In most of these words, the Y- part of the long U sound is lost. (See long U, p. 257.)

This is the entire list of words with UI.

These words are not counted under long U, p. 257.

See also:

-ER, p. 121
-IR, p. 164

UR as in fur

Exceptions:

purr
burr
  (2 R's)

turn	nurses	surprise
hurt	curved	hurry
church	curly	Thursday
burn	burnt	turtle
		Saturday
blur	suburb	turpentine
curb	return	furthermore
turf	surface	survival
purge	pursue	frankfurter
knurl	urban	reimburse
burgh	furlong	appurtenances
	nurture	

In these words, the R is at the end, is followed by a different consonant, or is doubled between vowels. U in the middle of the syllable is usually short, but the R changes it to the special English vowel sound of ER.

247 words have U changed by R.

These words are also counted under R, p. 219.

See also:
-VE, p. 267

No Exceptions

V as in valentine

five	driving	very
cave	gave	seven
leave	given	over
brave	arrived	evening
stove	heavy	everything
vine	advance	provision
voice	flavor	advocate
river	oven	overturn
never	diver	vacation
vote	vivid	behavior
verb	alcove	inveigled
vie	average	juvenile
vast	vinyl	adventurous
vein	viola	provisional
vile	evolve	conveyance

V is a consonant letter for the first sound in **valentine**. Ordinarily, it is necessary to double a consonant letter before a native English suffix in order to keep the vowel of the root short. But V is never doubled, because VV looks too much like W. **Never** would look like **newer**. The reader must be prepared to use either a long vowel or a short vowel, whichever makes sense.

1491 words have V as in **valentine**.

See also:

V, p. 266

No exceptions

VE as in have

give	moved	above
live	living	receive
love	loving	believe
twelve	proved	themselves
glove	calves	improve
carve	resolve	native
nerve	approve	active
groove	forgive	detective
sleeve	outlive	impulsive
shelves	relieve	talkative
cleave	movement	responsive
salve	deserve	productive
mauve	revolve	selective
waive	bereaved	comparatively
heave	conceive	subjective

-VE is a consonant team for V as the last sound in the word. We never use V at the end without silent E. (To keep the V from falling over?)

These are words where the silent E does not make the vowel before it long. Notice that O in these words has either a short U or a long OO sound. See page 266 for words where a single vowel before -VE is long.

287 words have -VE where it does not make the vowel before it long. Of these, 185 have the suffix **-ive**. Most of the rest have vowel teams or consonants before the V.

These words are also counted under V, p. 266.

The Letter W

Before the vowel, W is a consonant letter for the first sound in **win**. After the vowel, W is always part of a vowel team.

1. W as a consonant letter.

   a. W occurs before the vowel either by itself, or as the second member of a consonant blend, as in

   wax, **w**ait, **w**ent, **w**eed, **w**ine, **w**ish, **w**ant, **w**on, **w**arm, **w**ord, s**w**ing, s**w**arm, t**w**elve, t**w**ist, d**w**arf

   b. When W comes before A or O within the syllable, it changes the vowel sound. It changes the short A sound to the sound of short O and the short O sound to the sound of short U, as in

   want, **wa**sh, s**wa**p, s**wa**t, **wa**nder, s**wa**ddling, **wo**n, **wo**nder

   If the letter after the changed A or O is R or R followed by a different consonant, it changes these vowels one more step. The R changes the short O sound of the A to a long O sound: and it changes the short U sound of the O to the same sound as UR, as in

   war, **wa**rm, **wa**rden, s**wa**rthy; **wo**rld, **wo**rse, **wo**rthy

   These changes do not seem surprising if we notice what R normally does to short O and short U sounds:

   fond/ford, wand/ward; fun/fur, won/word

   But if the sound after the A or O is G, K or NG, the vowel remains short, as in

   wag, thw**a**ck, **wa**x, tw**a**ng, polliw**o**g

   Since the U in the consonant blend QU has a W sound, it has the same effect on A that W has, as in

   sq**ua**d, sq**ua**sh, sq**ua**nder, q**ua**ntity, q**ua**rt, q**ua**ck

   O does not happen to occur after qu in any syllables where it would normally be short.

c. W is the first member of the consonant team WH, as in **what**. This team occurs only at the beginning of the word, as in

> **wh**en, **wh**ere, **wh**ich, **wh**y, **wh**ip, **wh**eel, **wh**isper, **wh**ine

In some regions, WH is an unvoiced version of the W sound. But in many regions, it sounds exactly like W.

Before long O and OO sounds, WH sounds like H, as in

> **wh**o, **wh**om, **wh**ose, **wh**ole, **wh**ooping

d. W is the first member of the consonant team WR, as in **write**. This team occurs only at the beginning of the word or syllable, as in

> **wr**eck, **wr**ing, **wr**ap, play**wr**ight

2. After the vowel, W occurs only as the second member of the vowel teams AW, EW and OW, as in

> j**aw**, p**aw**, d**aw**n, cr**aw**l, h**aw**k, **aw**kward,
> n**ew**, f**ew**, ch**ew**, curf**ew**
> h**ow**, d**ow**n, g**ow**n, h**ow**l, gr**ow**l, sh**ow**er, t**ow**el, all**ow**
> sh**ow**, sh**ow**n, gr**ow**th, b**ow**l, wind**ow**, pill**ow**, shall**ow**

(See "The Letter A," p. 67; "The Letter E," p. 104; and "The Letter O," p. 182.)

W as in wagon

we	waiting	always
walk	wished	away
would	windy	between
with	wider	twenty
sweet	wildest	winter
wire	awoke	backwoodsman
twin	beware	wayfarer
waist	highway	interwoven
sweat	entwine	overweight
dwell	likewise	bewilder
wean	waiver	cottonwood
womb	welter	earthenware
wed	wicket	
wince	aware	
weld	forthwith	

W is a consonant letter for the first sound in **wagon**. W is a consonant letter only when it comes before a vowel letter. After a vowel, W is always part of a letter team for a vowel sound.

578 words have W as in **wagon**.

See also:

Short A, p. 71
WAR-, p. 272
WO-, p. 274

WA- as in wand

Exceptions:

wag
wagon
wax
swam
quack
swagger
waxen
wigwag
thwack
twang
aquatic
  (short A)

was	swapping	water
want	wanted	waterfall
watch	washer	wander
squash	squashy	whatever
what		
wad	waffle	waterproof
wasp	wallet	breakwater
watt	swallow	qualify
squat	quarrel	quantify
swan	squander	quality
squad	warrant	swastika
swab	waddle	quadruped
swamp	squabble	kilowatt
wand	equality	quadrangle
	washable	

In these words, the A should be short, because it is in the middle of the syllable. But W before the A changes the short A sound to broad A, with a sound like short O as in **hot** or **dog**. Since it is the **sound** of W which has this effect, QU- also changes short A to broad A.

Notice that most of the exceptional words have K, hard G or NG sounds after the A.

92 words have WA- or QUA- with a broad A sound.

These words are also counted under W-, p. 270 or under QU-, p. 214.

See also:

WA-, p. 271
WOR-, p. 275
-OR, p. 197

WAR- as in warm

No exceptions

		Unstressed
war	warmer	forward
warn	warning	backwards
swarm	quarter	afterwards
quart	reward	upwards
ward	award	headquarters
warp	forewarn	quarterback
wart	warden	quarterly
dwarf	warfare	

		Unstressed
thwart	warble	bulwark
quartz	wardrobe	windward
wharf	lukewarm	leeward

If **warm** did not have an R after the vowel, the W at the beginning would give the A a broad sound, equivalent to the short O sound of **hot**. But the R changes the broad A sound to a long O sound. (Compare **fond/for** and **wand/war.**)

40 words have WA- changed by R in a stressed syllable, where the long O sound is clear.

39 words have WA- changed by R in an unstressed syllable, where the vowel sound is often muffled.

These words are also counted under W-, p. 270, and under QU-, p. 214, and R, p. 219.

Exceptions:

who
whose
whole
whom
whoever
whoop
whore
(WH = H)

WH as in wheel

what	whack	whisper
when	whale	whisker
where	wheat	somewhere
which	white	whatever
why	whip	nowhere
while	whether	whereabouts
wheeze	whimper	anywhere
whew	whirlpool	whippoorwill
whiff	whistle	meanwhile
whiz	whittle	whirligig
whey	wherefore	whither
wharf	whit	wheresoever
whim	whetstone	wherewithal
whisk	whinny	whimsical
whet	whereupon	whereby

WH- is a letter team for the special English consonant sound in **wheel**. In many regions it sounds the same as plain W-. In other regions it sounds like the consonant blend HW-. This is the Old English sound of WH.

We use the team WH at the beginnings of question words. Most of the other WH- words have meanings conected with whistling or whining sounds.

91 words begin with WH.

See also:

WA-, p. 271
WOR-, p. 275
O, p. 188

WO- as in wonder

won	wolves	wonderland
wolf		wonderful
		woman
		saleswoman
	wondrous	womanly
	wolfish	womanhood
		washerwoman
		needlewoman
wont		wonderment
		unwonted
		gentlewoman
		womankind

Exceptions:

wobble
  (short O)

swum
swung
  (U after W)

women
  (short I)

In these words, W at the beginning changes the short O sound to short U, as in **nut** or **put**.

This is the entire list of words with WO- having a short U sound.

These words are also counted under W-, p. 270.

Those where the O sounds like short U in **nut** are also counted under O, p. 188.

See also:

WAR-, p. 272
WO-, p. 274

WOR- as in worm

Exceptions:

worn
sworn
  (normal sound
   of OR)
liverwurst
  (U after W)

worsted
  (silent R)

word	worker	workshop
work		worry
world		fireworks
worse		network
worst		silkworm
worth	worship	overwork
	worthy	unworthy
	worthless	workable
	teamwork	underworld
	crossword	handiwork
whorl	cutworm	worshipful

If **worm** did not have an R after the vowel, the W at the beginning would give the O a short U sound. But the R changes the short U sound to the special English vowel sound of ER. (Compare **fun/fur** and **won/worm**.)

51 words have WO- changed by R to sound like WER.

These words are also counted under W-, p. 270 and under R, p. 219.

WR as in write

wrist	writer	wrinkle
wrap	written	handwriting
wrong	wrapper	typewriter
	wrote	

wring	unwrap	writhing
wrench	wrangle	playwright
wren	wrestle	shipwreck
wreath	wretched	wreckage
wrath	wriggle	

wrack	wry	overwrought
wreak	wrought	
wrest	writ	

WR- is a letter team for the sound of R. It occurs only at the beginning of the word. This is a native English consonant team. Words beginning with WR have meanings connected with the idea of twisting.

48 words have WR-.

These words are also counted under R, p. 219.

See also:

-X-, p. 278
X-, p. 279

No exceptions

X as in fox

box	boxes	except
fix	fixed	excuse
next	mixing	exciting
wax	waxy	expect
six	sixth	sixteen
ax	axle	oxygen
coax	exile	saxophone
ox	oxide	experiment
relax	exclude	excursion
complex	expert	expensive
hoax	exchange	dexerity
lax	exhale	crucifix
lynx	expend	expansion
flax	prefix	extinguish
sphinx	suffix	inexperienced

-X is a single letter for the consonant blend -KS. When a word ends in this blend, the use of -X prevents the word from looking as though it had the suffix **-s** added to it. This enables the eye to distinguish between (one) **tax** and (many) **tacks**. -X also occurs at the end of the Latin prefix **ex-**.

Since -X represents two consonant sounds, it does not need to be doubled before a native English suffix.

350 words have X sounding like KS.

See also:

-X, p. 277
X-, p. 279

X as in example

exact	exhaust
	exactly
exempt	exasperate
exert	executive
exist	examination
exult	exhibit
	auxiliary
exhort	exemplary
exude	exhilarate
	exonerate
	unexampled

When the syllable ending in X is unstressed, and the next syllable begins with a vowel, or with silent H, the X is a single letter for the consonant blend GZ. This is a voiced version of the usual sound of -X, which is -KS. Compare the sound of unstressed X in **executive** with the sound of stressed X in **execute**.

43 words have -X- sounding like -GZ-.

These words are not counted under X, p. 277.

See also:

-X, p. 277

X as in xenon

Exceptions:

x-ray
  (We name
   the X)

Xerox   xenophobia

Xerxes   xylophone

X is a consonant letter. At the beginning of the word, X sounds like Z.

These words are so unusual that they do not figure in the word study on which the numbers in this book are based.

The Letter Y

The letter Y serves both as a consonant and as a vowel.

Y is a consonant letter only when it is at the beginning of the word or syllable, as in

you, **y**es, **y**ard, **y**el-low, can-**y**on, law-**y**er

There are only 57 words where Y is a consonant.

In any other position, Y is a vowel letter. As a vowel, Y has the same three basic sounds that I has. (See "The Letter I," page 149.) Ordinarily, we use Y at the very end of the word, and I within the word. If Y is within the word, it indicates a Greek origin. In fact, in other languages, the letter Y has no separate name of its own. Instead, it is called "Greek I," because there, too, Y within the word indicates a Greek origin.

The three basic sounds of Y as a vowel are long I, short I and long E.

1. Y is short within the syllable, as in **gym** and **sym**-bol.

   The short sound of Y is changed to the special English vowel sound of ER by final R, or by R followed by a different conso-nant sound, as in m**yr**rh and m**yr**-tle. But if the next sound is a vowel, it will capture the R sound, and leave the Y sound unchanged, as in s**y-ru**p and t**y-ra**nt.

2. Y is long, and sounds like the **name of the letter I** —

   a. When it is the only vowel letter in the root of the word, and is the very last letter of the word, as in

      b**y**, cr**y**, fl**y**, sk**y**, re-pl**y**, de-n**y**, sa-tis-f**y**

      But before suffixes beginning with vowels, the Y changes to I, as in

      cries, cried, cri-er, tri-al, dri-est, de-nied, de-ni-al

      However, if the suffix begins with I, the Y remains un-changed, since we never have two I's in a row in English:

      cry-ing, fly-ing, try-ing, re-ply-ing

   b. When it is the last letter in the syllable, as in t**y**-rant. But in the Latin style of spelling, these Y's are often short, as in cy-nic.

c. In the spelling pattern Y__E, as in **type**, st**y**le, a-na-**lyze**.

d. In the vowel team YE, as in **rye**, **bye**, at the end of the word.

e. When it is stressed before another vowel, as in cy-a-nide, h**y**-a-cinth.

3. Y spells the sound of long E—

a. When it is in a suffix, and is the very last letter in the word, as in

can-d**y**, hap-p**y**, quick-l**y**, ba-ke-r**y**, his-to-r**y**, li-bra-r**y**, a-bi-li-t**y**, ge-o-lo-g**y**, ge-og-ra-ph**y**, a-ca-de-m**y**

But before a second suffix, the Y changes to I, as in

can-dies, can-died, hap-pi-er, his-to-ri-an, hap-pi-ness, hap-pi-ly, merriment

However, if the suffix begins with I, the Y remains un-changed, since we never have two I's in a row in English:

car-r**y**-ing, hur-r**y**-ing, ba-b**y**-ish

The suffix -y is not changed to I in the middle of compound words like an**y**how, fair**y**land or clerg**y**man

b. When it is unstressed before another vowel, as in

hal-c**y**-on.

Of all these spellings, the two involving final Y, as in **by** and **candy**, are the only ones that need concern a beginner or a remedial student. These are standard English spellings. All the rest should be handled simply by sounding the Y exactly as one would sound an I in the same position.

Unstressed Y

Stress is of great importance to the final Y spellings. When it is stressed because of being in a root, Y sounds like long I, as in cry and re-ply. When it is unstressed because of being in a suf-fix, Y sounds like long E, as in can-d**y**.

Some linguists (and dictionaries) identify the long E sound of Y as a short I sound. But using the long E sound for these Y's seems to be the most useful approach for the novice reader who is attempting to decode a word that looks unfamiliar. In any case, the difference between unstressed long E and unstressed short I is nearly undetectable to the layman's ear, and the student reader is most certainly a layman.

Y in Teams for Other Vowel Sounds

Y is the second member of the vowel teams AY, EY and OY. These teams also have the alternative versions, AI, EI and OI. The versions which end in Y are only used when the team is final in the word or syllable, as in d**ay**, th**ey** and b**oy**. (See "The Letter A," page 67; "The Letter E," page 104; and "The Letter O," page 182.)

Exceptions:

Yvonne
  (Y is a vowel)

Y as in yellow

yard	yelling	yesterday
year	yanked	beyond
you	yours	farmyard
yes	younger	yourself
yet		Yankee
yarn	yelped	yonder
yearn	yielding	lawyer
yeast	youthful	dockyard
yoke	youngster	canyon
yacht	yearling	
yam	buoyancy	
yore	sawyer	
yew	vineyard	

Y- is a consonant letter for the first sound in **yellow**. Y has this sound only at the beginning of the word or syllable. Anywhere else in the word, Y is a vowel letter.

Only 57 words have Y as a consonant letter.

See also:

-I, p. 154
-IE, p. 158
-IED, p. 161
-Y, p. 285

-Y as in cry

No Exceptions

my	lying	good-by
try	trying	myself
sky	flyer	reply
why	drying	multiply
by	tying	
shy	spyglass	dragonfly
fry	rely	lullaby
pry	dryness	satisfy
deny	supply	terrify
defy	apply	magnify
ply	hereby	occupy
wry	thereby	amplify
sly	ally	certify
thy	comply	falsify
spry	bylaw	prophesy

At the end of the word or syllable, Y is a vowel letter. When Y is at the end of the root, it is stressed and sounds like long I.

128 words have long Y at the end of the root.

See also:

-I, p. 154
-IE, p. 159
-IED, p. 161
-Y, p. 284

-Y as in puppy

No exceptions

happy	hurrying	anyhow
baby	carrying	everything
country	finally	family
only	suddenly	nobody
pretty	nearly	fairyland
ninety	icy	heavyweight
envy	baggy	monopoly
hobby	greedy	ability
nasty	dirty	reality
angry	namely	oxygen
dreary	agency	abnormality
clergy	geology	visibility
victory	infinity	polygon
deathly	scientifically	sociability
jewelry	prophecy	radioactivity

At the end of the word or syllable, Y is a vowel letter. In these words, the -Y is unstressed because it is the suffix **-y** or in the suffix **-ly**. Suffix **-y** is pronounced like short I or long E, depending on what region of the country the speaker is from.

1628 words have the suffixes **-y** or **-ly**.

See also:

Long I, p. 152

No Exceptions

Y as in motorcycle

	stylish	bicycle
cyclone	hydrogen	hyena
thyroid	dynamite	psychologist
tyrant	dynasty	analysis
hygiene	hyphen	paralysis
zygote	cyclotron	myopia
thymus	typographic	hypothesis
stylus	pyromaniac	

In the middle of the word, Y is a vowel letter. It occurs in the middle in words of Greek origin, and spells the same sound that I would spell in the same position.

Y has a long I sound in a syllable that ends in Y. When there is a single consonant letter between vowels, the first vowel is long before the native English suffixes and certain Latin suffixes. The vowel is sometimes long in Latin words even when the next syllable begins with a consonant blend, as in **hydrogen**.

123 words have long Y within the word.

See also:

short I, p. 153

No exceptions

Y as in gym

myth	gypsy	mystery
rhythm	syrup	
gyp	crystal	cylinder
hymn	symptom	hypnotize
lynch	system	physical
	symbol	synonym
	pygmy	syllable
nymph	mystic	hypnosis
cyst	strychnine	hysterics
lymph	cynical	symbolic
		pseudonym
		amethyst

In the middle of the word, Y is a vowel letter. It occurs in the middle in words of Greek origin, and spells the same sound that I would spell in the same position.

Y is short in a syllable that ends with a consonant letter. When there are two consonants between vowels, the first vowel is almost always short. In many of the long, Latin words, the first vowel is short even when there is only one consonant between vowels, as in **cylinder**.

162 words have short Y.

See also:

I__E, p. 157
-IE, p. 158

Y__E as in type

Exceptions:

eye
   (see p. 295)

rhyme		typewriter
style		typewriting
bye		
rye		
dye	enzyme	stereotype
lye		analyze
scythe		paralyze
thyme	electrolyte	archetype
lyre	prototype	genotype
		neotype
		phenotype
		proselyte

In the middle of the word, Y is a vowel letter. It occurs in the middle in words of Greek origin, and spells the same sound that I would spell in the same position.

Vowel-consonant-silent-E is a special long vowel spelling pattern. The Y sounds like long I. The E remains silent when a syllable beginning with a consonant is added to the word.

The words ending in **-ye** are the only ones which are not Greek. These are Middle English spellings.

This is the entire list of words with Y__E.

These words are not counted under long Y, p. 286.

See also:

-IR, p. 164
-IRR-, p. 165

Exceptions:

myrrh
(double R
and H)

YR as in martyr

YR at the end, or before a different consonant	YR before a vowel
	syrup
martyrdom	lyric
	pyramid
	syringe
	tyranny
satyr	myriad
zephyr	panegyric
myrtle	porphyry
myrmidon	lyrical

In the middle of the word, Y is a vowel letter. It occurs in the middle in words of Greek origin, and spells the same sound that I would spell in the same position.

In the words in the left-hand column, the R changes the short I sound to the special English vowel sound of ER. In the words in the right-hand column, the Y remains short because the R sound goes off with the next syllable.

This is the entire list of words with Y changed by R, or with short Y before R.

These words are also counted under R, p. 219.

Those in the right-hand column are also counted under short Y, p. 287.

See also:
-S-, p. 227
Z, p. 291

Z as in zebra

Exceptions

rendezvous
(silent Z)

pizza
(first Z sounds
like T)

zoo	zipper	zigzag
zone	frozen	dozen
blaze	crazy	memorize
prize	fuzzy	recognize
size	cozy	magazine
daze	puzzle	realize
froze	razor	horizon
doze	zero	citizen
graze	amaze	organize
haze	drizzle	hazardous
zest	baptize	hypnotize
zinc	capsize	antagonize
zeal	trapeze	visualize
czar	analyze	naturalize
maze	gazette	oxidize

Z is a consonant letter for the first sound in **zebra** and the last sound in **blaze**. The sound of Z is the same as the sound of voiced S, but S is never voiced at the beginning of the word.

274 words have Z as in **zebra** and **blaze**.

Z as in waltz

chintz	howitzer	quartzite
quartz	eczema	

In these words, Z has the sound of unvoiced S.

This is the entire list of words in which Z sounds like unvoiced S.

See also:
-SE, p. 234

ZE as in sneeze

Exceptions:
Without E:
adz

freeze	freezer
squeeze	squeezing
breeze	wheeze
gauze	bronze
maize	breezy
ooze	
seize	
frieze	

-ZE is a consonant team for the sound of Z at the end of the root after a vowel team or a consonant letter. We never have Z alone at the end of the word. This team is used by analogy with the team -SE.

This is the entire list of words ending in ZE after a vowel team or a consonant letter.

These words are also counted under Z, p. 290.

See also:

-SI-, p. 236
-SU-, p. 239

Z as in azure

glazier
brazier

In these words, Z has the special consonant sound which is respelled ZH in dictionaries. The Y- element from the long U and the unstressed I's before a vowel cause this change in the Z sound.

This is the entire list of words that have Z sounding like ZH.

These words are not counted under Z, p. 290.

See also:

-SS, p. 237

ZZ as in buzz

fizz
fuzz
jazz

Exceptions:

quiz
whiz
fez
    (single Z)

-ZZ is a consonant team for the sound of Z at the end of the root after a short vowel. This team is used by analogy with -SS.

This is the entire list of words ending in ZZ.

These words are also counted once each under Z, p. 290.

Exceptions:

are
you
   (function
    words with 3
    letters)

go
pa
ax
ox
ad
el
em
id
   (main-idea
    words with 2
    letters)

Very Short Words

"Very short words" are words which contain only one or two speech sounds altogether. Some of them are main-idea words, which can be pictured, acted out, or precisely defined. Main-idea words must have at least three letters. When they are very short, they must be padded with silent letters to attain the three-letter minimum.

Certain other very short words are function words, with vague or variable meanings. These words serve chiefly to show how the main ideas of a sentence are related to one another. These function words need only enough letters to represent their sounds. They contain only one or two letters.

Function Words				Main-Idea Words			
am	of	a	oh	add	knee	buy	low
an	on	ah	do	egg	see	bye	know
as	or	fa	no	eye	die	rye	sew
at	up	la	so	sea	lie	hoe	due
if	us	be	to	tea	pie	toe	new
in		he	I	bee	tie	owe	knew
is		me	by				
it		we	my				
				inn	key	doe	tow
				odd	high	foe	cue
				ore	sigh	bow	sue
				pea	guy	mow	dew
				tee	dye	row	view
O	ho			ebb	gee	lye	rue
ay	lo			err	lee	roe	gnu
				awe	wee	woe	ewe
				aye	fie	sow	pew
				lea	hie	hue	yew
				fee	vie		

This is the entire list of very short words.

These words are also counted under the various vowel and consonant spellings they contain.

Appendix A

Dictionary Division of Syllables

If a word contains more than one syllable, there are two different kinds of reasons for separating the syllables from one another.

First, the **student** reader needs to divide up unfamiliar words so as to sound them out. For this purpose, we need a method which will yield the correct vowel sound for the stressed syllable as often as possible. A method of this kind is described in "Syllables, Stress and Word Structure," Appendix B.

Second, for the convenience of the **skilled** reader, printers need a method of dividing the longer words so that they may be broken with a hyphen at the end of one line of print, and carried on at the beginning of the next line. This method needs to give the reader accurate information about the vowel sound of the syllable just before the hyphen, especially if it happens to be stressed, and have a clear vowel sound when spoken. Since most of the vowel teams can have only one vowel sound in any case, the problem is serious only in connection with single vowel letters.

For the Latin-based words, dictionaries divide after the vowel if it has a clear long sound, as in **pa**-per, com-**ple**-tion, **ti**-ger, **ty**-rant, **pro**-gram, **stu**-dent; and after the consonant if the vowel has a clear short sound, as in **pan**-el, **dem**-o-**crat**-ic, **tim**-id, **tyr**-an-ny, **prod**-uct, **stud**-ied. Dictionaries also divide right after the vowel if the syllable is so lightly stressed that the vowel has no clear sound, as in de-moc-**ra**-cy.

However, dictionaries violate this system if the final syllable is a native English suffix added to a root word. Thus, the dictionary gives **bake/bak**-er, pre-**cede/**pre-**ced**-ing, **time/tim**-ing, **type/typ**-ist, **joke/jok**-ing, **tube/tub**-ing.

If there are two consonants between vowels, dictionaries, in general, divide between the two consonants, unless the first vowel is clearly long in speech, as in **ad**-vance, A-**pril**, rep-re-sent, re-**place**, **blis**-ter, vi-**brate**, **bot**-tom, **pro**-gram, **tun**-nel, lu-**bri**-cate.

But again, this system is violated before a native English suffix added to a root word which ends in two consonants, as in crack/crack-er, stiff/stiff-en, chill/chill-y, pass/pass-ing, buzz/buzz-er; land/land-ing, romp/romp-er, dust/dust-er; rich/rich-es, dash/dash-ing, etc., etc. If the consonant is doubled simply in the process of adding the suffix, only then does the dictionary show the division falling between the two consonants, as in hop/hop-ping.

But if the native English suffix is an integral part of the basic word, as in **paper**, then the dictionary follows the general procedure, and divides it **pa**-per. This is clearly a confusing system. It yields identical spellings for the first syllables of **tub**-ing and **tub**-bing, and gives the reader no warning that the U in **tubing** is long. In order to read such words without stumbling, the skilled reader must see them undivided.

If you, as a skilled reader, do not remember having been troubled by this sort of problem, it is because you have been carefully protected against these confusions by a convention of the publishing and secretarial worlds. The convention dictates that the native English suffixes must never be carried over from the end of one line to the beginning of another. If the lengthened form cannot be squeezed onto the upper line by crowding the type a bit, then the entire word must be placed on the lower line, and the letters or words of the upper line are spread out, if an even right-hand margin is required. This solution of the problem is universally incorporated into the style manuals of publishing houses, and into the basic training of stenographers.

With the advent of computer type-setting, there was a period of chaos in the process of dividing words at the end of the line. The computer programmers who work on this problem are at present restoring order to this process.

It is because the dictionary system of syllabication is so confusing that we have devised our own system for students to use in breaking down the unfamiliar words. Once students have finished learning how to read, they can learn how to divide words which must be broken at the end of the line.

Appendix B

Syllables, Stress and Word Structure

A syllable is a **vowel sound** and all the consonants that are pronounced along with it. A syllable may be composed of a vowel sound alone, or of a vowel sound carrying one or more consonant sounds, as in **I**, **by**, **spy**, **spry**; **out**, **pout**, **spout**; **sprout**, **sprouts**; **oil**, **boil**, **broil**, **broils**; **an**, **sand**, **stand**, **strand**, **strands**. In the last example, the short A sound is carrying six different consonant sounds. Notice that each of these examples contains only one vowel sound, even if it takes a team of two vowel letters to spell that sound.

Meanings of Syllables

There are three kinds of syllables, roots, prefixes and suffixes. The root contains the central idea of the word. A one-syllable word is a root with nothing added to it. It can have a variety of meanings, like **tie**, for instance. **To tie** is to make a knot, or to share a victory with another contestant. **A tie** is something to make a knot with, or an even score, or a beam holding railroad tracks together.

Longer words are made by joining syllables together. In a compound word two roots are joined for a very specific meaning, as in **necktie**. But most words have only one root, while all the other syllables are prefixes or suffixes. A prefix behaves like the root of a compound. It makes the meaning of the root to which it is added more specific, as in **un**tie or **re**tie. Suffixes usually change the form of the root, fitting it for different uses in the sentence, as in: one tie/two tie**s**; I tie/he tie**s**, he ti**ed** it/he is ty**ing** it; I drive it/I have driv**en** it/I am a driv**er**; fast/fast**er**/fast**est**; to sign/to make a sig**nal**.

As was mentioned under "Two Styles of Spelling," on page 22, Modern English comes down to us both from Old High German and from Ancient Latin. On the native English side of the language, the roots and prefixes are almost all common, everyday words, and the suffixes are so familiar that we respond to them automatically, without having to analyze how they are changing the word.

The roots on the Latin side of English, however, cannot usually stand alone as common, independent words. The few that can are rather technical, like **duct** or **vent**, and they are very narrow in meaning. But **-spect-** means nothing to us until prefixes or suffixes are added as in **re**spect or spect**acles**. Even then, we need a large collection of words with the same root, and some help from the dictionary, in order to see what the root contributes to the meaning of the familiar modern word.

But the Latin prefixes work just like the native English prefixes, narrowing the central meaning. Thus, **-spect-** means **look**, and **re**spect means to look at **again and again**. **In**spect means to look **into**, and **ex**pect means to look **out for**. Likewise, the Latin suffixes change the word's form. Spect**acles** are look**ers**, and inspec**tion** is a noun made from the verb **inspect**.

By consulting the dictionary, you can usually find an indication of the general meaning of a Latin prefix, or the usual function of a Latin suffix. It is often possible to find, also, the basic meaning of the Latin roots. One of the best dictionaries for this type of information is the paperback edition of Webster's New World Dictionary of the English Language. Such information can help to make the Latin side of our language much less formidable to the student than it is at first.

Stress

In English, we stress some syllables very heavily and hurry over others. The vowel sound of a stressed syllable is strong and distinct, while the vowel sound of an unstressed syllable is often weak and muffled, no matter what letter or letter team happens to be in use. For example, in the following words, the first syllable is stressed, and the second is unstressed: **final, cancel, pencil, pistol; Satan, kitten, satin, cotton, mountain; pocket, credit, carrot**. In each word, the vowel of the first syllable is loud and clear, while the vowels of the unstressed syllables all sound pretty much alike. The technical term for this muffled vowel sound is

schwa. In dictionary pronunciation guides, it is represented by an upside-down **e**.

Since we do not use accents or stress marks in our spelling system, these extremes of heavy stress and light stress can cause problems both for reading and for spelling. In reading, it is often hard for the student to tell where to place the stress in a three or four-syllable word; and in spelling, it is hard for many readers to tell what vowel to use when the vowel sound is schwa.

The habit of stressing one syllable very heavily, and slighting the rest, is characteristic of the German languages, and this habit has taken over throughout Modern English. However, the heavy stress is used in one way on the German (or native English) side of the language and in a very different way on the Latin side.

On the native English side, we follow the German habit of using stress to emphasize the point of what is being said. In a sentence the words that carry the main ideas are stressed, while the "little words" are hurried over: "The BOY was SICK." Putting extra stress on a "little word" gives the special meaning of that word special significance: "The boy WAS sick." Compare, also: "It FELL on the BOX," and "It fell ON the box," (not into it).

The same principle of stressing the main idea holds good for individual words. Since the main idea is contained in the root, the root is stressed no matter where it comes in the word: HAMmering, reMAKing, afterNOON, AFterwards, overTAKen, underSTANDable. The roots of these native English words are fairly easy to spot, so it is easy to place the stress correctly in words of this type.

In Latin and its descendants, French, Italian and Spanish, the stress pattern is entirely different. Instead of falling always on the root, the stress shifts back and forth as the word changes form. Compare poLITical and POLitics. In the purely Latin languages, the stress, wherever it falls, is fairly light, and the unstressed syllables are spoken fairly clearly—enough so that the vowels of the less-stressed syllables have maintained their characteristic sounds throughout two thousand years of language development.

When such a word first begins to enter English, its spelling reflects the original vowel sound for each syllable, stressed or unstressed. Moreover, the stress continues to shift in the Latin way as the word changes form. But now, wherever the stress falls, it is the heavy English type of stress. This quickly causes the vowels of the least-stressed syllables to become muffled.

Notice the varying vowel sounds in these sets: DEMocrat, deMOCracy, democRATic; ACtive, acTIVity, actiVAtion; MEDicine, meDICinal, mediCAtion; reSIDE, RESidence, resiDENtial; FInal, fiNALity; biOLogy, bioLOGical; and STAble, staBILity. Often the vowel of an unstressed syllable is still clear enough to be identifiable. But just as often, it is so muffled that the ear cannot tell what vowel letter to use in writing the syllable down.

Fortunately, we can often solve such spelling problems by thinking of a different form of the word. If we cannot remember what letter to use in the second syllable of DEMocrat, we have only to think of the form that tells what a democrat believes in—deMOCracy. Suddenly, the O speaks out clearly, and the problem is solved. If we don't remember whether to use **-ence** or **-ance** at the end of RESidence, we have only to think of the adjective form, resiDENtial, to realize that **-ence** is what we need for the noun form of the word. For the noun SUBstance, the adjective form, subSTANtial, solves the problem in the same way.

These two different types of stress pattern—stressed roots on the native English side, and shifting stress on the Latin side of the language—are closely connected to the two different spelling styles of Modern English.

On the Latin side of Modern English, we use the style of spelling that the words had in Ancient Latin, or in whatever modern form of Latin we took them from (most often, French, Italian or Spanish). On the native English side, we have a whole new style of spelling. Nowadays, this style may not seem so "new." In fact, it bears many traces of old-fashioned pronunciations which are long lost, like the K in **knot** or the E in **house** or **bite**. All of these silent letters represent sounds which once were in active use. But the "new" style was new when it became fully established some four or five hundred years ago.

In many ways, the two spelling styles are the same. All the consonant letters and consonant teams have the same sounds in both styles (except CH, which has three sounds on the Latin side, as in approa**ch**, **ch**aracter, and ma**ch**ine). The vowel teams work the same in both styles as in c**au**ght, appl**au**d; m**ea**t, rep**ea**t; **her**, p**er**fect. So do AR and OR, as in f**ar**, carnation; f**or**, fortune. The difference between the two styles shows up in different ways of using consonant doubling. The basic features of both systems are explained in the following pages.

Native English Style of Spelling

A. One-syllable words.

1. A vowel letter **within the syllable** is short:

   t**a**p, p**e**t, b**i**t, g**y**m*, n**o**t, c**u**t

2. A vowel letter at the **end of the syllable** is long:

   h**e**, h**i**, b**y***, n**o**, fl**u**, t**a**-ping, P**e**-ter, b**i**-ting, t**y***-ping, n**o**-ted

   The letter A, however, is broad when it is the very last letter in the word, as in f**a**, l**a**, l**a**, sod**a**

3. The pattern vowel-consonant-E:

   t**a**pe, P**e**te, b**i**te, t**y**pe*, n**o**te, c**u**te

   Here the vowel sound is actually within the syllable, since there is a consonant sound at the end. But the final silent E cancels the effect of the consonant letter, and warns us to take the vowel as long.

B. Compound Words

   Compounds are made up of two independent words. Each one is spelled the same way it would be spelled if it stood alone:

   milkman, housework, mailbox, teammate, fireplace, buttercup

   In both parts of a compound, the roots are stressed enough so that their vowel sounds remain clear.

C. Words with prefixes.

   The native English prefixes are usually syllables that can also serve as ordinary independent words. There are two groups of them:

---

* Y spells the same sound that I spells, depending on its position.

1. **a-, be-, for-, to-** and **with-**, as in **a**cross, **be**come, **for**get, **to**night and **with**stand.

   As prefixes, these syllables do not mean the same thing that they mean as independent words. But the words they appear in are so familiar that there is no real need to specify exactly what meanings the prefixes add to the roots. In words of this kind, the root is heavily stressed, and the prefix carries very little stress. That is why the **a** in **across** has such a muffled sound.

2. **in-, out-, up-, down-, under-, after-**, etc., as in **in**come, **out**go, **up**stairs, **down**stairs, **under**neath, **after**noon, etc.

   These prefixes, and many others like them, usually bring to the lengthened word the same meaning that they have as independent words. As a result, the lengthened words are very much like compounds, and the vowels of the prefixes retain their usual sounds.

   Fore-, mis- and **un-** as in **fore**cast, **mis**take and **un**tie are native English prefixes which work like these, even though **fore** is used very little nowadays as an independent word, and neither **mis-** nor **un-** can stand alone.

D. Words with suffixes.

   1. Suffixes beginning with consonants:

      These suffixes are: **-s, -ly, -less, -ful, -ness, -hood, -dom** and **-ward**. They are added without any change to the root:

      cats, **late**ly, **care**less, **care**ful, **sad**ness, **man**hood, **duke**dom, **up**ward

      The reader must understand that a silent E in the root remains silent in these words.

   2. Suffixes beginning with vowels.

      On the native English side of the language, these are: **-es, -ed, -ing, -er*, -est, -en, -et*, -ish*, -ow, -y***. These are added in different ways to roots of different types.

---

* As will be seen below, **-et** is originally a French suffix and **-ish, -y** and **-er** are often Latin suffixes, as well as being native English.

a. If the root ends in two consonant letters, the suffix is added without any change to the root:

   last**ed**, **bend**ing, **pitch**er, **wind**ow, **toss**es, **fuzz**y

b. If the root contains one vowel letter, and ends in one consonant letter, that consonant is doubled:

   written

   ta**pp**ing, re**dd**ish, bi**tt**en, gy**pp**ing, ho**pp**ing, cu**tt**er

c. If the root ends in silent E, the E is dropped before the suffix is added:

   ta**p**ing, ce**d**ed, wi**d**en, ty**p**ing, ho**p**ing, cu**t**est, dan**c**ing, lar**g**er, sen**s**es, del**v**ing, plea**s**ing, pau**s**ing

The vowels of the roots in these words obey the same rule that governs the vowels of one-syllable words—the vowel is short **within the syllable**, and long at the **end of the syllable**. The suffixes are added according to the single/double consonant rule, which is central to the native English style of spelling: One consonant between vowels makes the first vowel long; two consonants between vowels keep the first vowel short.

This rule works when the suffixes are added to one-syllable words, as above, and also when the simplest form of a word includes a suffix which cannot be dropped without changing the meaning, or making the word lose meaning altogether: la**d**y, la**dd**er; me**t**er, be**tt**er; ti**g**er, di**nn**er; to**k**en, bo**nn**et; du**t**y, bu**gg**y.

On the native English side of our language, we have a great many pairs of contrasting words like **taping, tapping, hoping, hopping, cuter, cutter**, where the meaning can be distinguished only by the sounds of the vowels in the roots. The single/double consonant rule is the device we use to solve this problem. It is important to understand what makes this device work.

The single/double consonant rule works because spoken English syllables ordinarily begin with consonant sounds, as in **he, be-gin, pa-per, pat-ter, de-moc-ra-cy**. Therefore, suffixes beginning with vowels are not complete as syllables. They become complete syllables only by capturing a consonant sound from the root to which they are added, and running off with it, as in han-**d**ing and loo-**t**ed.

In ordinary speech, we pronounce the consonant at the beginning of a syllable quite clearly, but we slight any consonant at the end. It takes deliberate effort to make a final consonant sound come out distinctly. But a vowel at the beginning of a suffix will pick up that consonant, and then the whole picture changes. Now, the last consonant of the root speaks out clearly, because it sounds with the second syllable, and has become the first consonant in that syllable.

Evidence that this is really so can be obtained by noticing the confusions of non-readers. Many of them are not even aware of the last consonant sound in a word like **hand**, for instance. It is necessary to prove the existence of the D to them by having them repeat phrases containing lengthened forms like **handy** or **handing**. Then they can hear the D in the second syllable, and see that it really comes from the original word.

The same kind of consonant-capture takes place when the root has only one consonant sound at the end. Compare **hope** and **hoping**. Notice that the P of **hope** can be severely slighted without loss of meaning; but in **hoping**, the P sound is much clearer, because here it begins the second syllable. If, in writing the word down, we place the P with the suffix, where it really belongs, then the O is left as the last letter of the first syllable, and is therefore long. (The final silent E of **hope** can be considered as a sort of false suffix, which takes the P far enough away to keep it from making the O short. If the E is a suffix, it is only natural to remove it before adding other suffixes that begin with vowels.)

It is fine for the last consonant to go wandering off like this, leaving a bare vowel letter at the end of the first syllable, if that vowel is supposed to be long. It works well, too, when the root ends in two different consonants, as in **hand**. Even when the D runs off with a suffix, as in han-**dy**, the N stays behind, keeps the A within its own syllable, and therefore keeps the A short. But in a word like **hop**, which ends with a single consonant letter, we have a problem.

The suffix will surely capture that final P. So we have to insert an extra P to stay behind with the first syllable and keep the O short. This is why we have to double the consonant when lengthening a short-vowel word that ends in a single consonant letter.

3. There is one more English suffix, **-le**, as han-d**le**, sad-d**le** and ta-b**le**. It begins with a consonant, but we pronounce it like the suffix **-el**, as in bar-**rel**, fun-**nel** and ves-**sel**. Because of this pronunciation, **-le** works like a suffix beginning with a vowel. It captures the last consonant from the root and runs off with it, and we use the single/double consonant rule in adding it to roots as in ba**b-ble**/ta-b**le**. (The suffix **-el** is really just another version of **-le**. Of the two versions, **-le** is much more common than **-el**.)

4. Two native English suffixes in succession.

   a. If the first suffix is **-y** or **-ly**, we change the Y to I before adding a second suffix, whether or not the second one begins with a consonant:

      likel**i**hood, happ**i**ness, merr**i**ment; cand**i**es, cand**i**ed, happ**i**er, happ**i**est

   b. If the first suffix is **-le**, we keep the E before a second suffix beginning with a consonant:

      settl**e**ment, handl**e**less, gentl**e**ness

   But we drop the E if the second suffix begins with a vowel:

      stra**g**gling, stra**g**gled, stra**g**gler, stra**g**gly

   The reader must realize that there is an **-le** suffix buried within the second syllable of each of these words.

   c. In all other combinations, the second suffix is added without any change to the first suffix, regardless of how the second one begins:

      upwards, careful**ly**, bitter**ly**, careless**ness**, brother**hood**, handed**ness**

      hammer**ing**, madden**ing**, pocket**ed**, fever**ish**, slander**er**

   In **hammering**, etc., it is not necessary to double the

consonant when adding suffixes beginning with vowels, because they are being added to unstressed syllables which have no definable vowel sounds, in any case. There is no need to use a doubled consonant to insist on the specific sounds for these vowels.

The Latin Side of English

It is possible to analyze the Latin style of spelling in some detail. An analysis of this kind is given in the next section. Anyone working with a student who is having problems with adult reading materials or with terms introduced into social studies or science readings, should become familiar with it, so as to be able to point out relevant features of it as they arise in the student's reading. But for those who are teaching beginning or basic remedial reading such a detailed analysis is unnecessary.

Fortunately, there are some simple rules-of-thumb which students can apply to the Latin side of the language until they are confident enough about the long words to become able to handle a more detailed understanding of them.

Students need to know better, however, than to try to force the native English tricks of consonant doubling and stress pattern onto the Latin side of English. Therefore, they need to know that the two styles of spelling exist, and they need to know the native English style of spelling very well. They need to master the single/double consonant rule very thoroughly; and they need to know the entire list of native English suffixes backwards and forwards, with special emphasis on the suffixes beginning with vowels.

Then they need to know three special things about the Latin side of the language:

First, stress is unpredictable on the Latin side of the language.

Second, a single vowel letter is usually short on the Latin side, even if there is only one consonant between vowels, as in

magic, metal, clinic, robin; paragraph, general, visible, probable

Third, even on the Latin side of English, the single/double consonant rule applies to any syllable that comes immediately before a native English suffix, as in generalizing, separated, permitted and combatting

The student needs to know at a glance, of course, which style applies to a given word. Fortunately, it is quite easy to tell, chiefly by the length of the word, as follows:

a. Words of one syllable present no problem. They are all spelled by the native English style, regardless of origin.

b. Words of two or three syllables may be either native English or Latin. If the word has a native English suffix, the native English style applies; but with any other suffix, the Latin style applies, and the first vowel is very likely to be short even if there is only one consonant between vowels. (Compounds, and words with prefixes, are generally easy enough to read so that the student need not learn anything special about them, at first.)

c. Words of four or more syllables are almost all Latin, and use the Latin style of spelling.

There remains the problem of what the student should do about the unpredictability of stress on the Latin side of English. The stress is unpredictable chiefly because it shifts back and forth within the same word as the word changes form, as in deMOCracy and DEMoCRATic. This often prevents students from recognizing words which are in fact extremely familiar in ordinary speech.

Students should approach the long words by stressing **all** the syllables **equally**, using short vowels throughout, and **starting each syllable with a consonant, or consonant blend**, even though this type of syllable division often violates the dictionary method of dividing words. (Even on the Latin side, however, U is often long before a single consonant and a vowel.)

An easy way to master this technique is to copy the syllables, one below the other, in a vertical column, and read them off like the separate items on a shopping list. After reading each syllable accurately, the student should repeat them, in order, accurately, getting the feel of them in the mouth. A few repetitions of this kind will soon bring to mind any familiar word which the letters represent. For unfamiliar words, it will produce a fairly accurate approach to the true pronunciation, which can then be checked with a dictionary.

Here are some words divided in this way:

de	de	con	a	pa	In	re	vul	sig
mo	mo	ti	ni	ra	di	pre	ne	na
cra	cra	nue	mal	graph	an	sen	ra	to
cy	tic					ta	bi	ry
						tion	li	
							ty	

This device works because most of the long vowels in Latin are in unstressed syllables, and the long vowel goes short when the stress shifts onto it, as in produce, product and reside, residence. To English speakers, the stressed syllable is the heart of the word. By using equal stress and short vowels, we can be sure of getting a good feel for the heart of the word, while the other syllables soon fade out of focus, and take on their ordinary sounds.

Obviously, however, a short vowel pronunciation will not help the student if it is forced onto the -ta- syllable in **representation**. But in copying off a word of this kind, the student will spot the familiar -ation element at the end, and be unable to stick to the short-vowel strategy for that particular syllable. Thus, no harm is done by treating these words like the rest.

This approach to the long Latin words has a further advantage. Students who have listed the syllables of a word and pronounced each one clearly have heard a definite vowel sound in each syllable. When they need to spell that word, these sounds tend to come back to mind, especially if the students have been given some practice in writing the words they have recently decoded in this way. They soon find that it is possible to spell any Latin word by ear, if they have taken time to sound it out by the syllable while they had it before them on the page.

As they become less hesitant about the long Latin words, students can benefit by another kind of exercise. Let the student keep a notebook with one set of pages devoted to Latin prefixes, another set devoted to Latin suffixes, and a third set devoted to Latin roots. Have the student set up one page for prefixes containing A, another for prefixes containing E, and so on, one page for each vowel letter. Then let the student select words with prefixes from whatever reading material is in use, and place them on the correct lists.

When the longest list on the prefix pages reaches about halfway down the page, let the student set up the pages for suffixes, again devoting a whole page to those containing A, another to those containing E, and so on. Have the student collect words with Latin suffixes to place in lists on these pages. When one of the lists on these pages reaches halfway down the page, have the student take words from the prefix pages and place them where they belong on the suffix lists; and have the student transfer words from the suffix pages to the correct lists on the prefix pages.

As the lists grow, have the student look up the prefixes in the dictionary, and write the basic meaning of each one at the head of the list for that prefix. (An excellent dictionary for this purpose is Webster's New World Dictionary of the English Language, in paperback. The prefixes and many of the suffixes can be found listed among the regular entries there.) Help the student to see how the meaning of the prefix contributes to the modern meaning of the word. For the suffix lists, have the student look up the suffixes and note at the head of each list whether the suffix makes the word into an adjective, noun or verb, and write down any basic meaning for the suffix that the dictionary suggests. Help the student to decide whether the words on the list really do belong to the indicated part of speech, and how the meaning of the suffix contributes to the modern meaning of the word.

After this much work with Latin prefixes and suffixes, the student will begin to be able to spot the Latin roots, the syllables which are neither prefixes nor suffixes. Then it is time to set up pages for roots, this time segregating the words according to the vowel letters contained in the roots. Have the student transfer to these pages all the words already entered on the prefix and suffix lists. Then continue to build up all the sets of lists, entering each new word on each list where it belongs.

As the lists grow, certain roots will begin to turn up repeatedly. Then have the student select one root that occurs frequently, and make a special list of words with that root. See what the dictionary says about that root, and help the student to see the connection between the root, the various prefixes and suffixes it has acquired, and the modern meanings of the resulting words. Do this kind of thing for each root that occurs frequently.

As the lists grow, one more thing will happen. Regularities in the way stress patterns change from word to word will begin to become apparent. When one list contains **reside, resid**ent, **preside, president**, and another contains **refer, reference, defer, deference, confer, conference**, it begins to look as though the suffixes **-ent** and **-ence** have a specific effect on the stress patterns of the words to which they are attached.

Then it is time to begin sharing with the student the detailed analysis of the Latin style of spelling which is presented in the next section.

The Latin Style of Spelling

This analysis of the Latin style of spelling parallels the analysis of the native English style of spelling, which was given in the section on "Syllables and Stress," beginning on page 299. The analysis begins with one-syllable words like **robe**, and goes on to words combining two roots, like **astronaut**. Next, it treats the Latin prefixes, dealing first with prefixes ending in vowels, like **de-**, and then with prefixes ending in consonants, like **ab-**. Finally, it treats the Latin suffixes, dealing with the different ways in which different suffixes affect the stress patterns and vowel sounds of the words to which they are attached.

Teachers may employ this analysis most effectively by using the following plan.

First, read the analysis through, simply for your own information, picking up items that happen to be of special interest to you as an individual, but not trying to master the analysis as a whole.

Then, from your own reading in other materials, pick out words that exhibit features which violate the native English style of spelling in one way or another. Practice referring to the different parts of the analysis to find out what features of the Latin style are affecting these words. At the end of the analysis are a few examples of such words, with suggestions on where to look for the particular feature of the Latin style which is affecting each one.

Finally, whenever you notice that one particular type of Latin word is continually tripping your student up, you can share with the student the special part of the analysis that is helpful in decoding that particular type of word.

Latin Spelling

A. One-syllable words.

The Latin style of spelling does not affect words of one syllable. The native English style governs them all, regardless of origin.

B. Compounds (combined words)

Strictly speaking, the term **compound** refers only to native English words like **milkman** and **housework**, where two native English roots are joined without change. But on the Latin side of English, also, there are many words formed by joining two roots, words like **astronaut**, star-sailor; **automobile**, self-mover; **geology**, earth-science; **geometry**, earth-measurement; **geophysics**, earth-physics; and **pseudonym**, false-name. In such words, the two roots are joined by a vowel which is short if it happens to be stressed. The joining vowel is very often an O.

This type of word formation is still very active in Modern English. It is even used to join native English roots to Latin roots, as in speed**o**meter, where the first root is native English, and astr**o**turf, where the second root is native English.

The stress shifts back and forth in these words, as it does throughout the Latin side of English. The shifts are in response to the various suffixes that are attached to the end of the second root. These shifts of stress will be considered under the heading "Latin suffixes," below. But if the combined word has no suffix, the heaviest stress tends to fall on the first syllable:

AStronaut, DEMocrat, Isotherm, THERmostat, PSEUdonym

Notice that the vowel of the stressed syllable can be short even when there is only one consonant letter before the next vowel, as in d**e**mocrat.

C. Words with prefixes.

The Latin prefixes are syllables which cannot stand alone in English as common, ordinary words. But to the ancient Romans they often did stand alone, and they meant the same kinds of things that our native English prefixes mean when standing alone. They were the Latin words for **to**, **with**, **down**, **under**, **for**, **out**, **in** and so on. The basic meaning of each one can be found in the dictionary.

As they affect English spelling, the Latin prefixes fall into four classes:

1. Prefixes ending with vowels: **de-**, **pre-**, **pro-**, **re-** and **se-**, as in

   demand, **pre**dict, **pro**duce, **re**main, **se**cede

   These prefixes are added to the root without any change, and their vowels can be counted on to be long if the stress falls on the root. It usually does fall on the root if the words are verbs, like the examples above. But if the word is not a verb, the stress often shifts back onto the prefix, as in

   decent, **pre**fix, **pro**gram, **re**flex, **se**cret

   In these particular words, the vowel of the prefix remains long, even when the root begins with a blend of two consonants. But, quite often, the stress falling on the prefix makes its vowel go short, without any doubling of the consonant that begins the root, as in

   deluge, **pre**sence, **pro**mise, **re**lic

   We have many words that function as verbs part of the time, and as nouns or adjectives the rest of the time. When they are verbs, they normally have the stress on the root; when they are nouns or adjectives, the stress often shifts back onto the prefix, and makes the vowel short, as in

   > to desert someone on the desert
   > to present a present
   > to progress with good progress
   > to record a record
   > to rebel like a rebel

These shifts of stress do not cause any problem to the reader, because the context prepares us for verbs or nouns before we reach them. If the sentence has prepared us for a verb, we automatically respond by stressing the root; while if we have been prepared for a noun, we tend automatically to treat the first syllable like a root and stress it, even if it does happen to be a foreign prefix.

But the tendency of the vowels in these stressed prefixes to go short can be a problem for students who have just mastered the single/double consonant rule and learned how essential it is on the native English side of the language. Fortunately, this shortening occurs mainly in the Latin words that are most common in ordinary English speech. Students have only to learn to switch to a short vowel sound, which will reveal the word as a familiar item of their own speaking vocabulary.

2. Prefixes ending in consonants: **ab-**, **ad-**, **con-**, **dis-**, **ex-**, **in-**, **ob-**, **per-**, **sub-** and **trans-**, as in

> **ab**stain, **ad**vance, **con**tain, **dis**pute, **ex**pect, **in**vite, **ob**serve, **per**suade, **sub**mit, **trans**mit

In these words the prefix is added without any spelling change because there is no difficulty in pronouncing the last consonant of the prefix right before the first consonant of the root.

But it is often difficult to pronounce the complete prefix before the first consonant of the root. Then we drop the last consonant of the prefix, and double the consonant that begins the root, as in

> a**ff**ect, a**ll**ow, a**nn**ounce, a**pp**ear, a**rr**est, a**ss**ist, a**tt**end, co**ll**ide, co**mm**and, co**rr**ect, di**ff**use, e**ff**ect, e**ss**ence, i**mm**ense, o**cc**ur, o**ff**end, o**pp**ose, su**ff**ix, su**mm**ons, su**pp**ose

This is one of the chief sources of doubled consonant letters on the Latin side of English. They also occur occasionally when the prefix happens to end with the same consonant that begins the root, as in

> a**dd**ict, co**nn**ive, di**ss**ect, i**nn**ate

But when **trans-** is added to a root beginning with S, the two S's merge, as in tran**s**cript.

When a doubled consonant follows an A in words like

affect, the original prefix is always **ad-**, meaning **toward.** **The word ab**, meaning **away**, could also be plain **a** in Latin speech, whenever that made for easier pronunciation. They did the same thing when it was a prefix, adding **a-** directly to the root when that was more convenient, as in **avert**. Very few words of this kind have come down to us, however.

We have a few words where there is only one consonant between the vowel of the Latin prefix and the vowel of the root, as in

abuse, adopt, disarm, exact, inert, obey, peruse, suburb

And in

avert, digest, dilate, edit, elect, emit, omit

In the first group of these words, the prefix has its original form. Here, the prefix has been added to a root beginning with a vowel. In the second group, the last consonant of the prefix has been dropped altogether for ease of pronunciation.

Other examples of prefix alteration for the sake of convenience occur in these words:

acquire, suspend, sustain, combat, compose, impress, embrace

(E sometimes takes the place of I in the prefix **in-**, as in **en**tire.)

Finally, when **con-** is added to a root beginning with a vowel, the N is dropped and the O becomes long, as in **co**ed and **co**erce.

The stress pattern for words with prefixes ending in consonants is the same one that applies when the prefix ends with a vowel. The stress normally falls on the root if the word is a verb. But if the word is a noun or an adjective, the stress can move back onto the prefix, as in

assets, **con**tents, **dis**trict, **ex**tra, **in**stinct, **ob**long, **per**fume, **sub**urb, **trans**it

Likewise, the stress can shift in the same word, as it switches from a verb to another part of speech, as in

to annex an annex
to combat in combat
to export an export
to import an import
to suspect a suspect

to discard onto the discard
to object to an object
to perfect something and
   make it perfect

3. Prefixes with two syllables: **circum-**, **contra-**, **extra-**, **inter-**, **para-**, **peri-**, **super-**, **tele-**, as in

circumstance, **contra**dict, **extra**dite, **inter**fere, **para**graph, **peri**scope, **super**vise and **tele**phone

In these words, the stress falls on the first syllable of the prefix, with another stress on the root. The first A in **para-** is always short and so are the first E in **tele-** and the E in **peri-**. But the U in **super-** is always long.

With these prefixes, the only peculiarity concerns **super-** Many of the words that contain it came to us after a long stay in France, where **super-** was slurred into **sur-**, as in **sur**prise and **sur**round. Otherwise, these prefixes are added directly to the root without change. Of course, this sometimes produces a doubled consonant, as in **inter**rupt.

4. Numerical prefixes: **hemi-**, **semi-**, **mono-**, **bi-**, **tri**, **quadr-**, **quint-**, **dec-**, **cent-**, **milli-**, **poly-** and **omni-**.

The first two mean **half**, as in **hemi**sphere and **semi**circle. Examples of the rest are: **mono**cycle (**one** wheel), **bi**cycle (**two** wheels), **tri**cycle (**three** wheels), **quad**ruplets (**four** children at one birth), **quin**tuplets (**five** children at one birth), **dec**ade (**ten** years), **cent**ury (**one hundred** years), **milli**pede (a **thousand**-legger) **poly**syllable (a **many**-syllabled word) and **omni**potent (**all**-powerful).

We have some other numerical prefixes which also come down through the Latin. But most of them go back to the Greek, and occur only in very technical terms. These are best learned in connection with the technical subjects to which they belong. An example is **hexa**gon, a six-sided figure in plane geometry.

5. Two prefixes in succession.

We have many words that begin with two Latin prefixes.

The first prefix is added to the second as usual, in accordance with convenience of pronunciation, as in

> **de**compose, **re**inforce, **dis**regard, **im**provise, **pre**digest, **inter**relate, **super**impose

In these words the stress sometimes moves back onto the first prefix, as in **com**promise and **re**present.

D. Words with suffixes.

We have a great variety of suffixes that come down to us from Ancient Latin, so many that here it is possible to deal only with the most important ones. But all of them are easily identified by anyone who can recognize the native English suffixes beginning with vowels (**-ed, -en, -er, -es, -est, -et, -ing, -ish, -y, -le, -ow**). Any other suffix beginning with a vowel belongs to the Latin side of English, and is added to the root according to the Latin style of spelling. The only Latin suffix that begins with a consonant is **-ment**. The suffix **-tion** is not really one beginning with a consonant, as will be seen below.

The Latin suffixes resemble the English suffixes in one important respect. All those that begin with vowels capture a consonant from the end of the root in order to become complete syllables, as in fa-tal. Furthermore, if the root ends in two consonants, the first consonant stays behind with the root, and keeps the vowel of the root short, as in plas-tic and cot-ton. But there the resemblance ends. In fact, it is the way these suffixes behave that makes the chief difference between the two styles of spelling.

The Latin suffixes fall into three main groups.

The first group consists of suffixes containing A, E, O or U. In this group, the most familiar suffix is **-al**, as in total and general. These suffixes have a particular influence on the stress patterns and vowel sounds of the words to which they are attached. The other suffixes that work like **-al** are listed below, at the end of the section on **-al**.

A second group of suffixes has unstressed I before another vowel. Familiar examples are **-ial** and **-ion**, as in serial and union. These suffixes influence the stress patterns and vowel sounds of words differently from the way the **-al** suffixes do. They are identified in the section on **-ial**.

Finally, another group of suffixes contains I by itself. The most common of these is **-ic**, as in com**ic** and exo**tic**. These suffixes have a third type of influence on the stress patterns and vowel sounds of the words to which they are attached. These suffixes are listed in the section on **-ic**.

1. Suffixes like **-al**.

In two-syllable words, **-al** usually takes a long vowel in the root, if there is only one consonant between vowels, as in fatal, penal, final, total and brutal. But there are some very familiar words where the root vowel is short, even though there is only one consonant between vowels, as in metal and pedal.

This is a very important feature of the Latin style of spelling—the first vowel is often short even when there is only one consonant between vowels. Examples of this came up earlier, in connection with nouns like desert and record. There will be many more examples of the same thing as the analysis of the Latin words proceeds.

The stress in all these two-syllable words is heavy on the root. Even in the rare case of a suffix containing a vowel team, as in cer**tain** or tort**oise**, the stress is heavy on the root, so heavy that the vowel team of the suffix loses all its character. A word like ca**nal**, where **-al** is heavily stressed is extremely unusual.

In longer words, however, the stress pattern has little to do with the root. It depends more on the length of the word and on what the suffix is.

With suffixes like **-al**, the stress usually depends on how many consonants there are before the suffix. If there are two consonants before **-al**, the stress is drawn to the syllable before the **-al**, as in ex**ter**nal, pa**ter**nal, au**tum**nal and co**los**sal. Notice that in **autumn**, the stress is on the first syllable. It is the addition of the suffix that draws the stress onto the **-tum**, and makes the N sound at the beginning of the last syllable. In three-syllable words like this, the stress is on the middle syllable.

In four-syllable words with two consonants before the suffix, the stress still comes right before the **-al**, as in hori**zon**tal, conti**nen**tal and monu**men**tal. In these words, there is also a secondary stress on the first syllable, and the first vowel is normally short, even if there is only one consonant before the next vowel.

But if **-al** has only one consonant before it, the stress moves back onto the first syllable in three-syllable words, and onto the second syllable in four-syllable words, as in **hos**pital, **ar**senal, **ter**minal; in**tes**tinal, mu**nic**ipal and o**rig**inal. The three-syllable words of this kind are very common, and a great many of them have only one consonant between the first vowel and the second. In those words, the first vowel is short, as in **an**imal, **gen**eral, **phys**ical and **nat**ural. Only a U tends to stay long in this position, as in **fu**neral. (In general, U has much less tendency to go short before a single consonant than any of the other vowel letters.) Notice that the A which is long in **na**ture goes short in **na**tural. This tendency of vowels, to flip from long to short as a word changes form, is a very common feature of the Latin side of English.

There are quite a few suffixes containing A, E, O or U that work like **-al**. The ones most frequently used are **-ant, -ance, -ent, -ence, -ate, -age, -or, -ar, -ure, -a, -us, -um, -o, -an, -on, -ous**. Three- and four-syllable words with these suffixes tend to display the same stress pattern as the three- and four-syllable words with **-al**. Words ending with the suffix **-ment**, the only Latin suffix beginning with a consonant, also tend to conform to the same stress pattern.

This stress pattern is illustrated in the lists below. The first word in each list has the stressed syllable for that list in bold.

3 syllables

			4 syllables
animal	e**ter**nal	o**rig**inal	conti**nen**tal
elegant	de**fen**dant	sig**nif**icant	disin**fec**tant
elegance	a**bun**dance	sig**nif**icance	

resident	dependent	equivalent	correspondent
reference	dependence	circumference	correspondence
delicate	consummate	inadequate	
average	percentage		disadvantage
creditor	director	solicitor	malefactor
popular		particular	caterpillar
furniture	adventure	expenditure	agriculture
camera	vanilla	anathema	propaganda
stimulus	consensus	sarcophagus	streptococcus
minimum	momentum	aluminum	memorandum
domino	contralto		inuendo
pelican	suburban	American	
unison	abandon	automaton	
barbarous	tremendous	monotonous	ambidextrous
document	apartment	development	readjustment

Gaps in these lists correspond to gaps in the language. We do not have any words to put in those places. For example, we have no three-syllable word ending in **-ate** and stressed like ete**r**nal.

In words like **disappearance**, however, the stress is on the root. Syllables with vowel teams in them tend to draw the stress in words with all these suffixes, just like the syllables that end in two consonants. In words like **fragrance** and **algebra** the consonant blends GR and BR behave like single consonants. The GR has a long A in the syllable before it, and the BR allows the stress to move back to the first syllable. This is because these blends can be used to begin syllables, as in **grand** and **brand**. Such blends often go off with the suffix in the Latin style of spelling, leaving the vowel before them long, if it is stressed, or muffled if its unstressed. The consonant teams TH, PH and CH sounding like K, all of which occur frequently on the Latin side of the language, also behave like single consonants in the Latin style of spelling.

Words with the suffix **-age** sometimes violate the usual stress pattern quite sharply, taking a heavy stress on the suffix, as in gar**age** and sabot**age**. This is because these words were borrowed relatively recently from the French, where there is a tendency to stress all final syllables. In such words, the vowels retain their French sounds, and have nothing to do with English spelling of any style. The suffix **-age** violates the **-al** pattern in another way also. It almost always takes a short vowel in two-syllable words that have only one consonant between vowels, as in m**a**nage and d**a**mage. It usually takes a vowel team to show a long vowel before **-age**, as in dr**ai**nage and l**ea**kage. Notice also that the Latin suffix **-age** is often added to a native English root.

Finally, the suffix **-ment**, unlike the other Latin suffixes, begins with a consonant, and it can be added to roots which contain long vowels shown by the pattern vowel-consonant-E, as in **base**ment. The reader must realize that the E remains silent in these words, just as it does before the native English suffixes beginning with consonants, as in **late**ly and **care**less. The suffix **-ment** is included here because it has the same effect on the stress pattern that **-al** has.

2. Suffixes like **-ial**.

We have a great many suffixes like **-ial**, as in ser**ial**. All of these are two-syllable suffixes formed by inserting an unstressed I before a suffix like **-al**. The I sounds like the Y in hap**py** and the I in happ**i**est. In a few cases these forms are actual examples of the suffix **-y** changing to I before a second suffix, as in env**y**, envious and fur**y**, furious. But ordinarily, we do not have **-y** forms corresponding to the words that have these suffixes. Thus, we have **native** and **nation**, but no such word as "naty."

If there is only one consonant between vowels, these suffixes make the vowel before them long, unless it is an I, in which case it is always short, as in r**a**dio, pr**e**vious, **i**diot, ph**o**bia and st**u**dious. This is a very reliable pattern. Among hundreds of words with these suffixes, there are no words with long I before the unstressed I, and only a handful of words where A or E is unaccountably short, as in companion.

These suffixes have another striking, and very reliable

feature. They always draw the heaviest stress onto the syllable right before the unstressed I. This is true regardless of whether the syllable taking the stress is a prefix, as in **pre**vious; a root, as in in**fur**iate, or a suffix, as in sol**ar**ium. It is also true regardless of the length of the word, as in **ra**diant, ma**lar**ia, plane**tar**ium, totali**tar**ian; **se**rious, in**ter**ior, inex**per**ience, encyclo**pe**dia; **triv**ial, re**cip**ient, equi**lib**rium; **o**pium, cus**to**dian, audi**tor**ium; **du**bious, en**thu**siasm.

It is helpful to remember that the unstressed I in these suffixes is equivalent to a Y. In the above examples, it has the same sound that **-y** has as a suffix. After certain consonants, however, it sounds more like **consonant** Y in canyon. Examples are: alien, region, bilious, million, junior; behavior, convenient, familiar and communion.

Understanding that the unstressed I can sound like a consonant Y helps one to see where we get the SH sound in a word like **racial**. Experiment with this word as follows: First, pronounce it very slowly as **race-yal**. Then say it the same way several more times, stepping up the pace at each repetition. You will end with the normal sound of the CI in racial. There are many words where this process has produced SH sounds when the spelling would ordinarily suggest a plain S sound, as in gracious, passion, tension, crucial; financial, delicious, atrocious, unconscious, compulsion.

With other consonant sounds, the same process produces slightly different results. On the Latin side of English, a Z sound is most often spelled by a single S between vowels, as in refusal and divisor. Before suffixes like **-ial**, these Z-sounding S's go to a special sound which is respelled ZH in dictionaries, as in confusion and division. Other examples are: occasion, amnesia, decision, erosion and conclusion. Simpler forms of the same words often end in D sounds, as in divide, decide, erode and conclude.

A similar process makes **-tion** sound like **shun**. Try the same experiment with **nation** that you did with **racial**. Say **nate-yon** very slowly, but use a special version of the T sound. We usually pronounce T by touching the tip of the tongue to the spot where the roof of the mouth meets the upper teeth. For this experiment, touch the backs of the upper teeth a trifle lower down than usual. This will make it easy to get quickly to the Y sound. It will also make the T approach fairly close to an S sound. We have plenty of evidence that the Latin vocabulary must have used this type of T for a long period at some time in the past. The evidence is provided by pairs of modern English words like politics, policy; agent, agency; delicate, delicacy, etc.

Using this special T sound, then, pronounce **nate-yon** slowly, and repeat it slowly a few times until you have the special T sound under good control. Then begin speeding it up at each repetition until you come out with the normal sound of na**t**ion.

As was mentioned earlier, **-tion** is not a suffix beginning with a consonant. Rather it is the suffix **-ion** combined with a T which it has captured from the end of a root, as in product, production; contort, contortion; ignite, ignition; demonstrate, demonstration; constitute, constitution. This is why **-tion** is not added to words in the same way as **-ment** and **-less**, which really do begin with consonants.

There are many words, however, where there does not seem to be any T in the root for **-ion** to capture, words like admire, admiration, and compose, composition. In such words, the inserted AT's and IT's are left over from lost forms of the Latin verbs. The Latin for admir**ed** is admir**atus**, so to make **admiration**, the Romans dropped the **-us** and added **-ion**. The Latin for compos**ed** was compos**itus**, and to make **composition**, they made the same substitution of suffixes. Even in such words, therefore, the T of **-tion** is really a captured consonant, and not the beginning of a special suffix. This is why it behaves the way all the other suffixes like **-ial** do, as in na**t**ion, mo**t**ion; vaca**t**ion, comple**t**ion, tradi**t**ion, devo**t**ion, pollu**t**ion; concentra**t**ion, repeti**t**ion, contribu**t**ion; accelera**t**ion, recombina**t**ion, centraliza**t**ion.

Finally, it should be noticed that most of the suffixes like -al can also form suffixes like -ial. Thus, we have the suffixes -iant, -iance, -ient, -ience, -iate, -ior, -iar, -ia, -ius, -ium, -io, -ian, -ion and -ious, as in radiant, radiance, convenient, convenience, appropriate, savior, peculiar, pneumonia, radius, radium, radio, physician, caution and curious.

3. Suffixes like -ic.

The suffixes containing I without a second vowel, like -ic, almost always take a short vowel in the syllable before them, even when there is only one consonant between vowels, as in static, panic, epic, critic, civic, logic and comic. In two-syllable words, the stress is heavy on the root, as usual.

In longer words, the stress pattern is the same as the stress pattern for words with suffixes like -ial. Regardless of how long the word is, -ic normally draws the heaviest stress onto the syllable just before it, as in organic, athletic, atomic; automatic, epidemic, paralytic, alcoholic; aristocratic, capitalistic. Notice how reliably the vowels go short, even when the original word had a long vowel in the last syllable, as in athlete and paralyze.

It is only in the most commonly-used three-syllable words that the main stress moves back onto the first syllable, as in politics, heretic and catholic. (Nowadays, we may not talk much about heretics. But there were at least two centuries during which heretics and the Catholic Church were discussed just as widely, and even more passionately than politics is discussed today.)

Other suffixes that work like -ic are -id, -in, -il, -it, -ice, -ile, -ine, -ite, -ive, and -ize, as in rapid, frigid, solid; cabin, robin; peril, civil, vigil; habit, credit, visit; novice, sterile, famine, respite and baptize.

In longer words, the suffixes -id and -it usually draw the stress onto the syllable before them, as in inhabit, inherit, exhibit, deposit and insipid. But the stress can sometimes move back onto the first syllable, as in benefit.

In three-syllable words with the remaining suffixes of this class, the stress pattern is like the one for suffixes like **-al**, as in **as**pirin, ac**com**plice, **pre**judice, **ju**venile, de**ter**mine, **mas**culine, **def**inite and **or**ganize. Notice that the I is long in orga**nize**, and that it may be either long or short in juve**nile**. But in the rest of the examples given here, the I is short.

However, in suffixes spelled with I__E, the sound of the I is quite variable. In **-ive**, it is normally short, and in **-ize**, it is always long. In most of the **-ile** words, long or short I is equally correct. With the others, it all depends on the individual word, as in sacri**fice**, armi**stice**; ca**nine**, doc**trine**; valen**tine**, disci**pline**; ter**mite**, dyna**mite**, favo**rite**.

Furthermore, most of the I__E suffixes occur at least once with a long E sound, which usually goes with a heavy stress on the suffix, as in na**ive**, po**lice**, automo**bile**, maga**zine**, e**lite**. These are Latin words that came to us through the French. By using the French sound of I, and by stressing the suffix, we retain their French flavor. In English, **-ine** is much more likely to behave in this way than any of the other I__E suffixes. But the student should be warned of the variability of these I sounds.

And again, no rule about the length of vowel sounds is entirely reliable on the Latin side of English. Suffixes like **-ic** occasionally take long vowels before them, as in **ba**sic, **mu**sic, **tu**nic, **hu**mid, **u**nit, **no**tice, **pro**file and **fi**nite.

Finally, there is an important two-syllable suffix that works like **-ic**.

It is the suffix **-ity**, as in char**ity**, capac**ity**, real**ity**, seren**ity**, public**ity**, timid**ity**, divin**ity**, civil**ity**, festiv**ity**, commod**ity**; relativ**ity**, electric**ity**, univers**ity**, insipid**ity**; municipal**ity**, instrumental**ity**, and reproductiv**ity**.

Notice that **-ity** always draws the heaviest stress onto the syllable just before it, even when that syllable started out as a suffix like -ic; that the vowel before it is always short; and that there is never a doubled consonant between the vowel of that syllable and **-ity**. Even when the vowel was long in the original word, as in ser**ene** and div**ine**, it goes short when **-ity** is added.

4. Suffixes containing long U spellings.

The most familiar of these is **-ure**, as in fig**ure**, fail**ure**, ten**ure**, nat**ure**, pict**ure**, advent**ure**, signat**ure**, manufact**ure**, temperat**ure**, meas**ure**, disclos**ure**, press**ure** and fiss**ure**. Notice that the end of the root in fig**ure**, **failure** and **tenure** is followed by a prominent Y- sound that is not reflected in the spelling. There is no need for a Y letter because the sound of long U is the **full name of the letter**, which might be spelled **yoo**. In an unstressed syllable like a suffix, much of the long U sound is muffled, but the initial Y- component of this sound is never lost. It is this Y- sound which converts the T's into CH sounds, S's into ZH sounds, and the SS's into SH sounds in words of this kind. This happens through a process very much like the one that distorts the T and S sounds in words like nation, musician and vision.

Other suffixes like **-ure** are **-ule, -une, -ue, -ual** and **-uous**, as in sched**ule**, fort**une**, stat**ue**, contin**ue**, us**ual** and contin**uous**. Again the Y- part of the long U sound is clearly heard after certain consonants, and acts to distort the T's and S's. In sche**dule**, it tends to distort the D sound into a J sound.

The vowels before the long U suffixes are often short.

5. Suffixes that are Latin as well as being native English.

These suffixes are: **-ish, -et, -le, -y, -er** and **-able**.

As a native English suffix, **-ish** makes the word into an adjective meaning "like a _____," with the root filling in the blank. **Slavish** means, "like a **slave**," and **mannish** means "like a **man**." But if the root is not a familiar native English word, **-ish** is a Latin suffix which shows that the word is a verb or a noun. It works like **-ic**, taking a short vowel in the syllable before it, as in vanish, relish, finish, polish and punish. In long words, it continues to work like **-ic**, drawing the stress onto the syllable before it, as in establish, replenish, diminish and astonish.

The suffix **-et** must be considered native English because so many of the words containing it, like bonn**et** and pock**et**, became thoroughly English so early that they were fitted into the native English spelling style when it was first established. But **-et** is really a French suffix, and it has continued to enter English throughout the modern period, bringing with it patterns that fit the Latin style of spelling, as in fac**et**, ten**et**, riv**et**, com**et**, cabin**et** and omel**et**. In these words, all the vowels are short, regardless of the single consonants. The stress pattern in the three-syllable words is the one that goes with suffixes like **-al**.

Words that have come into English more recently than those above may have some stress on the suffix, in imitation of the French fashion, as in bayon**et** and epaul**et**. In certain other words, we stress the **-et** heavily and pronounce it like AY, in an effort to retain the full French pronunciation, as in ball**et**, croch**et**, gourm**et** and Chevrol**et**. In such words, all the vowels, and the consonant team CH, retain their French characteristics.

The suffix **-le** is also really a Latin suffix. But again it came into common English use very early. Still, there are a few two-syllable words where consonant doubling is not used after a short vowel, as in **tre**ble and **tri**ple. In long words, **-le** behaves like the Latin suffix **-al**, as in **example**, **bicycle**, **capable** and **chronicle**.

The suffixes **-y** and **-er** came to us **both** by the Germanic route and by the Latin route. When the root before the suffixes **-y** and **-er** is not a common English root, these suffixes are Latin, as in **navy**, **duty** and **meter**. As a Latin suffix, **-y** often takes a short vowel without consonant doubling, as in v**a**ry, v**e**ry, c**i**ty, c**o**py and st**u**dy. The suffix **-er** sometimes does the same thing as in pr**o**per. In long words, **-y** and **-er** have less effect on the stress pattern of the original word than other Latin suffixes. The stress tends to stay where it was before the **-y** was added, as in injur**y**, bankrupt**cy**, certaint**y** and adulter**y**. Notice, however, how easily extra consonants creep into these words before the **-y**.

We also have longer suffixes ending in **-y**. Two of them are **-ary** and **-ory**. In three-syllable words, these tend to throw a heavy stress onto the first syllable, as in **sum**mary, **his**tory and **fac**tory. But often, the A or O of the suffix is also slightly stressed, and has a long sound, as in library, contrary, necessary, literary, voluntary, imaginary, vocabulary; category, dormitory, territory and laboratory.

The suffixes **-y** and **-er** are often added to combined words like **photograph**, drawing the stress onto the vowel that joins the two roots, and resulting in words like photography, telegraphy, calligraphy, photographer and telegrapher. All the **-ology**'s work the same way. The root **-log-** means "science," so that **biology**, **geology** and **psychology** mean "the sciences of life, earth and mind." The root -**crat**- means "rule by," so that **democracy** means "rule by the people," and **aristocracy** means "rule by the noblemen."

Keeping in mind the habits of **-y**, **-er** and **-ic**, and remembering that the combined words stress the first syllable if they have no suffix, one can make sense of the shifting stresses in such sets as **pho**tograph, photog**ra**pher, photo**gra**phic; **dem**ocrat, demo**cra**cy, demo**crat**ic; **tel**egraph, tele**gra**phy, tele**gra**phic; bi**ol**ogy, bio**log**ical; ge**og**raphy, geo**gra**phic; ge**ol**ogy, geo**log**ical; as**trol**ogy, astro**log**ical, as**trol**oger.

The suffix **-able** must be considered as a suffix which is native English as well as Latin because the suffix can stand alone as an independent English word, and because it leaves the stress undisturbed in most words, but behaves like **-al** in quite a few others.

This suffix is often added to native English words, as in **laugh**able and **understand**able, and in such words the stress remains on the root as is required by the English style of spelling. The stress also frequently remains undisturbed when **-able** is added to familiar Latin verbs, as in de**ba**table, pre**sen**table, recog**ni**zable and i**ma**ginable. But there are a few words made from familiar Latin verbs where **-able** throws the stress back onto the prefix, as in **pre**ferable and **com**parable. And then, there are words where the root is less recognizable, as in **cap**able, **prob**able and **vul**nerable. Here again, we tend to stress the first syllable.

Such words often have this suffix spelled **-ible**, especially after S, Z and J sounds, as in po**ss**ible, flexible, sen**s**ible, for**c**ible, vi**s**ible, le**g**ible; acce**ss**ible, divi**s**ible and diri**g**ible. Sometimes, this spelling also occurs after other sounds, as in ter**ri**ble, incre**di**ble and convertible.

6. Multiple suffixes.

In the native English style of spelling, we often have two English suffixes in a row, as in care**lessly** or hamm**ering**. On the Latin side of English, it is possible to pile up even more suffixes.

a. Native English suffixes added to Latin words.

Almost any word from the Latin side of English can take one or another of the native English suffixes, as in secret**s**, final**ly**, purpose**less**, purpose**ful**, conscious**ness**; prefix**es**, produc**ing**, committ**ed** and defend**er**. These suffixes are added strictly according to the English spelling style—maintaining silent E's where necessary, and adhering strictly to the single/double consonant rule if the suffix begins with a vowel. And, true to the native English style, they leave the stress pattern and vowels of the original word undisturbed.

b. Multiple Latin suffixes.

It is possible to have a series of three of four Latin suffixes added one after the other to a Latin root, as in **act**, ac**tive**, ac**tivate**, acti**vation**; vic**tor**, vic**tory**, vic**torious**; his**tory**, his**toric**, his**torical**; senti**ment**, senti**mental**, senti**mentality**; arti**fice**, arti**ficial**, artifi**ciality**; human, hum**anity**, hum**anitarian**. As each successive suffix is added, it has its own special effect on the stress pattern of what was there before. But the additions make no difference to the spelling of what went before.

However, when **-ity** is added after **-able** or **-ous**, it does affect the form of the previous suffix. Adding **-ity** to the simple word **able** yields **ability**, with an extra I thrown in between the B and the L. When the suffixes **-able** or **-ible** are lengthened by **-ity**, the same thing happens, as in cap**able** and cap**ability**, and poss**ible**, poss**ibility**. When **-ity** is added after **-ous**, the U is lost, and the O goes short, as in gener**ous**, gener**osity**, curi**ous**, and curi**osity**.

Finally, no matter how long or fancy the Latin word has become, a native English suffix can often be added at the end on top of everything else, as in victorious**ly**, historical**ly**, mysterious**ness**, and artificiali**ties**. But in these longer forms, there is one feature that should be noted. The native English suffix **-ly** is almost never added directly after the Latin suffix **-ic**. As shown above, it can be added after **-ic** plus **-al**, as in histor**ically**. But if we have no **-ical** form of the word, and we want to add **-ly**, we must throw in **-al** between the **-ic** and the **-ly**. Thus, we have emphat**ic** and emphat**ically**, but not emphat**ical**; we have athlet**ic** and athlet**ically**, but not athlet**ical**. We often suppress the inserted **-al** in pronouncing such a word, but when the word is written, the **-al** must put in a due appearance.

This concludes the analysis of the Latin style of spelling. It can be summarized very briefly as follows. When there is only one consonant between vowels, the first vowel is long only in three circumstances:

1. In many of the two-syllable words with suffixes like **-al**.
2. In the stressed syllable before suffixes like **-ial**, except that in this position, the letter I is short.
3. If the vowel letter is U.

Otherwise, stressed vowels are short, and the placement of the stress depends on what the suffix is.

This analysis can seem overwhelming when it is taken all in one dose. It is likely to prove more digestible when one uses it as a resource for the solution of specific problems, like the following.

1. Why is the first syllable stressed in **cosmonaut** when the

second syllable is stressed in **cosmology**?—See combined words, p. 313, and **-Y** as a Latin suffix, p. 327.

2. Why does the prefix **re-** have a short vowel in **refuge**? Why is the prefix stressed? Why are there not two F's to show that the E is short?—See prefixes like **de-**, p. 314.

3. Why are there two F's in **affect** when **afar** has only one?— See prefixes like **ad-**, p. 315; and remember that **far** is an ordinary English word.

4. Why is the first syllable stressed in **elephant**, when the second is stressed in **reluctant**? Why is the first E of **elephant** short?—See suffixes like **-al**, pp. 319-321.

5. Why is the E in **completion** long when the I in **rendition** is short?—See suffixes like **-ial**, pp. 322-324.

6. Why are the E and O in **Ethiopia** both stressed so heavily? —See suffixes like **-ial**, pp. 322-324.

7. Why does the SI in **tension** sound like SH?—See suffixes like **-ial**, p. 324.

8. Why is the O stressed in **prophet** when the E is stressed in **prophetic**?—See suffixes like **-ic**, p. 325.

9. Why is the A stressed in **totality** when one can hardly hear it in **total**?—See suffixes like **-ic**, p. 326.

10. Why does **banish** have only one N when **mannish** has two?— See suffixes that are both native English and Latin, p. 327.

Appendix C

Remedial Reading

In many schools where phonics is taught in first grade, each of the later grades includes a few pupils who have transferred into the school. Many of these children cannot keep up with the class because their former school favored word-memorization instruction. They cannot read well enough to manage the work which your regular pupils can do. They need special remedial work to bring their reading skills up to par.

As was mentioned in the foreword, *To The Teacher*, these children need different types of remedial handling, because poor readers go through distinct developmental stages in their attitudes toward reading and its problems. The one constant which unites these different stages is that the children are profoundly frightened by their reading problems.

Primary School Pupils

The second and third graders are still frankly facing the fact that reading is hard for them. If you simply use with them the same materials, you ordidnarily use in first grade, they can usually catch on quite quickly. Start at page one, and go straight on through the program. They will probably know quite a few of the consonant sounds already. But the vowels will be hard for them. So you need to work slowly at first, strengthening whatever they already know, and straightening out whatever misconceptions they have. You need to be very careful in helping them to learn how to blend sounds and how to sound out successfully. But once they can really sound out, they will gobble up the rest of the phonics lessons at a terrific pace. Their relief about being able to learn to read will work a remarkable reform in their general behavior, and will make the teacher realize how profoundly frightened they were before.

In addition to the special phonics lessons, these children need to be treated very gently at home. Parents, relatives and friends of the family often think these children are stupid, since they did not learn to read in first grade. But these children are almost never stupid. On the contrary, they are usually extra bright. They are bright enough to know that society has somehow broken its promise to teach them how to read. They are smart enough to know what a disaster this broken promise is. They will learn just as soon as someone shows them what the letters are for and how they work.

In the meantime, they must be encouraged at home, and praised for every bit of progress they make. Parents need to help them with reading of homework assignments from their regular classes until they get far enough along to manage the homework by themselves. Parents must refrain from ridiculing them or punishing them for their reading problems. They must also be careful to prevent other adults and older children from ridiculing them.

Similar precautions must also be undertaken in the regular classrooms where remedial readers are spending most of their day. Teachers must be supportive and encouraging, and they must lead the other children in the class to take the same attitude. The teacher must not call on the remedial readers to read out loud in class until she knows they can do it. In the meantime, she needs to help them read directions and written problems in math work; to let them work only on whatever spelling words they have already learned how to handle, and give them all the help they need with any reading work that is part of the daily activity. When other children are doing written work in class, the remedial readers should be working on phonics practice exercises.

Sometimes it is possible to have a classmate give a remedial reader the needed extra help. But if this is done, a careful eye must be kept on the relationship, to make sure that helper is really helping and is not making the remedial reader feel discouraged or defensive.

Older Children

The transfer children who come in at the fourth, fifth, sixth or early high school levels are quite another matter. They have already resigned themselves to being poor readers. They have convinced themselves that their reading skills are good enough for them, that reading is not really very important, and that they do not want to be boring, goody-goody bookworms, anyway. These children are likely to resist all offers of help with reading.

Nevertheless, there is one chink in their armor. They may be very snooty about reading. But they would like to be relieved of the bad spelling which is always getting them into trouble. For this age group, you should not even mention reading, or require special reading classes. No, not reading: spelling. Special help with spelling is something they can accept. Teach them what the letter-sounds, letter-combinations and letter-interactions are, and how to use this information for writing *words down according to their pronunciation*.

Then, once they are beginning to feel good about their spelling, you can get them to use their spelling knowledge to help themselves with reading. When they are stumbling in an effort to read a word you know they can spell, simply ask, "What would those letters spell if **you** had written them down?" Some consistent leadership of this kind will get them to transfer their spelling knowledge to reading. Then, in a few months, or a year, you can turn around and say, "See, you are not such a bad reader, after all, and reading has a lot of advantages."

How should you go about teaching spelling to these pupils? Where should you start, and what order of presentation should you use? The answer is easy. Use exactly what your school uses for first grade reading.

But don't let them know it is baby work. Use the first grade textbook as your source of spelling words, but keep it in your desk with a jacket which hides the book's own cover. Take one other precaution, also. Do not have them *memorize* spelling words. Instead, teach spelling as a *process*, as a matter of putting down the letters that show what the writer **pronounces** in order to **say** the word.

Like the younger remedial readers, these students will need help with reading for a while, both at home and at school. And again, they should be protected from riducule both at home and at school until they have learned to spell and read independently.

High School Transfer Students

Transfer students who enter a good school in the upper years of high school arrive with a great variety of reading levels, and a variety of attitudes toward reading. Some of them will be completely illiterate, and the rest will be able to score at anywhere from a third to a sixth grade reading level on a paragraph-meaning test.

Those reading at a 0 to 3.0 grade level have often matured enough to abandon the middle-childhood bravado about reading. They have gone back to facing the fact of their reading disability and are as pathetically anxious for help as the second-grade non-readers. With them, you can use the regular first-grade materials in the regular way. Just tell them frankly that they need baby materials because, when they were first-grade babies themselves, they were presented with a different kind of material which only confused them.

But do not expect these students to go through the first grade materials as fast or as easily as the second and third-graders can. The older students have been struggling for years to read by means of their misconceptions about words and letter-sounds. They will make the same types of errors over and over again, not because they are not trying, but because their erroneous habits are so deeply ingrained.

It takes these students a long time really to begin to believe in the reliability of letter-sounds. It takes a long time for them to learn *how* to sound words out, and even longer for them to form the habit of using sounding out for word-identification. Nevertheless, they will see themselves making progress; they will stick to the lessons with remarkable stubbornness; and they will learn to read, especially if, at every stage, you have them using their new knowledge for *spelling* as well as for reading.

But while they are in the process of learning to read, these students need the usual kind of special help to keep up with their regular classes. They need someone to read their textbooks aloud to them. They *must not* be called upon to read out loud themselves in ordinary classes. They should be excused from all writing assignments, and encouraged instead to answer questions orally, and to make reports orally. And all this must be done in a way which is not belittling to the student. All concerned, including the student, must realize and respect the fact that this student needs special help because he or she did not get the kind of reading instruction in first grade that your school gives.

Some of the older high school students who transfer to a good school while reading at a 0 to 3.0 level are still at the developmental stage of the fourth-grade non-readers. They are still pretending complete indifference to reading, but are sufficiently embarrassed about spelling to take special work in spelling. They should be taught by way of spelling, like the fourth-graders. But while they are learning to spell and read by this approach, they need the same kinds of special help and priveleges as the 0 to 3.0 remedial students who are frankly working on reading.

Finally, there are the high school students who enter a good school reading at levels from 3.0 to 6.0. Like the fourth-grade non-readers, these students usually do not want any help with reading, only with spelling. But you cannot help them with a spelling program based on the very earliest work of the first grade. They really *can* read and spell a lot of the simple, short-vowel words. Instead, you should work on their spelling by beginning at a slightly higher level. Their grasp of the sounds for single consonant letters is usually quite good, and they have some sense of the short vowel sounds, but need a great deal of practice with short vowels.

With these students, you should work on spelling by starting with words which contain short vowels only, but vary in the number of consonant sounds at the beginning and end of the word. Once they are able to handle short-vowel words with all the consonant blends at the beginning or the end, you should work on the consonant teams, SH, CH, TH, WH and NG. Then you can begin using the first grade text as a guide for presentation of the remaining phonic material.

Again, these students need special help to enable them to keep up with their regular classes while their spelling and reading skills are being dealt with. They need exactly the same types of special privileges as the non-readers, being allowed to answer questions and give reports orally, instead of doing written work. They should not be called on to read aloud in the regular classes. In dealing with their reading assignments for the regular classes, however, they need different handling, depending on their entering reading scores.

Those scoring at a 3.0 or 4.0 reading level should probably have someone read their textbooks aloud to them, and help them keep notes to use for reciting in class. Those reading at higher levels, should also have constant help. But the helper, instead of reading the textbooks aloud to them, should have the remedial student read aloud. The helper should follow the text, and straighten out the mistakes the student makes. In this way, the remedial student will get practice in reading, but will be prevented from becoming confused about the book's contents as a result of inadequate reading skills.

Finally, you should be warned that remedial students from fourth-graders on up will need more than a simple once-through journey on the plan of the first-grade reading course. After they have been through this, they need review. The review can be based on the spelling textbooks that your school uses for its regular classes, from second grade on up. This will give them mixed review of all the phonic elements. It will help the teacher see what they have really mastered, and what items still need extra work.

While this review is going on, remedial students should also be given lots of easy-reading, high-interest stories and biograpies to read. By this time, their reading will be good enough so that they can enjoy books of this kind. But they still need lots of practice with enjoyable reading because in earlier years they missed out on all the usual, recreational reading that makes good readers of the children who begin with phonics in the first place.

Remedial Students of all Ages

One general comment about remedial reading needs to be emphasized. The remedial teacher must keep one thing constantly in mind. The teacher must remember that it is *not* the fault of the students that they did not learn to read the first time around. They *failed because they were not taught* the things you are teaching them. They were not stupid or lazy or recalcitrant. They probably did not have any brain dysfunction. Their problem is first, that they were not taught *how to use the letters* for reading, and second that they were terrified by their failure.

They are still terrified whenever they make a mistake, no matter how suave their manner may be. You dare not let their mistakes go unnoticed, for any further confusion will cripple them completely. But each mistake must be handled in a positive and constructive way. Whatever the error, always mention *first* the one or two things that they did *right*. *Then*, point out the mistake, and help them understand which of their old habits crept in to cause that error, why it doesn't work to do it that way, and how to guard against that type of error in the future.

You need to combine the greatest firmness with a great deal of tender, loving care. Not "kindness," not condescension, not making excuses for the student. But true firmness and truly tender, truly loving care.

With this kind of treatment, the pupil who at first appears stupid, lazy, careless and scatter-brained will blossom into a bright, eager and industrious student.

Appendix D

The Hanna Research Project

In 1963, an educator interested in the problem of spelling instruction decided to use computer technology to examine enough of our words so as to settle the question of alphabet reliability once and for all. With the support of the United States Department of Health, Education and Welfare, the educator, Paul R. Hanna, of Stanford University, led the project. In 1966, Hanna and his colleagues presented their results in a massive tome entitled *Phoneme-Grapheme Correspondences as Cues to Spelling Improvement.** The data set forth in this report form the basis for the word counts in the *ABC's and All Their Tricks*.

The words selected for the Hanna study were drawn mainly from the Thorndike-Lorge *Teacher's Word Book of 30,000 Words*. This listing had been a standard source of school reading vocabulary for many years. Thorndike and Lorge compiled their list by determining how often each word occurred in the King James version of the Bible, and in a large selection of children's literature, school textbooks, children's magazines and magazines for the home. The *Teacher's Word Book* includes a list of 19,440 words which occurred one or more times per million running words in these sources. In a separate listing, it included an additional 10,560 words which occurred less than once per million running words in their source materials. The Hanna group used the 19,440-word list as their starting-point.

The list, however, had disadvantages as a basis for the Hanna study. For one thing, it was rather dated. Thorndike and Lorge completed their research in 1944. Several years of work were necessary between the choosing of source materials and final completion of the data, so that the list is based on books and magazines published considerably earlier than 1944. Scientific and social developments since that time have added many new words to our work-a-day language, and have pushed many others into the "rare" category. The Hanna group eliminated as irrelevant or unusable the Thorndike words belonging to the following categories: proper names, contracted, hyphenated, or abbreviated forms, slang, obsolete words, trade names, foreign words and words for which no pronunciation was provided in the dictionary chosen for the research. These operations reduced the list to 15,284 items.

They next culled the sixth edition of the *Merriam-Webster's New Collegiate Dictionary* for new words which the researchers could agree were sufficiently used to belong in the vocabulary of educated Americans. In this way, they selected 2,026 words to add to the basic list, yielding a grand total of 17,310. A close study of the final list would, I believe, convince most people that this research examines an adequate sample of English words.

The Hanna group then analyzed the words in detail. They used a computer program to compare the spelling of each word with the dictionary respelling that indicates how it is pronounced. This study produced lists showing (1) how many times each speech sound occured in syllables bearing primary or secondary stress, (2) how many times it occurred in unstressed syllables, (3) how many times it occured at the beginning, middle, or end of a syllable, (4) how many different spellings corresponded to the sound, and (5) how many times each separate spelling of the sound appeared in the various types of syllables and in various syllable positions. The lists thus generated are contained in the published results of the study.

The word counts given in the present volume are based on a detailed study of these lists.

* By Paul R. Hanna, Jean S. Hanna, Richard E. Hodges, and Edwin H. Rudorf, Jr., U.S. Government Printing Office, 1966.

More Phonics and Spelling Help

A MEASURING SCALE FOR ABILITY IN SPELLING by Leonard P. Ayres. An old Classic, now republished. One thousand frequently used words are arranged according to grade levels so that you can test any pupil and determine his or her level of spelling. The research and validation procedures are described in the book, as well as directions for testing. You may also use the lists for weekly spelling in your class. Pupils who can spell the thousand most common words are ready for most of the writing they need to do.

PHONICS MADE PLAIN by Michael S. Brunner. This set consists of flashcards and a wall chart for classroom use. On one side of each card is a phonogram to display to your class and on the reverse side is teaching information for you. The correlated wall chart does indeed make phonics plain, as you see everything organized into ten manageable groups. You CAN teach them. Your children CAN learn. Instructions included.

MRS. SILVER'S PHONICS WORKBOOK 1 by Claudine Silver. This course, the first in a series, is for beginners who need to learn consonant sounds and short vowel sounds. In the McGuffey system, it is used before the Primers. The teacher's edition contains complete instructions for using the workbook and for enriching the lessons with additional activities. With phonics, children can build a wide knowledge of words and ideas. To help with this, Mrs. Silver gives words for science, music, Bible, and other curriculum areas, and ideas for correlating them with each phonics lesson.

RICE CHRISTIAN READER AND SPELLER by Carolyn Rose and Karma Hudson. This unique teaching aid follows in the tradition of Webster's famous *Blue Back Speller*, providing word lists organized according to spelling rules. As children drill on these lists, they learn the power of letters. Useful at all levels from alphabet learning up to difficult four-syllable words.

PHONICS IN SONG by Leon V. Metcalf. Delightful, catchy melodies teach each letter of the alphabet and the most important digraphs—*ch*, *sh*, *th*, and *wh*. A sing-along tape is also available.

These books are available from:
MOTT MEDIA
Milford, Michigan 48042